PAUL M. BUTLER

Hoosier Politician and National Political Leader

George C. Roberts

Indiana University Northwest

NIVERSITY
PRESS OF
AMERICA

LANHAM • NEW YORK • LONDON

Copyright © 1987 by

University Press of America,® Inc.

4720 Boston Way
Lanham, MD 20706

3 Henrietta Street
London WC2E 8LU England

British Cataloging in Publication Information Available

Library of Congress Cataloging-in-Publication Data

Roberts, George C.
  Paul M. Butler, Hoosier politician and national
political leader.

  Bibliography: p.
  Includes index.
  1. Butler, Paul M. (Paul Mulholland), 1905-1961.
2. Politicians—United States—Biography. 3. Democratic
Party (U.S.)—Biography. 4. United States—Politics
and government—1953-1961. 5. Politicians—Indiana—
Biography. 6. Indiana-Politics and government.
I. title.
E748.B8895R62 1987   977.2'043'0924   87-6275
ISBN 0-8191-6295-7
ISBN 0-8191-6296-5 (pbk.)

All University Press of America books are produced on acid-free
paper which exceeds the minimum standards set by the National
Historical Publication and Records Commission.

For Bette and Emily

CONTENTS

PREFACE

Indiana has given the two major national political party committees six chairmen.* In spite of the importance of the state in the presidential election balance during the last quarter of the nineteenth century, it was not until 1904 that a Hoosier chairman was chosen. No Republican has served in such a capacity since 1934, but in the 1950s Indiana produced two Democratic national chairmen, Frank E. McKinney and Paul M. Butler, factional rivals. Butler's family background in South Bend directed his life toward a progression of party offices, responsibilities, and political experiences, yet he was the only one of the six Hoosier chairmen to hold neither an elective nor appointive public office before selection; in other ways he was also different. Butler will be remembered longer than any of Indiana's national chairmen, with the possible exception of Will Hays. He demonstrated the importance of politics in the Hoosier State. His style may have been altered by a broader experience, but the characteristics of Indiana's political system and the lessons it taught about duty, integrity, loyalty, and organization sustained him in a difficult period of leadership.

Paul M. Butler soon became a controversial chairman, and eventually it seemed he was involved continuously in contention. Even friends found an elusive quality in Butler's personality, and for many the manner in which they saw his personality was central to the way they approached the man. Whether Butler succeeded with programs and strategy, the way he affected party unity, and speculation as to what party leadership theories he was pursuing were all examined too immediately, too narrowly, in piecemeal fashion. Now, a quarter of a century after he left the chairmanship, is a better time for appraisal of his work.

This study of his political career will attempt to grasp the essence of his leadership in relation to background, in the context of the 1950s,

---

*Equally balanced between the parties, they were: Democrats Thomas Taggart (1904-1908), Frank E. McKinney (1951-1952), and Paul M. Butler (1955-1960); and Republicans Harry S. New (1907-1908), Will Hays (1918-1921), and Everett Sanders (1932-1934).

and in view of what has since been accomplished by his successors in an age not considered propitious for the democratic institution on which Butler's life centered—the political party.

Paul Butler was the last of the active, old-style Democratic national chairmen. His successors saw Democratic presidents acting as their own party leader and witnessed signs of disintegration of a party system Butler had known. His leadership was transitional, from the "old politics" toward the "new politics." Butler had never slighted communication concerns (he was aware of the possibilities of television, and appeared frequently), was an advocate of party reforms, and often opposed the old-line bosses. Several of his cohorts and younger party activists brought up under his leadership were active in later party reforms. However, his approval of democratization of the party nominating process does not mean he would have found all the McGovern reforms congenial. His disinclination to see parties weakened, especially when they appeared to be declining, would have limited his enthusiasm. He believed enough in the central importance of political parties in a democratic system, as well as in the high calling of politics, that he repudiated any approach to political reform that was essentially anti-party. Politics was a game, a way of life to be enjoyed—a lesson in humanity, friendship, loyalty, service. Butler was enough of a partisan to reject most proposals for non-partisanship in government, and was suspicious of bipartisanship, even in foreign policy.

Attention the Democratic Party paid to issues under Butler's leadership, at a time when issue concern among voters was supposedly slight, would have seemed more appropriate a decade later when volatile subjects seemed to dominate politics. Ironically, with his set of values, Butler would not have found himself on the liberal side of several of the later questions.

Butler served his party when his particular contributions were appropriate. That he left his imprint on the chairmanship is clear, and use of his devices by opposition party leaders was flattering. His party shows signs of rediscovering Butler, now that obsession with reform has ebbed.

Academic interest in Paul M. Butler, party leadership, party organization, and intra-party relations was stimulated long ago by Paul G. Willis, who made available for this study his papers, information, and experiences with Butler. He remains the inspiring teacher and scholar, sometimes in public service. My research was encouraged by my teachers, Louis E. Lambert and Maurice G. Baxter, by my colleagues, Lloyd A. Rowe and John M. Hunger, and most persistently by my wife.

I thank Indiana University for its generous research support, and Vice President Danilo Orescanin and Chancellor Peggy G. Elliott for their facilitations. Preparation of this book for publication was aided by the careful typesetting of Norma Michalski, advice from Joseph Pellicciotti, the technical assistance of Terrence Lukas and his staff, Richard Hewitt and Gloria Miller, and the manuscript work of the late Deborah Zak.

The staff members of the Archives of the University of Notre Dame and the Sam Rayburn Library were always helpful when called upon. For their special contributions I thank Anne Butler, Evelyn Chavoor, John Doran, the late Walter Johnson, Richard J. Murphy, the late Marshall Smelser, Neil Staebler, and James Sundquist. To all who helped me in any way to complete this work I am most grateful. Any error is on the side of the author.

Paul Mulholland Butler

Chapter One

A HOOSIER PREPARATION

Paul Mulholland Butler was born in South Bend, Indiana, June 15, 1905.[1] James P. Butler, his father, had also been born in South Bend (1864), while his mother, Mary E. Mulholland, had been born in Manchester, England (1867). The environment in which Paul Butler grew to maturity was more political than that of most South Bend families, and it was Democratic. In 1955, Butler's mother remembered that she had always been surrounded by politics in her home. Butler's father had been a railroad mail clerk twenty years, then a South Bend street commissioner, 1910-1914. In 1913 congressional Democrats provided in a rider to a deficiency appropriations bill for the removal of 1,300 deputy collectors of internal revenue, provided for in the Tariff Act of 1913, from civil service protection.[2] President Woodrow Wilson, who reluctantly approved this change, appointed James P. Butler a deputy revenue collector in 1914, with the support of United States Senator Benjamin F. Shively of South Bend. Paul Butler's grandfather, James Butler, born in Ireland, was in the transport business, and had served as South Bend's first street commissioner. Paul's uncle, John P. Butler, was also a street commissioner, and a cousin, William Butler, was active in city and county politics.

Paul Butler's father died in 1916, while Paul was still a student in St. Patrick's parochial school, from which he graduated in 1919. After attending the University of Notre Dame Preparatory School, for one year before its closing, he graduated from South Bend High School in 1923. He then returned to Notre Dame for four years to receive the Bachelor of Laws degree in 1927. He held a scholarship while attending Notre Dame. After Butler had become national chairman, his mother commented that her son was so frail as a child that she thought she would never raise him to maturity. He was afflicted with asthma, frequent colds, and digestive upsets which often kept him out of school.

While attending school, Butler worked part time at the Robertson Brothers Department Store, and from 1923 to 1925 was a reporter and proofreader for the South Bend *Tribune*. While serving as a store clerk, Butler was noticed by Vitus Jones, a South Bend lawyer and a

1

Republican, although not a political activist. Jones figuratively adopted Butler, who became a friend of Jones' son, Francis. Jones saw that recreational diversions were part of the young man's life. Jones apparently thought at one time that Butler would become a priest, rather than a lawyer; indeed, two of Butler's brothers did.[3] Not surprisingly, when Butler completed law school and was admitted to the practice of law in the St. Joseph County Circuit Court on June 17, 1927, at twenty-two years of age, he became an associate in the legal firm of Jones and Obenchain. In 1932, this firm was reorganized as Jones, Obenchain, and Butler, and was identified with corporation, banking, insurance, and municipal law. By the time Butler became national chairman in 1954, the firm represented such enterprises as the Singer Manufacturing Company, Greyhound Lines, American Mutual Liability Insurance Company, Hotel LaSalle, Holy Cross Hospital Association, Knute Rockne Trust, Jewel Tea Company, Socony Vacuum Company, Standard Oil of Indiana, and Capital Indemnity Company.

Butler was associated with the firm until 1956, when a Democratic National Committee spokesman announced his "routine" withdrawal because Butler had not been able to devote attention to law. A friend angrily recalled that Butler had been put out for absenteeism.[4] In 1940, Vitus Jones, the firm's senior member and Butler's benefactor, notified his partners that he might have to disassociate himself if they became too active in politics.[5] This warning was particularly directed to Butler, who had begun political activity in 1926, and had by this time become heavily involved. One partner, with the firm for twenty-two years, responded that he would have to side with Jones over Butler in a showdown, but also subtly reminded Jones that Jones himself had been anti-Franklin D. Roosevelt and strongly supportive of a conservative Democratic Congressman, Samuel Pettengill. Besides, some political activity brought business to the firm (bipartisan law firms exist in Indiana's partisan political environment for this very reason).[6]

Because Paul Butler never sought nor held an elective public office, he earned his living from the practice of law until he became national chairman. Butler authored a legal advice column in the South Bend *Tribune*, and established himself early in the legal profession, where he soon became known as a successful trial lawyer, in both civil and criminal proceedings. After eight years of practice the *Martindale-Hubbell Law Directory* gave him a "very high" rating.[7] He became eligible to practice before the Indiana Supreme Court, the United States District Court for Northern Indiana, the United States Court of Appeals, Seventh Circuit, and eventually the Interstate Commerce Commission. In 1934, the year of his marriage, Butler reported income of $4,742

2

from law practice. This partnership gross income rose to $9,878 in 1935, and to $10,384 in 1936.

On September 24, 1934, Paul M. Butler was married to Anne S. Briscoe in Springfield, Massachusetts. The bride, daughter of Stephen and Christian (Owsley) Briscoe of West Hatfield, Massachusetts, had met Butler while visiting in South Bend. The thirty year old lawyer and his wife started housekeeping at 112 South Notre Dame Avenue and thereafter owned or rented seven other houses in the South Bend area, appropriate to rising legal success and to accommodate a growing family. Their first child, Maureen Anne, was born a year after their marriage, Paul, Jr., in 1936, Karen Anne in 1938, Kevin James in 1939, and Brian Stephen in 1941. While Anne Butler was not a political activist, she was supportive of Paul's activities. When he was Indiana national committeeman she often drove him to political meetings. After national chairman Stephen Mitchell visited the Butler home in 1953, he marveled "at the prodigious and versatile abilities" of Anne Butler.[8] Family occasions were not forgotten by Paul Butler during pressing political engagements. On one wedding anniversary, he wired his wife, congratulating her for putting up with him for twenty-four years.[9]

Beginning in the late 1920s, and continuing until his election as national committeeman, Paul Butler engaged in a variety of religious, civic, and business activities. He was a member of South Bend Council 553, Knights of Columbus, and was made a Grand Knight in 1932. A loyal Notre Dame alumnus, he was chosen president of the St. Joseph Valley Alumni Club in 1932. In 1946 he was president of South Bend Catholic Charities. He was always active in whatever parish he was affiliated with. In 1947 he served as president of the South Bend Association of Commerce, as a Community Chest director, and as a volunteer for the Red Cross and Christmas For The Poor. He also served as a director of Reliable Coal and Ice, and as a board member of Serv-Art Wall Paper Manufacturing Company and of Paul Dillon Motors Company.

Butler was a popular public speaker, appearing before nonpartisan groups while building a political career, and incidently aiding that career by public involvement. Mrs. Butler has indicated that his extemporal speaking style relied on last-minute notes (although some speeches were certainly more formally prepared).[10] She also said he had what was then called "a good radio voice," and he used the radio for political campaigns, foreign policy discussion in 1941, and talks on such topics as public safety. Butler was a popular speaker before high school classes and for commencements. He spoke on "Opportunities in Law" and for the World War II effort, to Round Table, to which he belonged; to Americans for Democratic Action in Indianapolis; for dedications of school service flags and for National Brotherhood Week; on Memorial Day, St. Patrick's Day, Flag Day, and Columbus Day; and to the Daughters of the American Revolution, the Elks, Community Chest dinners, and nursing colleges. His speech topics ranged widely—"A New Deal at Home" (local government), "Labor in War Time," "The Supreme Court" (1930s), and "Your Share in America's Future."

After leaving school, Butler said he missed the culture and spirituality provided by the University of Notre Dame, even though he lived close to its activities. He urged the availability of its priests and professors to the community, suggesting that they limit their topics to those which could be discussed from the Catholic point of view. Butler spoke on the campus from time to time, for instance, to the Lay Faculty Discussion Forum in 1942, on "Post-War Political and Economic Objectives of the United States." His loyalty to Notre Dame went beyond attendance at football games. After he became national chairman he returned for an address to the Notre Dame Academy of Political Science and for Democratic mock conventions; he wrote a political appeal to the "college man" for the Notre Dame *Scholastic*.

From the notes and texts of Butler's speeches, from records of other activities, and from notes he took from reading materials used in speech preparation, a pattern of Paul Butler's philosophical approach to life can be constructed. To varied audiences Butler argued citizen responsibility commensurate with rights, the exercise of civic duties, and sacrifice (particularly during World War II). In anticipation of John F. Kennedy's Inaugural Address, Butler ended a 1943 high school commencement address, "In brief, your share in America's future is not only what you can get, but, more importantly, what you can give." Butler excoriated the professions (including the clergy) for less than ethical behavior and the selfishness of special interests (labor, as well as others) seeking money and pleasure at the expense of the public welfare. Still, he believed unions had the right to strike, even in wartime, since little actual damage to the war effort resulted. His postwar goals included cooperation among labor, management, and government; also more social security, and armament and universal military training for post-war peace.

Butler also publicized his concept of civil religion. In a 1941 Memorial Day address he lectured that the command of our dead heroes was "Next to God, be loyal to your country." True Americanism was God, followed by the valuing of rights and liberties; Christian philosophy was the essence of democracy, and to disregard that fact was to contribute nothing to America.

Butler often found the occasion to lash out at prejudice and to plead for toleration of an individual's right to whatever convictions held, arguing that intolerance was simply un-American. Communists and

4

others might use Americanism as a mask to mislead the populace, yet it would be mistaken to label opponents "un-American" without careful deliberation. Yet, perhaps not surprisingly, Butler believed "There need be no tolerance of deliberate error. There can be no tolerance whatever of that which is morally wrong." He cited Cardinal Francis Spellman's admonition that one should do what one ought, not what one pleased.

In addressing Catholic audiences, Butler might vary his theme: ". . . our American concept of government is so thoroughly Catholic in origin . . . ." In serving "God and His Church," one would serve country and fellow man. Catholic education added moral and spiritual dimensions to human development. In 1944 he told graduates of the St. Francis College of Nursing in Lafayette, Indiana, "The post-war era will present unlimited opportunities not only for the spread of Catholic doctrine but also for the beneficial influence of militant Catholic Action."

Butler was greatly agitated by the United States Supreme Court's decision, *People ex rel McCollum v. Board of Education*, 333 U.S. 203 (1948), in which the Court held that programs of religious instruction in public school buildings violated the First and Fourteenth Amendments to the Constitution. He consequently collected articles and books on this issue, which were used for speeches. In an address to the Daughters of the American Revolution, "Our American Heritage," he said some individuals were using the heritage of religious freedom to destroy the Christian concept of American government. "God belongs in our public schools and in our private and parochial schools. God belongs in the education of our children. God belongs in the American concept of civil government. Not even an erroneous decision of our Supreme Court can change this."

Just as other things foreshadowed Butler's general liberalism, it is not difficult to believe that issues of prayer and Bible-reading in public schools, proposals for aid to religious schools, and finally the abortion issue, arising for the most part after his death, would have divided him from many of the liberals who had been his political allies in the 1950s.

The issue involvement and speaking which put Butler most in contact with a major national public policy question was his local participation in Fight For Freedom, a pre-Pearl Harbor interventionist organization formed in April, 1941, by those who believed the Committee to Defend America by Aiding the Allies (the White Committee) was "equivocating and failing to lead public opinion as it had in the past."[11] Fight For Freedom argued that the United States was already at war, that Hitler would permit no peace, and that it was immoral to leave the burden of war to others while waiting for the inevitable. Force should be met with force; the Axis powers should be warred on. Fight For Freedom was also concerned with a just way of life at home, or winning at home while fighting overseas. This battle of mind and spirit called for the brotherhood of man, opposition to racial and religious discrimination, an America united without internal dissension, the right of workers to organize and bargain collectively, and protection from selfish and irresponsible interests. The group's chairman, the Reverend Henry W. Hobson, Episcopal Bishop of Southern Ohio, stressed concepts such as the children of God, world responsibilities, and evils worse than war. As indicated by his speaking activities, Paul Butler shared many of these ideas, and, in spite of an Irish background, was drawn to support of Great Britain's stand against Hitler, and to the company of the interventionists.

The University of Notre Dame seemed to be a focal point for divisiveness on the question of American intervention in World War II, and the Spanish Civil War (particularly the triumph of General Francisco Franco) was part of the broader question. As the Notre Dame debate raged, those supporting intervention could cite support from Bishop Lucey of Amarillo, Texas; Monsignor John A. Ryan, theologian; Alfred E. Smith, the 1928 Democratic presidential candidate; and *Papal Announcements and American Foreign Policy*, written by Bishop Joseph P. Hurley of St. Augustine, Florida, and published by Fight For Freedom. Three individuals, connected with Notre Dame, predominated in the acrimonious debate of that time, when religious people often thought of foreign policy in strong moral terms. These individuals were Professor Francis E. McMahon, Philosophy Department; Reverend John A. O'Brien, Department of Religion; and Clarence Manion, Dean of the School of Law.

McMahon, activated by the role played by O'Brien, had some support from his colleagues for his position of aiding those resisting the Axis powers, but overall, the Notre Dame community showed stronger support for the opposition, the America First Committee. McMahon was anti-Franco because Franco had been supported by the Axis, and, in turn, supported them. However, not all of McMahon's group supported aid to Russia. In 1939 McMahon had told a peace conference that world fraternalism was the only cure for war. In 1942 he was elected president of the Catholic Association for American Peace. In 1943 he was forced out of Notre Dame, particularly because of his views on Franco's Spain, continuing his career at the University of Chicago.[12]

O'Brien, an Oxford scholar, and a nationally known isolationist, who accompanied Charles Lindberg on speaking tours, was said to have easy access to the Chicago *Tribune's* columns, and was a welcomed speaker at America First rallies. Manion, with whom Paul Butler had been closely connected politically, became a member of the national committee of the America First Committee in October, 1941. A week before Pearl Harbor, he and McMahon had a South Bend radio debate on the war question.[13]

The Chicago chapter of the Committee to Defend America by Aiding the Allies, which Adlai Stevenson served as first chairman, had been a strong and prominent organization. But not until July 2, 1941, did Courtenay Barber, Jr., and Albert Parry, both of whom had been associated with the White Committee, organize Fight For Freedom in Chicago. Seemingly to make up for lost time, the group quickly became active, and looked to Indiana, where several chapters of the White Committee had been formed. A caravan of seven automobiles was organized in Chicago to tour northern Indiana on July 19, 1941, for the purpose of reaching the man in the street in industrial communities. This caravan was probably organized at Francis McMahon's insistence, since he was Indiana chairman for Fight For Freedom. He wanted to attract more attention to the group in South Bend. The climax of the caravan was an open air Beat-Hitler rally in South Bend's Howard Park. McMahon headed the local reception committee, which included Paul Butler. One hundred people gathered to hear McMahon appeal, "as a Catholic and as an American," for support of President Roosevelt's foreign policy. Butler also spoke, defending Roosevelt's Atlantic policy on hemisphere defense, freedom of the seas, and Britain's dependence on sea lanes, which the American Navy could protect. Butler told the audience that American liberty won by struggle was worth retaining by struggle:

> The liberty and freedom we enjoy, gifts of the Creator of all men, are recognized in a political philosophy based upon the brotherhood of free men under the fatherhood of God. Shall we now be content to sit idly by and witness the ever-increasing enslavement of free people throughout the world?[14]

The July, 1941 rally did not end Butler's efforts for Fight For Freedom and the ideals which it represented. In a September speech to a group of Democratic women, he attacked what he called the isolationist propaganda encouraged by pro-Axis forces in America, mentioning by name Charles Lindberg, Senator Burton K. Wheeler, Gerald Nye, and Father John O'Brien. Butler said there was no possible compromise with Hitler and his anti-Jewish Nazis. Butler also appeared for Fight For Freedom on a South Bend radio broadcast, October 22. Noting that he hated war, Butler nonetheless advocated preparation for war. He lamented the use of racial, religious, and nationality prejudices in the debate over American foreign policy. He particularly resented the appeal made by isolationists to German, Irish, and Italian groups in the

United States. He asserted that support of Christianity, love, and charity needed enthroning, while prejudice, hate, and fear needed uprooting. This theme was continued in a November speech to the Veterans of Foreign Wars: too much intolerance existed, and national unity and support of American leaders was necessary at a time when Britain and Greece stood almost alone against Hitler.[15] Butler had played an active local role in the struggle over American intervention in World War II.

We now turn to Butler's political party activity, without completely separating it from these other civic activities. From 1926 to 1954, when he was elected national chairman of the Democratic Party, Butler had participated in precinct, city, county, congressional district, state, and national politics. While holding several *party* offices,[16] he was never a candidate for *public* office, pointing out to his children that one could be deeply involved in politics, and could exercise considerable influence, without ever seeking public office.[17]   All this experience helped shape the philosophy which guided him as national chairman.

Paul Butler was not quite old enough to be a candidate for precinct committeeman in the 1926 May primary election; but after turning twenty-one in June, he became involved in the general election campaign by taking the poll of his native rural township (Clay) in St. Joseph County, and serving as poll book holder at the Roseland polls in November. He was symbolically rewarded with the election of a Democratic township trustee, an unusual event in such Republican territory.[18]   There has been some doubt as to whether Paul Butler was ever elected a precinct committeeman (what national chairman would not want to claim such distinction?), and official records are scanty, but the newspaper record does show that he was an unopposed candidate for precinct committeeman for Clay Township in the 1928 Democratic primary election, the same year he was elected president of the St. Joseph Young Democrats.[19]   This may be the only time he was elected precinct committeeman (he was probably appointed in 1936 and 1948, because he was active in county reorganization meetings); but in 1938 and 1940, he was elected delegate to the state conventions.[20]

Paul Butler reached political maturity and became a political activist during a period of political transition, when St. Joseph County was shifting from Republican to Democratic support, a movement abetted by the 1929 Depression and New Deal voter mobilization. Socialized into an urban-industrial political system during a brief period of prosperity, then one of depression and recovery, he found himself functioning in a local party factional milieu which differed only slightly from state factional politics, with which the young enthusiast also became acquainted before long.

8

In 1926, the year Butler first served as a poll book holder, St. Joseph Democrats began to break the Republican hold on the courthouse. George Schock, an attorney, former deputy prosecutor, and newsman, won a contest for county chairman after his followers had worked ten years to restore the party organization. In winning the chairmanship, Schock defeated a candidate supported by the South Bend city organization, headed by Mayor Chester Montgomery, who had been elected in 1925. In November, 1926, Democrats carried their county ticket into office, aided by Republican identification with the Ku Klux Klan.[21] In 1928, Democratic organizational candidates won primary election nominations, but lost all county contests in the Herbert Hoover-Alfred Smith general election contest.[22] The Democratic Party had three different county chairmen between 1928 and 1930, but was successful in the 1930 general election.[23]

In 1932, Democratic factionalism featured a county courthouse-city hall division (as foretold in 1926), and the courthouse group won the county chairmanship. November brought the first complete Democratic victory in a presidential election year in St. Joseph history. In the 1934 primary election a New Deal Democratic Club unsuccessfully challenged the county organization, headed by Chester Montgomery, former mayor of South Bend, and Rudolph Ackermann. But in November, Montgomery was defeated for mayor and all county office contests were lost, except for two judgeships.[24]

Paul Butler, developing a successful legal career, was by this time becoming more involved in political activity. He helped support friends seeking patronage positions from the New Deal, giving his approval to the successful candidate for postmaster at South Bend. When the South Bend *Tribune* attacked Franklin Roosevelt in 1932, Butler wrote a letter causing the newspaper to print Roosevelt's acceptance speech. In 1936, Butler, speaking for the Young Democrats in a radio debate, supported reelection of the president Butler believed had saved the nation from revolution. Butler's efforts were praised.[25]

Butler experienced a disappointment in state politics in 1934, when Clarence Manion, a member of Notre Dame's law faculty and Butler's former teacher, failed to win the Democratic nomination for United States Senator in the state convention. Paul V. McNutt, formerly Dean of the Indiana University Law School and National Commander of the American Legion, had been elected Governor of Indiana in 1932. He vigorously led the state into a little New Deal, with a new revenue structure, executive branch reorganization, and a patronage system which collected two percent of the salaries of state employees for political party treasuries (a system which developed downwardly to local politics). His enemies often labeled his methods dictatorial. Clarence Manion was part of the core of American Legion

Democrats working for McNutt's gubernatorial nomination in 1932; Manion delivered the state convention's keynote address. In St. Joseph County the dominant faction had prevented election of all but four McNutt delegate candidates. In 1934, Manion, who had been serving as Indiana Federal Emergency Relief Director, sought the senatorial nomination, claiming Governor McNutt's backing. Manion was opposed by McNutt's former state party chairman and Sherman Minton, Public Service Counselor for the Indiana Public Service Commission. Minton won with McNutt's support, while Manion ran third.[26]

Butler was Manion's devoted follower, and helped another Democrat congratulate Manion as the "newest and best dealer of the New Deal." Manion desired to see Butler city judge in South Bend.[27] Chagrined over his loss of the senatorial nomination, Manion gradually developed a different political orientation, and emerged a Republican. As shown above, he was a leading spokesman for America First, then became a prominent figure in rightist political circles. Manion recalled that Butler and he divided over local factionalism, Franklin Roosevelt, and the question of America's involvement in World War II, and that "Paul stayed with Roosevelt." Although the two drifted apart politically, the teacher and his student remained friends.[28]

By 1936 Butler had been drawn more and more into county politics. Many Democrats resented the 1934 general election losses, and the results of the 1936 primary election were heralded as the defeat of bossism. Butler was part of a group of "new-breed" Democratic leaders opposed to the Chester Montgomery-Rudolph Ackermann leadership. Butler, speaking as a Young Democrat and member of the Young Men's Democratic Club, summarized the arguments of the self-styled reformers against the "old machine and bosses" in a radio broadcast. The "self-appointed dictators," who had tried to dominate the Young Democrats, were using the WPA (there were allegations of scandal in local WPA administration) for political purposes; the Democracy of St. Joseph County was bigger than any man, needed a new deal, and must nominate candidates free "from the taint of machine candidates." While both factions organized Roosevelt clubs, the old guard supported Governor McNutt's candidate for Governor (Lt. Governor Clifford Townsend), and the reformers did not. Butler argued that the issue was not gubernatorial politics but local bossism, and that reform augured well for Roosevelt's reelection.[29]

For the next twelve years, at the end of which time Butler was elected chairman of the Third Congressional District, the factionalism of 1936 persisted in generally the same form, except for some shifting of individuals from one group to another. Those who won in 1936 were dominant, although occasionally the primary nominations were

10

shared by the factions. When the "organization" shifted, those once called "reformers" became known as "bosses."

A plethora of groups came into existence to oppose the dominant organization—Democrats for Good Government, Democratic Victory Ticket, and the Democratic Association, among others. By the late 1930s, Polish-Americans and other ethnic groups were demanding more recognition from the Democratic Party, and particularly nominations for county office. Such dissatisfied individuals on South Bend's west side were often found in the faction opposed to the regular organization.[30]

While factional bickering was often intense, the city hall-courthouse split did not exist, because the organization controlled both. In 1946 the two leading factions joined in the primary election to defeat a third faction, only to divide again over election of the county chairman. Butler said the dissidents were directed by selfish people.[31] Louis Chapleau, an attorney and long-time friend of Butler, was chosen county chairman in 1944. In 1948, John Shively, a newcomer, was nominated for chairman by Butler, and in a harmony move, elected unanimously.[32]

While these factional struggles were unfolding, Paul Butler continued his varied party activities, supporting friends for patronage appointments, and particularly engaging in general election campaigns. In seeking balanced tickets, Butler worked at getting Masonic lawyers placed on the Democratic ticket to secure some Protestant support.[33]

By 1938, the incumbent Democratic congressman, Samuel Pettengill, conservative in his politics, had turned definitely against Franklin Roosevelt. He particularly opposed Roosevelt's plan to reorganize the Supreme Court. Butler, an earlier supporter of Pettengill, had decided by 1938 that the congressman no longer represented his constituents. Butler did not accept Pettengill's charge that Roosevelt undermined constitutional government.[34] When Pettengill decided not to seek reelection, the Democratic nomination was won by George N. Beamer, like Butler, born in Clay Township, and a graduate of Central High School and the Notre Dame Law School. Beamer, who had once practiced in the same law firm as Butler, was appointed South Bend city judge in 1933 and elected St. Joseph prosecuting attorney in 1936 (he would later be appointed Attorney General of Indiana and a United States federal district judge in 1962). Butler served as Beamer's congressional campaign manager and constructed an admirable campaign organization, but Beamer lost to Robert A. Grant, a friend of both Beamer and Butler. Allegations persisted that the county organization failed sufficiently to support Beamer because he had been too zealous in enforcing gambling laws while prosecuting attorney. Beamer ran in a year not overly favorable

11

to the New Deal, nationally or in Indiana; Roosevelt's name was not on the ballot, and Indiana Democrats had factional problems.[35]

Butler was active again in the 1940 and 1944 campaigns, making radio broadcasts for the Democratic ticket. His 1940 approach was to honor Thomas Jefferson and to attack potential Republican presidential candidates before the Republican convention. After Wendell Willkie became the nominee, Butler accused the incumbent Third District congressman of not supporting Willkie on national defense issues. Franklin Roosevelt was hailed as the man who had saved American democracy, the champion of the "Christian philosophy that it is the duty of a nation to care for its stricken people" until economic conditions improve. Roosevelt had the nation's confidence in regard to the world crisis, and inexperienced Republicans should not be trusted with administration of progressive legislation enacted by the New Deal. With slight variation, Butler told his 1944 radio audiences that the incumbent Republican congressman was a "mouthpiece" for isolationists and special interests, and that extraordinary times demanded Roosevelt's reelection.[36]

Paul Butler entered a different phase of his political career in May, 1948, when he became Democratic chairman of the Third Congressional District, and consequently a member of the Democratic State Committee. The district contained four counties, each having two votes in the district reorganization meeting, regardless of population; a candidate for district chairman from St. Joseph County (assuming support there) needed three more votes to win, or if the vote tied, the incumbent chairman could decide the outcome. The incumbent chairman was not a candidate for reelection, and Butler's choice was unanimous.[37]

How was Butler able to secure the district chairmanship? Certainly Butler had no personal political power base in 1948, with patronage and other appurtenances. He had never been county chairman. In a sense, he rose in politics by latching onto other political leaders (local leaders, a governor, a presidential candidate); and, if they lost power, Butler found others. But if he had no real power base, he had a voice and influence in political circles—he was a respected member of a political organization and was consulted by other leaders on questions of party importance. One colleague remembered meeting Butler for the first time in 1946, at a political meeting in a private home, where Butler was the "dynamic speaker," who greatly impressed the audience.[38] By 1948 Butler was an active county Democratic leader of wide experience "with a fine personality, integrity, and the guts to make decisions."[39] He also had a superb knowledge of voter names and family associations, as well as the workings of the local political process. He counted as friends, public officials, party officers and many

12

precinct workers.[40]   St. Joseph County and South Bend party and public officials offered him broad support in his quest for the district chairmanship, and exerted influence on members of the district committee. As a prelude to party factionalism at the state level, in which Butler would soon be involved, his candidacy was also aided by those who wanted changes in state party leadership.

Butler's political experience, ranging from precinct politics to congressional district politics, had shown him bitter factionalism and disappointments, but also the pleasures of the game of politics and the reciprocal loyalty of friends in political ventures. In keeping with the Indiana political culture, he had developed a strong partisanship. He tended to see nonpartisanship as evil because it was designed to destroy the two-party system and wreck party responsibility.[41]   He also stressed the importance of party organization, balanced tickets, and loyalty to the party organization in both strong terms and actions. He later informed one Democratic official, "You know from long experience that the strength and vitality of our Party in St. Joseph County is the orderly and democratic discipline that is maintained by the Party organization in the community which could very well create such imbalance on our ticket as to defeat us every time if we did not provide such discipline. Generally, that capacity of our organization has provided honest and constructive government."[42]   In regard to patronage and organization prerogative, Butler stated his creed:

> I make no pretense of being anything but an organization Democrat. If the city organization and a county organization has made a selection and I know nothing detrimental in a substantial way about the person the party has recommended I go along and add my personal endorsement and work for the appointment of that person. I do not consider myself bigger or more important than the political committee which, by its votes, has honored me with its chairmanship. I think that is the least that is to be expected of any political committee official or any elected official who must depend upon a party organization for support.[43]

Butler once opined that a person who had lost a primary election contest, and wanted to run as an independent candidate in the general election, should be quietly informed that such a course would deprive him of any party organizational support in the future.[44]   In fact, in the 1950s, several St. Joseph Democrats who had won primary nominations against the organization were defeated, with the help of Democratic voters, in general elections. Butler spoke to private audiences of Democrats to help defeat these anti-organization

Democrats.[45]   In a county where Democrats employed a slating process for primary elections, and where all precinct committee members had a vote, Butler saw no impropriety in helping defeat Democrats who had beaten the organization in primaries.

But, of course, Butler was with the "organization" when expressing these views.   Earlier, he, too, had opposed the "organization."   That activity represented his reform philosophy, directed against "selfish bosses," who thought themselves more important than their party and its organization.   This aspect of his reform views actually supported his emphasis on the importance of party government and organization.   Butler's reform traits never strayed far enough toward "goo goo," "good government" concepts to threaten his attachment to partisanship and party organization.

Butler was prepared ideally, practically, and psychologically for his new role in Indiana politics.   While he had some contact with state-level politics, much of what he was to encounter would be new.   The political environment of the state as a whole was not greatly different from that of St. Joseph County in most particulars, but a general description of Indiana's political culture and realities will be helpful in understanding the wider area in which Butler would be functioning.

Butler rose to political prominence in a competitive state—competitive in the sense that Republicans and Democrats enjoyed mobilizing their identifiers for electoral struggle, also competitive in that Indiana was not a one-party state.   These conditions carried over from the nineteenth century, but after 1892 Republicans had an electoral advantage until the 1930s brought at least temporary success for Democrats, which Butler had seen erode by 1948.   Indiana had no dominant urban center, such as Chicago in Illinois; nor did either major party hold exclusive influence over urban or rural areas.   At the local level, a vast majority of Indiana's counties were one-party. Indiana was a partisan state, where partisan feelings also carried over from the nineteenth century.   Hoosier politicians frowned on governmental arrangements which were nonpartisan, and the election code was clearly restrictive of third party ballot access.   Democrats and Republicans agreed to share control of some governmental agencies through formal bipartisanship, otherwise leaving an unusually large number of offices to be filled through a patronage process which paid scant attention to any merit principle.   Strong party organizations for professional politicians and activists, and a nominating system at the state level dominated by professionals made Indiana stand out from many states.   A statewide, mandatory primary election law had not been enacted until 1915, and, except for earlier experimentation with the primary, statewide candidates were nominated in a state convention. Both major parties frequently exhibited factionalism, most often based

14

on a combination of personality and desire for power and patronage (or some would have said, general contrariness), seldom based on ideology altogether, and even less on geography.[46]

There was never any compulsion for Paul Butler to reject the general outlines of the Hoosier political culture, which he already knew in St. Joseph County; indeed his views on political parties, partisanship, and party organization supported the general political arrangements of his state. He saw nothing in Hoosier politics which denied access to those who wished to become activists. What he would come to find wrong was a lack of vigor and effectiveness at the state level of leadership, which he traced in part to a bipartisan establishment which went beyond the sharing of the personnel of state agencies. It was a condition which had made him a reformer in his younger days—selfish individuals placing personal interests ahead of their party, and, with bipartisanship, doing so in an act of collusion across party lines.

Butler's immediate attention, as the new Third District chairman, was drawn to the biennial reorganization of the Democratic State Committee in May, 1948, at which meeting Pleas Greenlee was replaced by Ira Haymaker as chairman. Butler supported this change, while favoring reelection of Frank McHale as national committeeman. He also supported the appointment of Frank McKinney as treasurer.[47]

Changes in state party offices were related to the gubernatorial candidacy of Henry F. Schricker, a former state senator and lieutenant governor who had survived a 1940 Republican trend to become Indiana's war-time governor, but who could not seek reelection in 1944 under state constitutional provisions. Instead, Schricker sought a United States Senate seat, but was narrowly defeated. Born in Starke County in 1883, Schricker had been farmer, banker, newspaper editor and publisher. A popular politician, with an image of fiscal conservatism, Schricker was drafted to become the first governor to be elected twice under the 1851 Constitution, and easily secured the state convention nomination, as well as a comfortable margin in November, while President Harry S. Truman narrowly lost Indiana. The new state chairman, Ira Haymaker, had been active in the Schricker draft.[48]

Always a Schricker admirer, Butler encouraged the 1948 revival of Schricker's political career. During the next four years, the two would increasingly become allies in a factional dispute that would lead to Butler's election as national committeeman.

As the new district chairman, Butler prodded county chairmen outside St. Joseph County to activate viable campaigns in 1948. He politely offered instructions for precinct workers if county chairmen thought they would be helpful.[49] St. Joseph Democrats drew up a campaign budget of $47,450 (a considerable increase from $4,736 in

15

1944), and actually raised $38,061, and spent $36,304—$11,045 for general expenses, $8,330 for advertisements, and the remainder for securing automobiles and 1,000 campaign workers for getting out the vote.[50] These types of expenditures were typical for the time. Butler continued his usual practice of radio and rally speeches, asking support for Truman, Schricker, the congressional candidate, and the local ticket.[51]

With Truman and Schricker winners, and with the election of the first Democratic congressman in a decade, Butler received thanks from district Democrats for his leadership and work.[52] With state government patronage now available, he also received many requests for jobs, and patronage matters required attention for several months. Butler also became co-manager of the county auto license bureau for two years.[53] Butler was less successful in negotiating federal patronage because he was not on good terms with the new Democratic congressman, Thurman C. Crook. Crook, slated by organization Democrats and unopposed in the primary, had been an unexpected winner in November.[54] Since Indiana had no Democratic senators, the national committeeman, Frank McHale, had an important role in dispensing some Truman Administration patronage, and the bulk of Butler's correspondence with McHale concerned patronage. On some appointments, the two agreed; where they did not, McHale was usually successful.[55]

State party factionalism, of a type already known to Butler, reasserted itself in the Schricker Administration. Governor Schricker had been drafted as a candidate on a condition of complete reorganization of the State Committee. Schricker gradually became displeased with what he perceived to be the closeness of state chairman Ira Haymaker to national committeeman McHale. McHale and Schricker had been factional opponents since the 1930s, when McHale, who had become national committeeman in 1937, emerged as a powerful figure in the administrations of Governors Paul McNutt and M. Clifford Townsend. Schricker was particularly chagrined at the slowness with which he felt McHale supported his nomination for governor in 1940.[56]

Born in Logansport in 1891, McHale was Cass County president of the newly formed Young Democrats and was organizing for a presidential campaign by the time he was twenty-five. After service in World War I, and a few battles with the Ku Klux Klan, he moved to Indianapolis and became active in American Legion politics, like several successful Hoosier politicians of his time. He was elected state commander of the Legion in 1927, and managed McNutt's 1932 gubernatorial campaign. A graduate of the University of Michigan Law School (and a football star), McHale had also pursued a legal and business career. By 1952, he was vice-president and a director of

16

Southern Indiana Railroad, Incorporated, and a director of the Nickle Plate Railroad (eventually becoming chairman of the board); he had also founded the National Bank of Logansport. His law firm was general counsel for several railroads, the Indiana Brewers Association, Cummins Engine Company, Commonwealth Edison Company, and several other firms. It was also national counsel for Central Newspapers, Incorporated, owners of the Indianapolis *Star* and *News*, along with other Indiana and Arizona newspapers. Indiana Democrats viewed the *Star* as the state's leading Republican newspaper; consequently Butler and other Democrats resented the Democratic national committeeman representing this newspaper.[57]

Paul Butler was naturally drawn to Governor Schricker's side in the factional dispute with McHale. First of all, Butler's local political experience in the 1930s had usually found him aligned with a faction at odds with the state McNutt-McHale organization, which had not been favorable to Schricker nor to Butler's friend, Clarence Manion. And Butler not only admired Schricker as a political leader, but both had an image of politics and politicians which did not fit McHale. Butler's local dislike of selfish party leaders who put self above party was transferred to Frank McHale.

Butler, in contact with Schricker, and others were planning the 1952 ouster of McHale as national committeeman as early as the August, 1951, meeting of the Indiana Democratic Editorial Association at French Lick.[58] Schricker himself was mentioned as a replacement for McHale, but was instead drafted again as a candidate for the United States Senate. Schricker accepted, as had been his manner in 1948, on the condition that McHale would be ousted, along with state chairman Haymaker, who had increasingly displeased Schricker.[59] Paul Butler emerged as the candidate to oppose McHale. Not only had Butler been an active district chairman, but his colleagues saw him as an energetic and valued member of the State Committee, for whom Butler had chaired a committee on rules and reorganization.[60]

McHale's enemies took advantage of what they thought were his weaknesses, which included Democratic losses in the 1950 election and the 1951 city elections, and identification with the scandals of the Truman Administration. McHale publicly attacked what he called "certain scurrilous articles regarding me," which appeared in the New York *Herald-Tribune* and the St. Louis *Post-Dispatch*, labelling McHale a "ten-percenter" in regard to an arms contract secured by Empire Ordnance Corporation. Both McHale and Frank McKinney, who since October 31, 1951, had been chairman of the Democratic National Committee, secured profits of $68,000 on an investment of $1,000 made in 1946. McHale urged party officials to support him, while Butler's reaction was to collect articles and editorials from the

17

Indianapolis *Times* on the "two Franks," and send them to selected members of the State Committee with the admonition not to disclose that he had sent them. Butler noted that "The papers also contain many articles about the Empire Ordnance deal in which both Franks were involved."[61]

Butler reported to Schricker a telephone call from McHale to an Elkhart Democrat, in which McHale labelled Butler a good young fellow "being terribly misguided by Henry Schricker." Phillip Murray of the CIO was supposedly pressuring State Committee members on behalf of McHale. Butler asked Schricker to "call upon the organization people from the precincts on up to bring about a thorough and complete reorganization of the officers of the State Committee and Indiana members of the National Committee." To accomplish this goal, twelve of the twenty-two votes on the State Committee would be needed, and Butler told Schricker these votes were already secured, and perhaps five more.[62]

The 1952 congressional district reorganization meetings, which chose members of the State Committee, were indeed favorable to the Schricker-Butler forces, and particularly in the Second and Eighth Districts, which were pivotal. Ira Haymaker and his vice-chairman did not seek reelection. Haymaker was replaced as state chairman by Charles E. Skillen, who had served Schricker in two administrations, most recently as personnel director of the Indiana Highway Department, with its adequate patronage. Skillen had never held public office, but had been a county chairman, district chairman, and secretary of the State Committee.[63] McHale decided to meet the challenge rather than retire, and issued a pamphlet pointing out his party service, his immigrant parents, and his patronage for former members of the armed services. It was separately asserted that President Truman wanted McHale retained.[64] Butler defeated McHale, 14-8, and McHale promptly claimed he had been defeated by a machine "led by a Governor whom I twice helped nominate and elect." Butler said his election was "a triumph for rank and file Democrats of Indiana."[65]

Response to the upheaval in Indiana politics was quick and widespread. Congressman Ray Madden informed Butler the change in leadership had been delayed too long for the party's good. Judge Warren E. Martin of the Indiana Supreme Court felt the "reorganization timely and will be very wholesome for the party." Former member of Congress James Noland referred to "the fight you waged to improve and strengthen the party." H.J. Noel, Political Action Committee director for the Indiana CIO, reported satisfaction.[66]

Fred Bays, a former state chairman, believed the most important event for the Democratic Party in fifty years had been "getting rid of the selfish, bipartisan influence of Frank McHale," with "his manipulations in the beer, whiskey, and blacktop rackets," the receiverships that McHale and others "grabbed the last dollar from." Summing up the arguments of those who truly detested McHale, Bays added:

> Few men know Frank McHale as I know him and few understand how detrimental his activities were to the great purposes of the Democratic Party in this state. As you remember, four years ago it was my purpose and intense desire to throw him out and make you the National Committeeman. It should have been done then; I am grateful it has been done now. The days of the bi-partisan, greedy McHale are over for which I am truly thankful.[67]

Butler thanked the "Faithful 14" on the State Committee for their part in his victory, and particularly those who had worked at county level reorganization, which was crucial in the First and Eleventh Districts, where the county chairmen named the district chairmen.

Frank McHale's influence in Indiana politics certainly did not disappear after his loss to Butler, but his importance declined relative to that of Frank E. McKinney. Both worked together factionally, held similar outlooks, and were identified with similar interests during the remainder of Butler's life and beyond, although they sometimes sponsored different candidates for office in friendly rivalry. McKinney, born in Indianapolis in 1904, began a business career at the age of fourteen as a bank messenger boy. He was elected treasurer of Marion County in 1934. As county treasurer he was entitled to a percentage of all delinquent taxes collected, a not inconsiderable opportunity in a depression period, and was able to invest in the banking industry. He became president of Fidelity Trust Company, which eventually evolved into the American Fletcher Corporation, of which McKinney was executive committee chairman when he died in 1974. McKinney was also involved as a director of several business firms, and was at times part-owner of three baseball clubs; he was also a civic organization activist and World War II veteran. When he became chairman of the Democratic National Committee in 1951, he had served as a precinct worker and as city, county, and state party treasurer.[68]

The Butler-McHale relationship was one of mutual hatred and remained so.[69] Butler had better social and personal relations with McKinney; partly because a son of each became school friends.[70] Those Hoosier Democrats who looked to Butler for leadership generally shared Butler's reaction to McHale and McKinney. Of course, as McKinney became more prominent in the anti-Butler faction, he became more the object of wrath of Butlerites.

19

At a point in history, Indiana Democrats produced three strong party leaders, two of whom became national party chairmen. All three were Roman Catholics with Irish ties. Yet, while similar in ethnicity, Butler, contrasted with McHale and McKinney, was never so involved in business ventures, and they certainly saw politics differently. But for the next decade, Frank McKinney and Frank McHale would have to share their party leadership with a newcomer, who would function on a national scale, even before becoming national chairman. At the age of forty-seven, twenty-six years after entering politics, Paul Butler was Indiana's Democratic national committeeman.

NOTES

1. Biographical material concerning Butler has been obtained from the Paul M. Butler Papers, University of Notre Dame Archives, Notre Dame, Indiana (hereafter cited as Butler Papers, for which box numbers are location numbers and are subject to change), particularly in Boxes 2, 7, 18, 75, 81, 102, 172, and 204; from the local history files of the South Bend Public Library (the Butler material contains biographical information filed with the Citizens Historical Association of Indianapolis, July 27, 1935); from an interview with Anne Butler, June 10, 1975; and from a letter to the author from Paul M. Butler, July 5, 1961. Also of use have been: Timothy E. Howard, *A History of St. Joseph County Indiana* (Chicago and New York: Lewis Publishing Company, 1907, reproduced 1971, by Unigraphic, Evansville, Indiana), I; John D. Barnhart and Donald F. Carmony, *Indiana: From Frontier to Industrial Commonwealth* (New York: Lewis Publishing Company, 1954), IV; Hugh Morrow, "The Democrats' No. 1 Optimist," *The Saturday Evening Post*, July 28, 1956, pp. 28-29, 67-69; and the South Bend *Tribune*. Other sources will be specifically cited.
2. Laurin L. Henry, *Presidential Transitions* (Washington: The Brookings Institution, 1960), pp. 85-86.
3. Vitus Jones to Roland, Paul, Francis, and Roland, Jr., December 2, 1940, Butler Papers, Box 75.
4. Sam Brightman, newstype strip, August 30, 1956, Butler Papers, Box 172.
5. Vitus Jones to Roland, Paul, Francis, and Roland, Jr., December 2, 1940, Butler Papers, Box 75.
6. Roland Obenchain to Vitus, Paul, Francis, December 4, 1940, Butler Papers, Box 75.

7. *The Martindale-Hubbell Law Directory* (New York: Martindale-Hubbell Publishers, 1935), I, 252, 379.

8. Mitchell to Butler, 1953, Butler Papers, Box 81.

9. Paul Butler to Anne Butler (telegram), September 24, 1958, Butler Papers, Box 18.

10. Speech texts, 1938-1948, are in the Butler Papers, Box 197, for the most part. See also Boxes 44, 46, 75, and 102.

11. The Committee to Defend America had been formed a year earlier. It was often called the White Committee after William A. White, Kansas editor and one of its organizers. White resigned as chairman on December 26, 1940, amid charges the committee was leading the United States into war. See Walter Johnson, *The Battle Against Isolation* (Chicago: University of Chicago Press, 1944); and Walter Johnson, with Carol Evans and C. Eric Sears (eds.), *The Papers of Adlai E. Stevenson* (Boston: Little, Brown, 8 vols., 1972-1979), I, 453-563 (hereafter cited as *Stevenson Papers*).

12. Thirty-five years later, McMahon indicated that if he had known then what he knew now (particularly in regard to communism after World War II), he would have pursued a different course (telephone interview with Francis McMahon, January 31, 1975); telephone interview with Courtenay Barber, Jr., January 29, 1975; the Notre Dame *Scholastic*, September 29, 1939, and April 15, 1942.

13. Telephone interview with Francis McMahon, January 31, 1975; telephone interview with Clarence Manion, June 10, 1975; the Notre Dame *Scholastic*, September 26, 1941, October 10, 1941, and October 17, 1941.

14. Telephone interview with Courtenay Barber, Jr., January 29, 1975; telephone interview with Francis McMahon, January 31, 1975; South Bend *Tribune*, July 17, 18, and 20, 1941; speeches in Butler Papers, Boxes 102 and 197.

15. Butler Papers, Box 197.

16. Precinct committeeman, county president of Young Democrats, state convention delegate, congressional district chairman and state committee member, national committeeman, and national convention delegate.

17. Interview with Anne Butler, June 10, 1975.

18. Paul Butler to the author, July 5, 1961; South Bend *Tribune*, November 3, 1926.

19. South Bend *Tribune*, April 8, 1928, and its Notice of Primary Election, April 24, 1928.

20. Ibid., April 14, 1938, and May 5, 1940.

21. Ibid., May 9, 1926, and November 3, 1926.

22. Ibid., May 9 and 13, 1928, and November 7, 1928.

23. Ibid., May 11, 1930, and November 5, 1930.

24. Ibid., May 4, 1932, November 9, 1932, May 6 and 9, 1934, and November 7, 1934.

25. Butler to F. Kenneth Dempsey, August 10, 1933, and B.J. McCaffley to Butler, May 27, 1936, Butler Papers, Box 75; South Bend *Tribune*, July 15, 1932; radio debate, October 23, 1936, and Benjamin Piser to Butler, November 4, 1936, Butler Papers, Box 75.

26. I. George Blake, *Paul V. McNutt: Portrait of a Hoosier Statesman* (Indianapolis: Central Publishing Company, 1966), pp. 107-108, 149. For a description of McNutt's success, factions, and the 1934 contest, see also James H. Madison, *Indiana Through Tradition and Change: A History of the Hoosier State and Its People 1920-1945* (Indianapolis: Indiana Historical Society, 1982), pp. 140-143.

27. Telephone interview with Clarence Manion, June 10, 1975; Paul Butler and George Beamer to Manion (telegram), February 23, 1935, Butler Papers, Box 75.

28. Telephone interview with Clarence Manion, June 10, 1975; interview with Anne Butler, June 10, 1975.

29. South Bend *Tribune*, May 3, 1936, undated 1936 radio speech, Butler Papers, Box 197.

30. South Bend *Tribune*, April 24 and 26, 1938, and April 4, 1940. Newspaper comments on the primaries for several elections cited such groups as Slavish Democratic Clubs and Colored Democratic Clubs.

31. South Bend *Tribune*, April 7, 1940, May 5, 1940, and May 5, 8, and 12, 1946; Butler to William Plodowski; March 24, 1944, Butler Papers, Box 75.

32. South Bend *Tribune*, May 7, 1944, and May 2, 5, and 9, 1948.

33. Butler to Frederick Van Nuys, July 30, 1941, Butler Papers, Box 75; interview with Marshall Smelser, September 24, 1974.

34. Butler to Frank E. Gannett, January 27, 1938, Butler Papers, Box 75.

35. Louisville *Courier-Journal*, October 22, 1974; Paul C. Bartholomew, *The Indiana Third Congressional District: A Political History* (Notre Dame: University of Notre Dame Press, 1970), pp. 155-157.

36. Updated radio text, 1940, and radio texts, November 2 and 6, 1944, Butler Papers, Box 197.

37. South Bend *Tribune*, May 13, 1948.

38. Interview with Marshall Smelser, September 24, 1974; John P. Doran to the author, November 6, 1974.

39. Interview with Louis Chapleau, June 11, 1975.
40. John P. Doran to the author, November 6, 1974.
41. Kansas City *Times,* April 26, 1960; Toledo *Blade,* May 26, 1957.
42. Butler to Edward F. Voorde, April 25, 1958, Butler Papers, Box 17.
43. Butler to Thurmond Crook, August 20, 1950, Butler Papers, Box 84.
44. Butler to Edward F. Voorde, May 18, 1959, Butler Papers, Box 17.
45. Interview with Freda Noble, September 24, 1974; interview with Marshall Smelser, September 24, 1974.
46. For a description of the nature of factionalism after Butler entered state politics, see George C. Roberts, The Democratic Party of Indiana, 1952-1958 (Ph.D. dissertation, Indiana University, Bloomington, 1962).
47. Butler to McHale, June 28, 1948; and Butler to McKinney, June 23, 1948; Butler Papers, Box 84.
48. For insight into Schricker's political career, see Charles F. Fleming, *The White Hat: Henry Frederick Schricker: A Political Biography* (n.p., 1966). Also see Donald Richard Smith, The Political Speaking of Henry F. Schricker of Indiana (Ph.D. dissertation, Purdue University, West Lafayette, 1960); interview with Marshall Smelser, September 24, 1974.
49. Butler's letters to county chairmen, August 10, 1948; and Butler to Lloyd Martin, August 25, 1948; Butler Papers, Box 84.
50. St. Joseph County Democratic Central Committee Budget, Receipts and Expenditures, Fall Campaign, 1948, November 2, 1948, Butler Papers, Box 84.
51. See Butler Papers, Boxes 84 and 197.
52. Marshall E. Hanley to Butler, May 19, 1952, Butler Papers, Box 101.
53. See Butler Papers, Box 84; telephone interview with Charles F. Fleming, April, 1975.
54. Butler to Crook, August 20, 1950, Butler Papers, Box 84; Bartholomew, *Indiana Third District,* pp. 172-174.
55. Butler Papers, Box 84. Yet in Michigan, Truman gave federal patronage to the governor to keep it from a national committeeman friendly to James Hoffa, and Truman said he believed in patronage going to a governor (interview with Neil Staebler, February 22, 1981).
56. The South Bend *Record ,* January 4, 1952; South Bend *Tribune,* May 17, 1952.

57. Logansport *Pharos-Reporter*, September 9, 1916; Indianapolis *Star*, January 27 and 28, 1975; Barnhart and Carmony, *Indiana*, III, 224.

58. T.J. Costello to Butler, November 3, 1951, Butler Papers, Box 84; Paul G. Willis, "Urges Democrats to Take Offensive," *Chanticleer*, December 12, 1951; Butler to Henry Schricker, January 12, 1952; and Schricker to Butler, January 14, 1952; Butler Papers, Box 84.

59. The South Bend *Record*, January 4, 1952.

60. James R. Noyce to Butler, February 18, 1952; and Butler to State Committee members, February 4, 1952; Butler Papers, Box 84.

61. Butler to Florence Smith, March 24, 1952, Butler Papers, Box 84. Butler to Stephen Mitchell, May 18, 1954, Butler Papers, Box 7, credits the Indianapolis *Times* with exposing McHale and McKinney in 1952, and with helping elect Butler national committeeman. Irving Leibowitz, *Times* reporter was admired by Butler and communicated with him. McHale to Butler, November 29, 1951 (with copy of telegrams to New York *Herald-Tribune* and St. Louis *Post-Dispatch*), Butler Papers, Box 84; South Bend *Tribune*, May 17, 1952. Butler and his friends referred to McHale and McKinney as the "Two Franks" and the "Two Macs," and to McHale as "Keg Head McHale."

62. Butler to Schricker, May 1, 1952, Butler Papers, Box 84.

63. Indianapolis *News*, May 14, 17, and 19, 1952; interviews with Charles Skillen, April and September, 1959; Louisville *Courier-Journal*, August 26, 1960.

64. South Bend *Tribune*, May 17, 1952; Statement of Frank McHale Released to the Press, Saturday, May 17, 1952, Butler Papers, Box 101.

65. Indianapolis *News*, May 19, 1952; South Bend *Tribune*, May 17, 1952.

66. Madden to Butler, May 19, 1952; Martin to Butler, May 20, 1952; Noland to Butler, May 21, 1952; Noel to Butler, May 20, 1952; Butler Papers, Box 101.

67. Bays to Butler, May 20, 1952, Butler Papers, Box 101.

68. The Indianapolis *Star*, January 11, 1974; Barnhart and Carmony, *Indiana*, III, 98; *The Official Program of the 1952 Democratic National Convention* (Chicago: Democratic National Committee, 1952); Frank McKinney to the author, June 28, 1961.

69. Interview with Freda Noble, September 24, 1974; verified by Paul G. Willis.

70. Butler to McKinney, January 17, 1949, Butler Papers, Box 75; Butler to McKinney, June 18, 1952, Butler Papers, Box 101.

Chapter Two

TRANSITION TO NATIONAL POLITICS

The two and one-half years[1] Paul Butler served as national committeeman from Indiana, before his election as national chairman, can most usefully be viewed as a period of transition for him from a local Hoosier politician to a national political leader. The new political friends he made, the broader political horizons he observed, the ideas he encountered, the activities he engaged in, the responsibilities he was charged with, and the innovations he became identified with all helped prepare him politically and intellectually for his service as national chairman, and indeed helped him secure election to that office. While his local political apprenticeship and political outlook influenced the manner in which Butler would respond to problems as national chairman, this transitional period was of even greater importance.[2]

All of these environmental factors reflecting the greater universe will be carefully examined, but attention must first be directed to a parochial matter of great concern to Butler—the seemingly persistent factionalism of the Indiana Democracy, described above, and its effect on his political career. Butler had a natural interest in South Bend and Indiana politics which diminished only gradually because of distance and preoccupation with national affairs after he became chairman. This natural interest was reinforced by his felt need to maintain a local political base. He needed to maintain his coalition on the Indiana Democratic State Committee if he were to win reelection as national committeeman in 1956, and he needed to minimize factional problems which might limit his effectiveness as a member of the Democratic National Committee. This meant attention to the 1954 State Committee reorganization, nominations to be made at two state conventions, and the general mending of political fences after the bruising factional battle of 1952. Butler attuned himself to political developments at the county and district levels by his widespread travels throughout the state, and by extensive correspondence with a network of factional allies, who served as local intelligence agents.[3]

Butler's concern with factionalism required surveillance of the activities of Frank McKinney and Frank McHale. In speeches to

25

Indiana Democrats, Butler continued to castigate "personal selfishness" in party affairs.[4] He successfully urged former Governor Schricker, and others, who desired the maintenance of an active and militant organization in Indiana, to attend a New York party dinner because "the two Franks" would be there, and had no right to be perceived as official party representatives from Indiana.[5]

Party dinners and other fund-raising activities were a continual problem for Butler. In 1953 Butler supported National Chairman Stephen Mitchell's establishment of a National Advisory Council, utilizing localized state fund raisers to help each state meet party financial quotas imposed by the National Committee.[6] Butler coordinated the program in Indiana. Financial quotas had to be met to prevent his embarrassment, yet many traditional contributors were reluctant to assist Butler because they were tied to McKinney and McHale. In 1954 the National Committee sponsored a national conference on the congressional campaign in Indianapolis, an event which attracted many important national Democrats. Staff people were sent to Indiana to work on this $100-a-ticket affair, and Adlai Stevenson, Harry Truman, Lyndon Johnson, and Sam Rayburn were listed on the program. Indiana Democrats had not sought the honor, and Butler, who wanted to sell 500 tickets, saw the "two Franks" holding their hands. Butler told his friends that his blue chips were on the table so that he would be either made or broken—"I believe that McKinney and McHale realize this, and therefore, will do all in their power to sabotage the whole program."[7] One prominent Democrat responded that "My old friend, Frank, should not be that way."[8] Butler hastened to approach his friends for lists of possible ticket purchasers, and invited all the Democratic mayors to attend the conference, while complaining that even those aligned with him factionally sometimes failed to cooperate.[9] In the end, Indiana Democrats responded adequately, and Butler was not embarrassed in the eyes of national party leaders.

In spite of Butler's anxieties, the state party also met its financial quotas in 1953 and 1954, oversubscribing the latter year. Records indicate that Butler made a $500 contribution to the National Committee in 1952, but more importantly his hard work and perseverance in fund-raising, helped along in part by his anxieties, were instrumental to success.[10]

Following soon after Butler's selection as national committeeman, the 1952 Indiana Democratic state convention presented opportunities for factional struggle. Two congressional districts, nominally allied with Butler's faction, defied outgoing Governor Schricker by offering their own candidates for state office. Uninvited, the McKinney-McHale group joined them, and succeeded in winning nominations for two

26

lesser offices, even though Schricker's candidate secured the gubernatorial nomination.[11]

Butler was drawn into congressional factional politics in the 1954 primary election campaign when the Vanderburgh County party chairman, R. Vance Hartke (later mayor of Evansville, and United States Senator), decided that Winfield Denton, an incumbent defeated in 1952, should be denied the congressional nomination. Having already feuded with Hartke over another matter, Butler knew that Denton had supported the Schricker-Butler faction in 1952, and Butler believed that McKinney and McHale were involved in this dispute.[12] Partly because Hartke had several enemies in his own (and Denton's) county, Denton won the nomination.

There were three contests for nomination at the state convention in 1954. The two major factions again opposed each other, and Butler's group prevailed. Butler also served as keynote speaker.

Butler's relations with the state Democratic chairman, Charles Skillen, and Skillen's success, so long as Butler was identified with him, were important to Butler's success in factionalism. As shown below, Butler soon had disagreements with Skillen over campaign methods, and several observers recognized the Butler-Skillen alliance as a marriage of convenience.[13] In February, 1953, Skillen announced plans for retirement because of physical ailments and his doctor's advice. But in a month, still complaining of illness and family problems, Skillen had changed his mind.[14]

The McKinney-McHale group hoped to replace Skillen at the May, 1954 party reorganization meeting, but Skillen was reelected.[15] Butler forgot his differences with Skillen in informing Adlai Stevenson that the faction favoring Stevenson's presidential nomination in 1956 had retained control of the party machinery in Indiana.[16] This control would also favor Butler's retention as national committeeman.

A study of the Democratic National Committee, made in the 1950s, classified Indiana as a state where the national committeeman (Butler) was dominant over the state chairman (Skillen) in party control. Butler's difficulties in Indiana make this dominance seem weak, and the analysis overlooks the role of Governor Schricker in getting both Butler and Skillen into office. Skillen had not entered office as a Butler candidate, but as a Schricker candidate. In response to a questionnaire used in this study, Butler had responded that he considered the state chairman to be the state's political organization leader, since the national committeeman was really a liaison officer between state and national party organizations.[17]

A principal influence on Paul Butler, as he gained a new perspective on politics, while entering a new political world, and one that would facilitate support for his election as national chairman, was his involvement in the draft of Adlai Stevenson as the 1952 presidential candidate, and the subsequent campaign and associations. In April, 1952, Butler wrote Stevenson, informing him he supported him for president.[18] But while Governor Schricker had some contact with those organizing a Stevenson draft, Butler had little until the national convention met in July. The Indiana delegation, with twenty-six votes, selected Butler as its chairman. On July 16 the national committee of the Stevenson organization opened convention headquarters; two days earlier Governor Schricker, a Stevenson admirer, had expressed a desire to make the nomination speech for Stevenson. On the convention's opening day, July 21, Schricker agreed to nominate Stevenson. He and Butler had met with the draft leadership the night before. In a short time, many politicians wanted on the Stevenson bandwagon, and Jacob Arvey, the national commiteeman from Illinois, informed Schricker that Governor Elbert Carvel of Delaware would have the nominating honor. Butler, who knew the draft leaders wanted Schricker for the job, played an important role at this juncture. Butler told Arvey that Schricker would be allowed to make the nomination or Butler would raise the issue before the National Committee. Butler pressured Arvey to agree that in the roll call for nominations Delaware would yield to Indiana, Schricker would nominate Stevenson, and then Carvel would make a second nomination speech. This agreement held and Schricker had the honor.[19] After the convention's adjournment it was speculated that Butler was one "new face" candidate that Stevenson had under consideration for Frank McKinney's replacement as national chairman.[20]

Following the 1952 convention Butler maintained his ties with members of Stevenson's campaign entourage. He had known Wilson Wyatt of Kentucky, Stevenson's personal campaign manager, since 1948.[21] Butler first met Walter Johnson at the convention, but corresponded with him frequently thereafter. When the National Committee met in Chicago in September, 1953, Johnson invited Butler to attend a reunion of the Stevenson draft group, and Stevenson suggested the possibility of "a leisurely talk" at the same time.[22]

In 1954, Johnson, anxious to start rewriting on a manuscript later published as *How We Drafted Adlai Stevenson* , pressed Butler to check matters he had witnessed at the 1952 convention, and offered to come to South Bend for a conference. Johnson finally sent a substantial part of the manuscript to Butler, who entered some corrections in the margin, but did not return the manuscript, which is in the Notre Dame collection of Butler's papers. However, Johnson went to South Bend to discuss the manuscript with Butler.[23]

Butler also successfully urged Stevenson to come to South Bend for a 1954 weekend visit featuring an informal talk at a reception, a press conference, lunch at Butler's home, visitation of a Young

Democrats meeting, and attendance at Presbyterian services. Kidney stone surgery for Stevenson prevented a scheduled April visit, but Stevenson arrived June 26, just after Butler's forces had won complete control of state convention nominations. Butler and Stevenson were joined by Henry Schricker, Chairman Skillen, and the Democratic State Committee. It was speculated that Stevenson's visit would enhance Butler's prospects of succeeding Stephen Mitchell as national chairman. Stevenson expressed high esteem for Butler, but not presuming to state his choice, suggested that there were several acceptable candidates.[24] Butler was widely praised for bringing off the event, one admirer telling him it reflected Butler's "outstanding leadership to the Democratic Party of Indiana."[25]

While Butler had been focusing on such high-level politics and tending to the tedious matter of Indiana party factionalism, he had also been settling into a rigorous pattern of activity, both in Indiana and with the National Committee. This activity required attention, time, and financial outlay. On one hand, the practice of law promised time to pursue politics; on the other hand, his law partners might become concerned with absenteeism, or raise the kinds of objections heard years before about the effects of political activity by members on the firm. But Indiana law firms were often bipartisan in their organization, so as to benefit themselves no matter which political party controlled offices. Therefore the concerns of Butler's partners were not noticeable until he left South Bend for Washington. Court appearances could be shuffled, office absences adjusted for, and some law firm resources put to Butler's political uses.

However, the financial outlay was Butler's alone; there was no state nor national party subsidy for national committee members. In travelling throughout Indiana, and to neighboring states, Butler spent a considerable sum on fuel, automobile depreciation, and lodging. Unless he was the prime speaker at a local event, he might be expected to purchase tickets. He was also expected to make state party contributions and to purchase state dinner tickets. As a member of the National Committee he was also expected to be a contributor and dinner ticket purchaser; he also had travel and other expenses for two or more meetings of the National Committee each year, and for national conventions. These outlays would mean little to wealthy party officials, but could disrupt a family budget for a Paul Butler. Little wonder he welcomed the newly established plan for a steady salary for the national chairman when he assumed that office.

There is no evidence to indicate that any of Butler's predecessors (or successors) as national committeeman equalled his pattern of travel throughout Indiana, 1952-1954. His Indiana mileage during this intense period of party activity was 50,000, with 100-150 meetings a year.[26] He often had the benefit of Mrs. Butler's company and driving skills on these trips.

Butler saw his job as going to as many party meetings as possible and meeting party workers in every county. His energy was described by a district chairman:

> He would drive, fly, or otherwise travel to a Democrat meeting, deliver a stirring speech, confer with local leaders until 2:30 a.m., and pop into the hotel dining room for breakfast at 8, apparently fully refreshed and rested.[27]

In doing what he saw as his job, Butler worked out his theory of intra-party communication and maintained some awareness of factional matters as seen from the local standpoint. Without benefit of any political consulting firm, and as systematically as time and events would permit, he compiled telephone and mailing lists, and carried on a voluminous correspondence with a varied cadre of party and public officials, as well as party workers without title. This arrangement reinforced Butler's notions of the value of widespread participation by party rank and file. Like so many aspects of this transitional period, it would have its effect on his chairmanship.[28]

While Butler tried to bring enthusiasm and encouragement to local party gatherings, he had no national or state patronage to reward the party faithful after January, 1953, when Republican administrations settled in at Washington and Indianapolis. Late in 1952 he tried to get as many postmasterships for Democrats as possible.[29]

Butler had cooperated with political scientists studying the 1952 presidential nominating process; then on his own initiative he surveyed the Indiana national convention delegation, asking for suggestions for improvement in convention operations, which he could bring to the attention of the National Committee.[30] On issues of concern to the Executive Committee of the National Committee, he also sought views of Indiana party leaders.

In 1953, a new version of the *Democratic Digest* was promoted by the National Committee. Like other party workers, Butler took his subscription books to meetings and made *Digest* sales a priority activity, which he urged on other Hoosier Democrats. In South Bend he had young Democrats and others selling subscriptions, while he personally picked up unsold copies of the *Digest* (with the cover torn off) from a news agency for distribution as samples to prospective subscribers. He urged members of the State Committee to promote sales. In large part because of Butler's zeal, Indiana placed third on a quota list for *Digest* subscriptions. Even so, Butler complained, "I am

30

sorry to say that there are many places in Indiana where our organization has not done its job."[31]

Digest sales was not the only area where Butler began to find Indiana party organization unsatisfactory. Butler's increasing dissatisfaction with the dynamism level of the Hoosier Democracy was sharpened by five factors: (1) his experience in South Bend, where party activity, while factional, was nevertheless vigorous; (2) the juxtaposition of the perceived state party situation and his own flurry of activities; (3) his observations of other state party organizations and discussions with other party leaders, which gave him a broader environment within to compare party organizational effectiveness; (4) the concern of Adlai Stevenson and others with the state of national and local Democratic organization from the standpoint of the 1952 election; (5) the emphasis given party reorganization and revitalization by the national chairman, Stephen Mitchell.[32]

As Butler travelled about Indiana, he observed some variety in party organization, activity, and effort at the county level; consequently he soon noticed, if he did not already suspect, that not all county organizations functioned like the one in St. Joseph County. However similarly treated in the election laws, the rural and small town party environment was different from that in large urban places. Keen party competition might best guarantee party vigor. A basic measure of party vitality is the presence of a precinct committeeman, and perhaps one with longevity, yet in some Indiana precincts no candidates filed for the office in the early 1950s, nor were the vacancies always filled by appointment. One-party Republican domination could lead to Democratic atrophy; but even in strongly Democratic counties, the elected precinct committeeman might be incapacitated, yet allowed the title so long as factional realities were suited. In other cases, collusion with Republicans was suggested.[33]

Butler did not expect much help from the state organization in trying to revitalize local party organization because he found little vigor at the state level. This caused him to think more and more about the advantage of a direct relationship between the national party and local organizations. Local political conditions in Indiana were giving Butler a more nationalistic party outlook.

Permanence of party organization in Indiana was found only in the state party headquarters, or office of the State Committee in the Claypool Hotel in Indianapolis, where, around 1952, a suite of rooms was rented for $4,500 a year. About $38,000 was expended annually for salaries of six employees and other headquarters expenses. During campaign periods additional facilities were rented and more employees added (during the 1952 campaign twenty additional employees were paid, and fifteen workers donated time). The state chairman was paid

$7,500 a year, the vice chairman (who worked in headquarters) $4,092, and the chairman's secretary $3,000. Salary cuts were proposed after the 1952 election.[34] For a later period, from June, 1956, through December, 1958, Democrats spent about $72,000 for headquarters personnel salaries, while Republicans spent about $101,000 during six months of the 1958 campaign.[35]

The State Committee itself generally met once a month. It planned party dinners and the state convention program, concerned itself with fundraising, attempted some communication and publicity efforts, and tried to coordinate general election campaign activity. It received auxiliary support from the Indiana Democratic Editorial Association, which held meetings in conjunction with other party events; the Young Democrats of Indiana, organized in some counties and on most college campuses; and the Indiana Women's Democratic Club.

For a year after May, 1951, the State Committee published a free newspaper twice a month for party activists, and at one point, in 1953, distributed *Fact Sheet* for members of the State Committee only. Otherwise, the party depended on local Democratic weekly newspapers, subsidized by legal notices, required by law to be published in newspapers of opposite party affiliation. Democrats had no support comparable to that given Republicans by two Indianapolis daily newspapers, the *Star* and the *News*. Not until 1958 did the State Committee employ a publicity director.

Indiana Democrats had no systematic research facilities in 1952, especially between campaigns, but this is one area where Paul Butler briefly attempted to bring about improvement. In 1952 he recruited Paul Willis, an Indiana University political scientist, to plan a research bureau, looking ahead to the 1954 and 1956 elections. Some money was provided for travel and supplies while the experiment lasted.[36]

Campaign coordination by the State Committee could be an elusive matter, such as in 1956, when the Democratic gubernatorial candidate, alienated from the state chairman, opened separate campaign headquarters and to some extent went his own way in the campaign. Yet in the general election the State Committee published its usual campaign handbook, distributed campaign materials, and coordinated speaking activities and candidate travels.

For fundraising Indiana Democrats depended first on assessments made against county committees, secondly on party dinners, and thirdly on assessments of candidates for nomination at state conventions. Transfers from other committees (state and national) were also helpful. Limits were imposed on the Democratic Party's program in the early 1950s by the extent to which funds could be raised. With no gubernatorial patronage available to Democrats from 1953-1961, the traditional two percent assessment of state employees could not be levied. During the 1958 campaign period, May through November, the Democratic State Committee raised $141,000, while Republicans collected $576,000.

This description of state party activity does not illustrate everything Butler found wrong with the Indiana Democratic organization. He was also concerned with general strategy, technique, and attitude not conveyed by an account of activity and expenditure. Much depended too on Butler's perception of state chairman Charles Skillen, his factional ally of the 1952 reorganization victory, with whom Butler, at first, kept in close contact.[37] Butler, the unsalaried activist, soon developed "basic differences as to political organization" with Skillen, the salaried leader at party headquarters. Skillen "was wedded to the old-fashioned game of power politics and was unwilling to adopt the new, modern techniques of political organization so successfully developed and used in other states politically similar to Indiana."[38] Butler never stopped identifying effective political methods with the type of politics he believed in practicing. He saw his role in Indiana politics as an "effort to develop a responsible and responsive Party organization, based upon effective precinct work, outstanding candidates for public office, honest and decent leadership at all levels, freedom of elected public officials from control by selfish, self-appointed leaders, and the complete elimination from positions of power and influence of men who deal across Party lines to gain their selfish ends."[39] And the antiquated methods of old-style politics and bipartisan, selfish politics went together. Those who resisted modern political techniques, and persisted in serving themselves, had weakened party organization, then wrecked it with factionalism. In the end, Butler's real disgust with Skillen stemmed from Skillen, the beneficiary of Henry Schricker's support, using McKinney-McHale aid when his position became threatened.[40] Ironically, McKinney also believed that the activity and campaign efforts of the Indiana Democratic Party had been inadequate in the 1950s, but he was more inclined to blame Democratic loss of public offices than Skillen for this condition.[41]

In finding Indiana Democratic Party organization wanting, Butler liked to point to Michigan to show what Indiana could be like. He believed the two states had similar political environments—a long period of Republican domination, large industrial centers with strong labor organizations, and broad agricultural areas. Actually, Indiana had been somewhat competitive, Michigan a one-party state for years after the Civil War; and Indiana's urban population was more dispersed, while strong union organization was often lacking in urban areas. Nevertheless, Butler insisted on the similarities, while finding much to admire in Michigan party organization.[42] Butler spoke to Michigan Democratic audiences during his early years on the National

Committee, becoming acquainted with the state chairman, Neil Staebler, in what would become a lasting relationship, and particularly productive in terms of party organization. Michigan Democrats felt they had something to learn from Paul Butler also. Neil Staebler found Butler, as a new member of the National Committee, a person with excellent ideas on party organization, which impressed his colleagues. In 1954, Staebler became one of Butler's leading supporters for national chairman.[43] While Michigan Democrats could better execute some of the organizational ideas Butler had in mind, he still cherished hopes for Indiana, in spite of the futility he often felt.

As a member of the Democratic National Committee, Butler soon gained a reputation as a party organization specialist, as Neil Staebler has observed, by persisting on such matters as handbooks for precinct workers. Butler probably remembered a pamphlet on precinct activity which a Clark County Democratic chairman had written, and which had been distributed to Indiana party workers by the State Committee around 1948.[44] Yet Butler found this, and similar precinct activity guides prepared by the National Committee, inadequate for the politics of the 1950s. In May, 1954, he began pressuring National Committee officials for a handbook on the real duties of a precinct committeeman, arguing that county chairmen and precinct workers wanted such a guide because many did not know their duties and were not getting helpful suggestions from ineffective state party leaders. National Committee officials responded by calling his attention to two publications, *Vote Winner's Note Book* and *The Key to Democratic Victory*. They questioned the need for any other type of publication.[45] Butler liked *Vote Winner's Note Book*, which had just been prepared, but still wanted something better. Lack of enthusiasm on the part of party officials confirmed Butler's views on the inadequacy of party organization (a current concern of Adlai Stevenson also) and increased his impatience with specific individuals at national party headquarters. In two years, after Butler had become national chairman, Neil Staebler's Advisory Committee on Political Organization gave him his handbook, *Democratic Precinct Handbook: Official Manual*, along with a party fact book.

As a member of the National Committee, Butler had other opportunities to exhibit his energy and to demonstrate innovation. As an intelligent political leader, Butler had many ideas concerning political parties and leadership, which came from his rich experience, but he also "soaked up ideas," and he readily admitted not all the ideas he offered were original with him.[46] His ability to discover ideas, accurately analyze situations, listen, and rely on others kept him from remaining just another local politician.

Paul Butler's relationships with several people in Academe helped him at this stage in his career; this is particularly evident in two of the innovations he unsuccessfully championed as a National Committee member in 1953—his proposal for a 1954 midterm convention, and his proposal for a party constitution. These academic relationships can best be illustrated by his association with Paul Willis at Indiana University, and with John Kennedy, Devere Plunkett, and Marshall Smelser at the University of Notre Dame.

In July, 1952, Paul Willis, then an assistant professor of government at Indiana University, asked for Butler's assistance in a study of Indiana's national convention delegation, undertaken under the auspices of the American Political Science Association and with the blessing of the Democratic national chairman, Frank McKinney. Butler promptly cooperated.[47] Although Willis had been active in Monroe County and Seventh District politics against Butler's factional enemies, and in the Stevenson draft movement, and although his wife, Ann Willis, was president of the Monroe County Wilson Club, neither Willis nor his wife had met Butler, who now expressed a desire to meet them. The meeting occurred at a picnic sponsored by the Wilson Club in August, 1952, to which Ann Willis had invited Butler as speaker.[48]

Most of the Notre Dame professors, with whom Butler was acquainted, were involved in local politics, and meeting them was less complicated, particularly with Butler's frequent contacts with Notre Dame. Butler first approached Professor Marshall Smelser, Department of History, in 1953, for help with the midterm convention proposal.

Early in 1953 Butler became a member of the National Committee's Executive Committee, formally established in 1951, and by 1953 an eleven-member group with eight members elected from regions and three chosen as at-large members by the national chairman. Stephen Mitchell appointed Butler, who responded that he was honored by the appointment and the confidence Mitchell had in him, and was privileged to accept appointment from a chairman of such "integrity, ability and unselfish devotion to service of our country through the instrumentality of our party." Butler warned Mitchell he could not be a "yes" man, but he knew Mitchell was "not looking for that type in the regeneration and rejuvenation of our party organization." Since Butler expected only open, direct, and honest differences over method and technique, and not over principles, he pledged cooperation.[49]

Butler first attended an Executive Committee meeting on March 31 and April 1, 1953, being introduced to some important party policy matters on which he had already been briefed. At this meeting the National Advisory Council (on finance) was approved, organizational ideas for the 1954 congressional elections were discussed, and a committee to review party rules and by-laws (to which Butler would be

35

appointed) was authorized. As an item of new business, Butler presented his proposal for a 1954 party convention.[50]

Butler's midterm convention proposal was reported on the front page of the New York *Times*. What stimulated Butler's interest in a midterm convention? As Butler told the Executive Committee, the idea did not originate with him. He cited the recommendations of the American Political Science Association's Committee on Political Parties, President Harry Truman, former national chairman Frank McKinney, and Senator Hubert Humphrey.[51] Others had also suggested the idea to Butler. With Democratic Party fortunes at a low ebb, Butler wanted "a vehicle likely to attract wide notice," which would assist his party and advance his own political career. The convention proposal seemed to best meet these objectives at the moment.[52] But even if there had been discussion of a convention, Butler seized the idea and put it squarely on the party agenda. Even before his appointment to the Executive Committee, Butler was working on a midterm convention plan. Perhaps he had planned to offer it to the full National Committee, but he then saw greater opportunity with the Executive Committee.[53]

He solicited assistance. At Notre Dame, Professor Smelser, assisted by his colleagues John Kennedy, Stephen Ronay, and Devere Plunkett, prepared a draft which anticipated possible objections.[54] It pointed out historical advantages for the out party in midterm elections, focused on the need to give Democrats all possible advantages in 1954, and argued that shifts in control of the House of Representatives had always taken place on a "basis of broad, national issues." With the media's assistance, a convention would attract the attention of voters to the forward-looking party of initiative and action. With a national platform for the campaign, individual candidates could concentrate on local issues, yet benefit from national publicity. The convention would express "dedication of national party responsibility" to the importance of the legislature and the improvement of government. Anticipating the main objection to the convention, that it would produce party disharmony, the draft cautiously argued that a convention could be a vehicle of harmony constructed on a broad base of agreement. Practical consideration was given to time and place, financing, efficient use of media, speakers, entertainment, the conduct of business, and selection of delegates in a manner which would assure effective representation.

The draft, which Professor Willis of Indiana University produced, stressed even more pointedly the national party responsibility concept.[55] Butler was aware of that concept. During one of Butler's Bloomington visits in late 1952 or early 1953, Willis mentioned the American Political Science Association's report on responsible parties, during a discussion of political organization. Butler borrowed the report, which

36

is now in the collection of Butler papers at Notre Dame, with red pencil markings (probably those of Paul Willis), stressing sections on biennial conventions, a party policy council, relationships between national party committees and congressional campaign committees, and the national committee as a reflection of actual party strength in states. At this point in his academic career, Professor Willis offered seminars which focused on party structure, discipline, and finance, and how centralizing devices could overcome the localism resulting from legal-constitutional provisions affecting the party system. Attention was given to a proposed Democratic Party constitution, which provided for a foundation of national party structure and regulations. Party membership, based on both individuals and state parties, was proposed. Such devices could make for national party supremacy.[56] Willis discussed such matters with Butler, but has cautioned that he doubts Butler was consciously pursuing a well integrated philosophy of party responsibility.[57]

The Willis draft of a midterm convention proposal stressed changeless party machinery while America had rapidly become urbanized with national social and economic problems. Parties must follow the example set by interest groups, and realize that the focus of political power was national. Campaign issues should be national in scope, and a midterm convention would draw national attention to the Democratic Party. By taking advantage of the absence of presidential coattails in 1954, a convention could overcome a lack of money and publicity, personify the party, and enable it to speak clearly. Disagreement within party ranks should be identified well in advance of the next presidential election. Like the Smelser draft, the Willis draft concerned itself with time and place, delegate selection, cost, staging, and anticipated objection to the convention idea. Finally, the convention should "formulate a simple, comprehensive statement of party policy," with room enough for candidates to maneuver. The convention should also concern itself with the development of "more effective permanent national party organization."

Butler very effectively combined the Smelser and Willis drafts for a 1954 midterm convention proposal, using the best of each, for his own strong and coherent version presented to the Executive Committee.[58] The national committeewoman from California was very much impressed with Butler's presentation. His notes from his meeting also furnish some insight into the nature of the opposition immediately encountered. The convention would be costly, unappreciated by the rank and file, and publicize party disagreements. Chairman Mitchell suggested less difficulty of acceptance if the notion of a convention could be changed to that of a party conference.[59]

Butler did not ask the Executive Committee to decide the midterm convention issue immediately; instead he asked that the proposal be publicized and referred to a committee of Democratic members of Congress, which would make recommendations to the Executive Committee for further recommendations to the National Committee. Actually, a resolution referring the proposal to a joint congressional-National Committee group was adopted. Chairman Mitchell quickly appointed the committee, noting that "This novel proposal was considered too important for unstudied . . . discussion."[60]

Butler did not want Stephen Mitchell to get involved directly with the midterm convention proposal because of the opposition it soon aroused, but Mitchell had indicated his support privately.[61] One of Mitchell's associates at this time remembers that Mitchell knew that many party professionals did not support the biennial convention concept; he was unwilling to call it his own proposal, but he privately encouraged Butler to develop the idea for presentation to the Executive Committee.[62]

The research division of the National Committee widely distributed copies of Butler's convention proposal to all Democrats in Congress, many newspapers, and party leaders, with requests for comments. Butler was advised that newspapers and news commentators had given the idea much publicity, and that a number of members of Congress had publically discussed the proposal. Apparently this media attention confirmed a practical argument for holding a midterm convention. In letters to Indiana Democrats and to newspapers, Butler expressed his desire to obtain opinions on the convention proposal, favorable or unfavorable, for presentation to the committee studying the matter. He reminded Frank McKinney of his earlier approval of the idea and solicited his frank views of the proposal, while admitting to McKinney that there were "some real problems in connection with such an idea." Butler wrote Paul Willis:

> Of course, it would be much easier for a Congressman to run in an off-year election without being tied down to a party platform. A good many of them are not much concerned about the improvement of governmental processes through the development of greater party responsibility to the voters.[63]

Butler detected particular objections from "Dixiecrats and hard-shelled conservatives from the South," and from Republicans and the South Bend *Tribune,* who feared a 1954 convention would assist Democrats.

Support for the convention was generated from Senators Hubert Humphrey and Estes Kefauver, Jack Croll of the CIO's Political Action

Committee, The American Political Science Association's Committee on Political Parties, Walter Johnson, the Indiana CIO, and some members of the Indiana Democratic State Committee.[64]

Butler learned that the Executive Committee would meet in Chicago, September 14 and 15, 1953, in conjunction with the National Committee, to receive committee reports, including the report on his midterm convention proposal.[65] Stephen Mitchell suggested that Butler inquire as to exactly how the proposal would be considered. Butler found out he would appear separately before the congressional and the National Committee sections of the committee studying his proposal; he was also told that Sam Rayburn was opposed. Butler promised to outline his plan, without lobbying, and to accept the decision.[66] In Chicago the two sections of the committee met jointly, with Sam Rayburn and Governor William Marland of West Virginia presiding. Their decision was accepted by the Executive Committee. Butler was complimented "for his excellent presentation of the proposal," which would continue to be studied, it was hoped. The report continued:

> . . . the problems of cost and of many state party regulations make it inadvisable that the National Committee contemplate holding a Mid-term Convention in 1954 . . . our own party should concentrate on conferences and meetings of a regional and topical nature to bring the issues clearly to the people and to plan programs and efforts leading to the strengthening of our party in our States and Nation.[67]

After six months of effort, Butler probably found little consolation in these words.

A month before the Chicago meeting, Robert Riggs, writing for the Louisville *Courier-Journal*, noted that while many Democrats might be interested in a 1954 platform for congressional candidates, the civil rights problem might cause the country to see Democrats fighting on issues, thus negating the practical argument that a midterm convention would attract media attention.[68] Indeed, the midterm convention issue was related to concerns about party loyalty, civil rights, and the South. In fact, Butler was at the time a member of a committee studying party rules, and the more he became interested in rules the more he was taken by the midterm convention idea, as well as general ideas of party centralization. All these notions, in turn, raised Southern fears, and the dominant tendencies at the Chicago meeting had been directed toward the amelioration of Southern feelings about the Democratic Party.

The roots of concern with loyalty went back at least to the 1948 Dixiecrat revolt, and certainly to the 1952 convention, which had adopted the Moody Resolution (sponsored by Senator Blair Moody of

39

Michigan).[69] The Moody Resolution, in effect a credentials resolution, provided that delegates not willing to give assurance that they would use their official capacities to secure ballot placement for the convention's presidential nominee (or for electors) would not be seated. Exceptions were made in 1952 if state law or instructions from party bodies would have to be contravened. The convention eventually voted to seat three Southern delegations held to be in violation of the Moody rule, and the forces supporting Adlai Stevenson gave strong assistance to the South (the Indiana delegation, chaired by Paul Butler, voted to seat the Virginia delegation).

After the 1952 election, when some Southern Democrats supported the Republican presidential candidate, the loyalty oath remained as part of the rules applicable to the 1956 convention. However disloyal some Southern Democrats had been, moderate Southern party leaders were rankled by the requirement for a loyalty oath for convention delegates. Because these moderates had shown loyalty, their pleas for repeal of the Moody rule were listened to. The moderates were particularly heard by the Stevenson-Mitchell wing of the Democratic Party, which saw Southern reconciliation as part of the task of harmonizing, rebuilding, and financing the party. Southern moderates trusted Mitchell, who gained more trust while touring the South.

At Mitchell's request, the Executive Committee of the National Committee, at the first meeting Butler attended, executed authority granted by the 1952 convention and authorized appointment of a committee to study National Committee rules. It became known as the Committee to Review the Rules and By-Laws Governing the Democratic National Committee, and Butler was a member. Why was this committee established? Ostensibly, Mitchell was troubled by "deficiencies and ambiguities" in the existing rules, and was interested in formalizing and streamlining the rules.[70] In 1951, chairman Frank McKinney had pointed out that the Democratic Party had "no constitution, by-laws, organizational structure, or rules of procedure, except for a compilation of precedents prepared every four years . . . for use at the National Convention."[71] Mitchell was also confronting the problem of the legality of the National Committee unseating its own members who had failed to support Stevenson. In this way, the matter of loyalty intruded, and would eventually dominate consideration of party rules.[72]

However much Butler may have desired party harmony (and he did wish to please Stevenson and Mitchell), his interest in party rules and his membership on the rules review committee appeared to inevitably drive him toward party nationalizing proposals which implied loyalty. Butler's interest in party rules afforded him a means of becoming

40

exceptionally well informed on rules—a political advantage—and identified him with progressive objectives.[73]

Butler lost no time in moving on the rules question. The day after his appointment to the review committee had been announced, he informed Mitchell that he wanted to collect the rules of all state committees to see what these rules prescribed for party memberships; he was interested in how far the national party could go in touching such matters as party membership—an approach certain to raise concerns of those troubled by focus on the loyalty issue.[74] About this time, Butler sent Paul Willis a proposed party constitution of unknown authorship, which Willis eventually revised and shaped into his own version of a party constitution.[75] The constitution Willis received was prefaced with a citation of the American Political Science Association's Committee on Political Parties report on party responsibility; its provisions were extremely nationalistic. A state party could affiliate with the "Democratic National Party of the United States" only if the national party bodies found the state party's purpose compatible with that of the national party and if its structure and operation were democratic. National party purpose paralleled the Preamble of the United States Constitution. National conventions would meet biennially, and a loyalty oath would require delegates to pledge support of presidential nominees. Supreme party authority would be vested in the national convention, with the National Committee authorized to act between conventions. National Committee members, serving two-year terms, could be expelled "for cause," and opposition to presidential nominees would constitute grounds for expulsion. This proposed constitution could be approved and amended by a majority of convention delegates. Butler and Willis discussed party membership and loyalty, including the possibility of dropping the term "loyalty" from both rules and discussion of rules.[76]

Willis also received a request from James Sundquist, then assistant to Chairman Mitchell. While Sundquist's main responsibility was in the areas of research and policy, he was also privy to headquarters discussion of party organization and rules. He advised Willis that Mitchell had asked the American Political Science Association to solicit its members for ideas on party membership and loyalty. Willis responded that he and Butler had been discussing such matters "in relation to the problem of adopting rules governing the national party," and that he would prepare, at Butler's request, a report on this problem. Willis also suggested the possibility of the national party registering its name and emblem (Willis preferred the Indiana Democratic Rooster) so that recalcitrant state parties could be barred from their use.[77] Sundquist remembers discussions of the loyalty question with Mitchell and deputy chairman Hy Raskin at this time; Willis believes Butler was also involved in similar discussions with Mitchell and Raskin. Since Mitchell and his associates were not discouraging those who considered nationalistic party rules, which would have provoked even moderate Southerners, it seems likely that Mitchell was forced into a more conciliatory position publicly than he preferred privately.[78]

The more Willis worked at preparing a report on party membership and loyalty for Butler in the summer of 1953, the more he was inclined to take a broader view of his task. After all, the Democratic Party was one of the few national institutions without a body of fundamental rules governing it; therefore, it had an uncertain politico-legal existence. Such a legalistic assessment impressed lawyer Butler, who then asked Willis to draft a party constitution.[79]

Professor Willis sent Butler his draft constitution late in August.[80] Among its "basic assumptions" were these: (1) it was consistent with Butler's midterm convention proposal; (2) the National Democratic Party (truly representative) was to be federal, not confederate, in structure; (3) with dual citizenship in the United States, the national party would be supported by both state party organizations and the people; (4) the constitution would be flexible, yet provide stability; (5) an organization must exist in perpetuity, facilitate compromise, and expect basic agreement and acceptance from its members once disagreement had been resolved by majority decision. Willis cautioned Democrats to remember:

> Once before in the Party's history a Southern minority seized control of the Party largely because alternative leadership abdicated its responsibilities. As a consequence the Party was wrecked and fifty years, a half century, was required to rebuild it.
> This must not be permitted to occur again!

Willis proposed this constitution for THE DEMOCRATIC PARTY, with the Rooster as symbol; the name and symbol to be reserved exclusively for party members, either state parties or individuals. The constitution called for biennial national conventions (Butler's proposal to the Executive Committee was cited) with delegates required to sign a loyalty oath. Delegates would be partially selected by a state's National Committee members, who also would be required to sign a loyalty oath (cleverly, these oaths were justified by reference to primary election laws and regulations, applying to voters and candidates in ten Southern states). The National Committee would be expanded by the addition of members of Congress and appointees of a Democratic president or the national chairman. The constitution would be effective with affirmative votes of two-thirds of the delegates at a national convention; amendments, once approved by thirty members of the National Committee, would be ratified by a majority of delegates at a national convention.

Butler went to the September, 1953 National Committee meeting in Chicago, knowing that the Executive Committee would receive reports from both the rules review committee, of which he was a member, and the committee studying his midterm convention proposal. By bringing along a proposed party constitution, Butler had gone far beyond mere revision of existing party rules. However, there is no record that Butler unveiled his constitution in Chicago, or anywhere else. The compromise atmosphere on matters of rules and loyalty, prevailing in Chicago, probably made Butler feel it prudent to withdraw from innovation for the moment, and especially after his convention proposal had been rejected. The National Committee's counsel, Harold Levanthal, later recounted the situation, noting that the function of the committee established to review National Committee rules was greatly misconceived, so that the 1952 convention rule affecting loyalty, rather than rules of the National Committee, became the focus.[81] At any rate, Southerners pressed for repeal of the Moody rule, and the result was creation of yet another committee by the rules review committee. It would make recommendations for the 1956 convention, and study what was now labelled the "mis-called loyalty oath."[82] Not until 1957, by which time Butler had become national chairman, did the National Committee adopt its own rules.

While the issues of a midterm convention and a party constitution would not be revived, as such, during Butler's time as national chairman, the Democratic Advisory Council, a between-conventions policy-pronouncing body, was established in 1957. Twenty-one years after Butler's unsuccessful venture with conventions and constitutions, the 1974 Kansas City Democratic midterm convention, or conference, adopted a party charter.

NOTES

1. He continued to serve as Indiana's Democratic national committeeman until the 1960 convention, having been reelected in 1956, holding this office simultaneously with that of national chairman.
2. An undated story in the local history files of the South Bend Public Library, from the South Bend *Tribune*, said that Butler's

professional control in South Bend had been observed by national party leaders before he was selected national chairman.

3. See letters, clippings, scrapbooks, and telephone lists in Butler Papers, Boxes 2, 75, 80, 83, 105, 106, 169, and 170.

4. Von Eichhorn to Butler, May 27, 1953, Butler Papers, Box 81.

5. Butler to Schricker, January 29, 1953, Butler Papers, Box 81.

6. See material in Butler Papers, Boxes 74, 76, and 103. Butler had between thirty and forty members of the Indiana Advisory Council to assist him.

7. Butler to Hugh Vandiver, August 20, 1954, Butler Papers, Box 104. For anxiety over the dinner results, see Butler to Stanley H. Woodward, October 1, 1954, Butler Papers, Box 104.

8. Eugene B. Crowe to Butler, August 16, 1954, Butler Papers, Box 104.

9. Butler to Mrs. Kenneth Luckett, July 3, 1953, Butler Papers, Box 80.

10. Financial information and fragments of reports can be found in the Butler Papers, Boxes 15, 82, 103, and 104.

11. Indianapolis *News*, June 24, 1952; Paul G. Willis, "Indiana, The Democratic Delegation," *Presidential Nominating Politics in 1952*, ed. Paul T. David, Malcolm Moos, and Ralph M. Goldman (Baltimore: The Johns Hopkins Press, 1954), IV, 91.

12. See letters to district committee members from Butler, March 22, 1954, Butler Papers, Box 106; Butler to Frances Luckett, November 5, 1953, Butler Papers, Box 80; Evansville *Courier*, April 10, 19, and 27, 1954.

13. Mace Broide to Butler, December 7, 1954, Butler Papers, Box 2.

14. Skillen to Butler, February 18, 1953; and Democratic State Headquarters Press Release, March 26, 1953; both in Butler Papers, Box 80.

15. Indianapolis *News*, May 11, 12, 13, 14, and 16, 1954.

16. Butler to Stevenson, May 18, 1954, Butler Papers, Box 80.

17. Bancroft C. Henderson, The Democratic National Committee (Ph.D. dissertation, University of Minnesota, Minneapolis, 1958); Butler to Henderson, March 21, 1957, Butler Papers, Box 7.

18. Butler to Stevenson, April 12, 1952, Butler Papers, Box 101. John B. Martin, *Adlai Stevenson of Illinois: The Life of Adlai Stevenson* (Garden City, New York: Doubleday and Company, 1976), p. 484, indicates Stevenson made a favorable impression on Butler, and others, at the August, 1951, Midwest Conference of Democrats held at French Lick, Indiana.

19. Walter Johnson, *How We Drafted Adlai Stevenson* (New York: Alfred A. Knopf, 1955), pp. 64, 101, 111, 137-140.

20. South Bend *Tribune*, August 8, 1952.

21. Probably through Americans for Democratic Action, which Wyatt served as President. See Butler Papers, Box 75.

22. Butler to Walter Johnson, September 3, 1953, Butler Papers, Box 81; *Stevenson Papers*, IV, 268.

23. Johnson to Butler, March 15 and 30, 1954, Butler Papers, Box 74; Walter Johnson to the author, October 29, 1974.

24. South Bend *Tribune*, June 23, 24, and 27, 1954.

25. Richard Cornes to Butler, June 28, 1954, Butler Papers, Box 80.

26. Butler to Bancroft Henderson, March 21, 1957, Butler Papers, Box 7. See Butler's Appointment Book for 1953, and as projected for 1954, called "Week at a Glance Jr."—the book was printed for 1952, but has dates adjusted for 1953, Butler Papers, Box 7. In November, 1953, he attended eight meetings in five congressional districts, in December, five in four districts, and in February and March, 1954, nineteen in several districts.

27. Paul Hillsamer, Marion *News-Herald*, January 5, 1962; Butler to Joseph Eichhorn, May 13, 1953, Butler Papers, Box 80; Butler to David Eilert, November 17, 1953. Butler also spoke to Americans for Democratic Action in Indianapolis, Roosevelt Day, January, 1953 (Butler is supposed to have affiliated with ADA at the state level, about 1948, on the urging of some colleagues in South Bend), Butler Papers, Box 76.

28. See telephone cards, Butler Papers, Box 197; correspondence in Boxes 80, 101, 104, 105, and 106; and address cards, Box 82.

29. See Box 102, Butler Papers.

30. Paul T. David (ed.), *Presidential Nominating Politics*; Paul Willis to Butler, July 5 and 14, 1952, Butler Papers, Box 102; letters to delegation, August 26, 1952, Butler Papers, Box 10.

31. Butler to John Hoving, August 12, 1954, Butler Papers, Box 82. In Box 82 are also receipts for *Digest* subscriptions sold at a June, 1953, district meeting. Stephen Mitchell to Butler, February 14, 1954, Butler Papers, Box 82.

32. On concern with party organization see Edward P. Doyle (ed.), *As We Knew Adlai* (New York: Harper and Row, 1966), pp. 84-86; Stephen Mitchell, *Elm Street Politics* (New York: Oceana Publication, 1959); Adlai Stevenson to Alicia Patterson, November 6, 1952, *Stevenson Papers*, IV, 193, mentioning "the moribund Democratic organization"; Harry Truman to Adlai Stevenson, November 7, 1952, ibid., IV, 198, wanting Stevenson to revitalize the National Committee; Stevenson to Stuart G. Brown, November 28, 1952, ibid., IV, 204-205; Stevenson to Dwight Palmer, December 7, 1952, ibid., IV, 215-216; Stevenson to Stephen Mitchell, December 8, 9152, ibid., IV, 216-217, in which Stevenson mentions Butler as one of the party leaders who might come to Washington for a few weeks of survey and analysis of state party organizations. Stevenson had come to see Michigan and Wisconsin as examples of Democratic Party revitalization which other states could follow, and Butler came to have similar feelings (see Stevenson to Richard J. Daley,

March 1, 1953, ibid., IV, 261-262; also Stevenson to James E. Doyle (telegram), December 9, 1952, IV, 218-219.

33. See Roberts, The Democratic Party of Indiana, on the Democratic Party in three Indiana counties in the 1950s, particularly p. 185 on incapacitation, and p. 146 on collusion. See also Mitchell, *Elm Street Politics*, p. 83.

34. Information for 1952 in Butler Papers, Box 101, along with a letter from a State Committee staff member to Butler, November 17, 1952.

35. Roberts, The Democratic Party, Chapter II, shows the financial condition for this period. Party records are usually considered personal property by party officers, and are often destroyed when leadership changes occur; scholars are not often allowed access to such records, although financial reports are supposed to be filed in public offices. Unfortunately, little financial data on Indiana Democrats exists for the 1952-1955 period.

36. Butler to Willis, November 17, 1952, Butler Papers, Box 101; Russell Wise to Willis, January 24, 1953; and Willis to Butler, June 4, 1953; Butler Papers, Box 80.

37. Butler said he talked on the telephone to Skillen two or three times a week during campaign periods (Butler to Bancroft Henderson, March 21, 1957, Butler Papers, Box 7).

38. Paul Butler to the author, July 5, 1961; *Minutes*, Indiana Democratic State Central Committee, August 25, 1956 contains Butler's remark on the outdatedness of billboards—in 1952 about as much was spent on posters and billboards as on radio and television.

39. Paul Butler to the author, July 5, 1961.

40. Ibid.

41. Frank McKinney to the author, June 28, 1961.

42. Robert L. Sawyer, Jr., *The Democratic State Central Committee in Michigan, 1949-1959: The Rise of the New Politics and the New Political Leadership* (Ann Arbor: Institute of Public Administration, The University of Michigan, 1960), pp. 124-128.

43. Neil Staebler to Butler, September 24, 1953, Butler Papers, Box 80; and Butler to John Hoving, August 12, 1954, Box 82; interviews with Neil Staebler, December 15, 1980, and February 22, 1981.

44. Interview with Elmer Hoehn, August, 1959.

45. The *Note Book* was devised in 1954, and the *Key* revised that year. Hugh A. Bone, *Party Committees and National Politics* (Seattle: University of Washington Press, 1958), p. 109, reports that the Office of Women's Activities served the entire headquarters in preparation of materials on campaign organization and techniques. See also Butler to Hy Raskin, May 18, 1954; Butler to Katie Louchheim, May 19, 1954; and Louchheim to Butler, May 25, 1954; Butler Papers, Box 104.

46. Telephone interview with John Kennedy, June 29, 1977; Paul G. Willis to the author, February 8, 1975.

47. Willis to Butler, July 5, 1952; copy of McKinney to Paul T. David, March 28, 1952; Butler to Willis, July 14, 1952; all in Butler Papers, Box 102.

48. Paul G. Willis to the author, February 8, 1975.

49. Butler to Mitchell, March 24, 1953, Butler Papers, Box 76.

50. Stephen Mitchell to Butler, March 20, 1953; Mitchell to Butler, April 9, 1953; Butler's notes for March 31 and April 1, 1953; Mitchell's report to National Committee members, April 22, 1953; all in Butler Papers, Box 76.

51. A Democratic National Convention in 1954?, a paper presented by Paul M. Butler to the Executive Committee of the Democratic National Committee, March 31 and April 1, 1953, Butler Papers, Box 204. Appendix B cites a letter from President Truman to Representative Jacob Javits (New York *Times*, March 2, 1952), with Truman calling the off-year platform for congressional candidates an "excellent idea"; McKinney to Senator Hubert Humphrey (New York *Times,* May 4, 1952), finding merit in a biennial national convention. Butler also noted that two sets of Republican leaders had issued party principle statements in 1950. The APSA report mentioned Woodrow Wilson's interest in a similar convention, and Butler might also have cited Alfred E. Smith's belief that the National Committee should have spoken out on important issues between 1928 and 1932. See also *The Development of National Party Policy Between Conventions* (Washington: Republican National Committee, 1966); Oscar Hanlin, *Al Smith and His America* (Boston: Little, Brown, and Company, 1958), pp. 151-152;*Toward A More Responsible Two-Party System* (Washington: American Political Science Association, 1950).

52. Paul G. Willis to the author, February 8, 1975.

53. Butler to Robert Hoover, March 26, 1953, Butler Papers, Box 76.

54. A National Convention in 1954?, Butler Papers, Box 81. Also Smelser to Butler, March 27, 1953; Butler to Kennedy and Smelser, April 23, 1953; in Butler Papers, Box 81; interview with Marshall Smelser, September 24, 1954; telephone Interview with John Kennedy, June 29, 1977.

55. A Democratic National Convention in 1954?, Butler Papers, Box 81. See also Willis to Butler, March 26, 1953 (an outline of the convention proposal), Butler Papers, Box 80.

56. Seminar notes in author's collection.

57. Paul G. Willis to the author, November 17, 1975.

58. The Notre Dame draft people and Willis did not know each other at this time, and all were unaware that Butler had sought advice elsewhere. Yet both drafts cover enough similar points to suggest that Butler may have provided the same guidelines for

each draft. Strangely enough, neither draft cited the widespread use of biennial conventions in the states, nor other state party institutions used to issue platform declarations. For instance, Indiana parties nominated candidates for state office every two years and adopted a platform. In any such election year, one hundred and twenty-five of one hundred and fifty state legislators faced reelection.

59. Clara Shirpser to Edward Litchfield, June 26, 1953, Butler Papers, Box 81; Butler notes in Box 76.

60. Mitchell's Report to Members of the Democratic National Committee and State Chairman, April 22, 1953, Butler Papers, Box 76.

61. Butler to Walter Johnson, July 10, 1953, Butler Papers, Box 80; Edward Litchfield to Butler, April 27, 1953, Butler Papers, Box 81.

62. James Sundquist to the author, October 23, 1974; Mitchell to Butler, April 8 and 9, 1953, Butler Papers, Box 76.

63. Butler to Ann and Paul Willis, April 17, 1953, Butler Papers, Box 81. See also Butler to Frank McKinney, April 20, 1953, and similar letters to others.

64. Butler Papers, Box 81.

65. Stephen Mitchell to Butler, August 14, 1953, Butler Papers, Box 81.

66. Butler to Kenneth Burkhead, September 2, 1953, Butler Papers, Box 81.

67. Press release, Democratic National Committee, September 14, 1953, Butler Papers, Box 81.

68. August 18, 1953.

69. For an excellent discussion of the loyalty problem during Butler's 1952-1960 period, see Abraham Holtzman, *The Loyalty Pledge Controversy in the Democratic Party* (New York: McGraw-Hill Book Company, 1960).

70. Mitchell to Butler, March 20, 1953; Mitchell's Report to Members of the Democratic National Committee and State Chairmen; both in Butler Papers, Box 76.

71. Document, dated October 31, 1951, in Butler Papers, Box 83.

72. Holtzman,*The Loyalty Pledge Controversy*, pp. 6-7.

73. Paul G. Willis to the author, February 8, 1975.

74. Butler to Mitchell, May 19, 1953, Butler Papers, Box 83.

75. This document must have come from those associated with the National Committee concerned with membership and loyalty questions, and perhaps from Harold Leventhal, Counsel. See Willis to Butler, May 30, 1953, Butler Papers, Box 83; Paul G. Willis to the author, July 23, 1977.

76. Willis to Butler, June 4, 1953, Butler Papers, Box 80; Willis to Butler, May 30, 1953, Butler Papers, Box 83.

77. James Sundquist to the author, October 23 and December 10, 1974; Willis to Butler, May 30, 1953, Butler Papers, Box 83;

Paul G. Willis to the author, February 8, 1975, and July 23, 1977.

78. See National Committee Counsel Harold Leventhal's comments: *Official Report of the 1960 Democratic National Convention and Committee* (Washington: National Documents Publishers, 1964), pp. 378-379.

79. Paul G. Willis to the author, July 23, 1977.

80. Willis to Butler, August 28, 1953; and Constitution of the Democratic Party of the United States; both in Butler Papers, Box 83.

81. *Official Report of the 1960 Democratic National Convention and Committee*, pp. 378-379.

82. Holtzman, *The Loyalty Pledge Controversy*, pp. 7-10.

Chapter Three

ELEVATION TO NATIONAL LEADERSHIP

It is difficult to say how disappointed Butler was with the fate of his innovations at Chicago, September, 1953, and he was still aligned with the Stevenson-Mitchell forces which were conciliatory toward the South on the loyalty issue. Perhaps the next several months were not conducive to more innovation on Butler's part; party unity, party successes in special elections, and the approaching 1954 congressional elections attracted attention. Butler was less identified in 1954 with some of the kinds of activity he had undertaken earlier.

At the same time, Butler's name began to be mentioned frequently as a successor to national chairman Stephen Mitchell. After the 1952 election, the anti-Stevenson wing of the Democratic Party, and some Stevenson supporters, began to find fault with Mitchell's leadership. In August, 1953, Stevenson found it necessary to proclaim his support of Mitchell, in the face of efforts to replace him.[1] By mid-1954, Stevenson believed Mitchell would resign after the congressional elections, and Stevenson did not feel he could persuade Mitchell to remain because it might give the appearance of Stevenson trying to control the party organization for his own benefit.[2]

As early as November, 1952, Walter Johnson, complaining of "tired, sick, and old leaders," such as Jacob Arvey and David Lawrence, had suggested to Butler that men like James Finnegan of Philadelphia and Butler were good national chairman material.[3] At least as early as April, 1954, Butler was thinking about the chairmanship and responding favorably to suggestions in the press and in letters that he should be chairman.[4] He informed one supporter that Mitchell was his close friend, and that Mitchell believed he had the qualities a party leader needed. He wondered, though, how far Mitchell could proceed in recommending a successor. Butler concluded that he was not a candidate and was not counting on being chosen chairman.[5]

As in 1952, when he chose Mitchell, Stevenson in 1954 wanted to continue the recent practice of having an Irish Catholic national chairman, and Butler was one of those advising him to continue the tradition.[6] Stevenson kept ranking Butler, a "new look" type whom he

51

was "coming to know well," at or near the top of his list of preferences, although he believed Butler "physically not strong," and worried about "some difficulties in the Indiana organization."[7] Wilson Wyatt wrote Butler, "Adlai and I have talked on several occasions about you—and I can assure you that you could have eavesdropped with pleasure."[8]

Butler gradually became more serious in his quest for the chairmanship. By the end of September, 1954, when responding to an offer of assistance from a Montana judge and Notre Dame alumnus, Butler asked for a friendly word to be passed on to the Montana national committeeman. While Butler was "not an active candidate," he would not decline if it were "the will of a majority of the members" of the national committee that he be Mitchell's successor.[9]

The more serious Butler became about the chairmanship the more he worried about the difficulties in the Indiana organization which Stevenson had noted. Butler had intimated that the McKinney-McHale alliance had sent money to South Bend to aid Butler's local opponents in the May, 1954, primary election. After the success of the September congressional dinner in Indianapolis, sponsored by the National Committee, the opposing faction had supposedly circulated the idea that a large crowd had been attracted only because $100 tickets had been reduced to $7.50. The State Committee admitted that about two hundred tickets had been distributed to local organizations.[10]

Butler certainly saw McKinney as the explanation for what was reported to be former President Truman's opposition to him as chairman. Butler addressed his concern to Stanley Woodward, treasurer of the Democratic National Committee, who planned to resign with Mitchell, so that the new chairman could name his choice as treasurer. Butler pointed out that Joseph and Stewart Alsop's newspaper column had reported Butler's unacceptability to Truman, but believed the Alsops had been misled into thinking this message had come from Truman personally. Butler thought some of McKinney's friends were really responsible. He indicated interest in the results of any conversations between Woodward and Truman. Butler told Woodward that while Butler was expendable as a politician, the new political look of the party should continue.[11] Woodward had, coincidentally, written Truman four days earlier, reporting his observations on the Indianapolis National Committee meeting and conversations he had engaged in there. Michael DiSalle of Ohio, James Finnegan of Pennsylvania, Congressman Hale Boggs of Louisiana, and "Paul Butler, our much respected, genial and untiring host, and National Committeeman in Indiana" had been mentioned for chairman, and "Butler's name seemed to head the list." Woodward bluntly stated that Frank McKinney did not like Butler and this was Butler's "only 'imperfection.'" Woodward hoped Truman would not veto Butler's selection as he feared McKinney would request.[12] Woodward then forwarded a copy of this letter marked PERSONAL to Butler (as well as to Mitchell and Stevenson), and praised Butler effusively for his role in making the Indianapolis gathering such a party financial success.[13] In spite of the anxieties the Indianapolis affair had caused Butler, its success had enhanced his reputation among the party leaders who had assembled to hear Adlai Stevenson open the 1954 campaign with an anti-McCarthy speech.[14]

Former National Chairman Frank Walker also wrote to Truman and sent Butler a copy of the letter. Butler then asked Walker to approach Carmine De Sapio, New York's national committeeman, for support of Butler for chairman. Butler felt he already had the support of Averell Harriman, the Democratic gubernatorial candidate. Butler attributed Frank McKinney's opposition to the defeat of McKinney and Frank McHale in one state committee meeting and two state conventions, and to McKinney's distaste for another Hoosier Democrat succeeding him as chairman so soon.[15]

Democratic success in the 1954 congressional elections (although not in Indiana) brought more Democratic governors and restored Democratic control of both houses of Congress; it also brought praise for Adlai Stevenson. Party success and a desire for unity, as well as hope for continued gains in 1956, created the atmosphere for the meeting of the National Committee in New Orleans, December 4, 1954, held there as part of the continuing courting of Southern Democrats.[16] Mitchell announced his resignation at the meeting, so the main order of business became the election of a national chairman.[17] The meeting was opened to the press and the public. When the roll of the states was called for nominations, Alabama yielded to Louisiana, whose Congressman Hale Boggs praised Mitchell before nominating Butler. Boggs lauded Butler for having an "appreciation of the national scope of the Democratic Party," and noted that Butler was known to all the committee members. Two members of the National Committee seconded Butler's nomination. Alabama's national committeewoman reiterated Butler's fairness to all elements in the party. Members of the National Committee had been provided with a reprint from the Indiana *Democrat*, urging Butler's election and attesting that he was popular with party workers, fair and unprejudiced, for unity, and willing to work hard. Only the "has-beens" in Indiana politics were jealous.[18] The names of Michael DiSalle of Ohio, F. Joseph Donohue of the District of Columbia, and James Finnegan of Pennsylvania were also presented. On the roll call, Butler received seventy of the one hundred five votes cast.

In acknowledging his election, Butler praised Mitchell and his defeated opponents, and told his colleagues he was proud to have been supported by all sections:

I believe that our Party is a national Party, and I believe it with all my heart. I am against any sectionalization of our Party by any issue, activity or any proceeding in the Democratic Party, and I shall attempt to serve the Party and all members of the Party, all sections of our country, with the same degree of understanding and appreciation of problems in their local areas as they certainly are entitled to at all times.

Butler, pleased by almost solid Southern support, informed the press that he was glad the loyalty oath from the 1952 convention would be abandoned, and in response to a question concerning segregation, he responded, "That's not a political issue."[19] He also charged that President Eisenhower lacked the capacity to govern and unite the country, and that a military career was not a full preparation for public office. This type of criticism would make Butler stand out among Democratic politicians, who were not then known for such irreverence.[20] In a few days, Butler was also quoted as saying Adlai Stevenson would not be drafted in 1956, but would have to fight for the presidential nomination.[21]

How had this feisty leader been elected chairman? Was he the Southern candidate? Twenty-seven of his seventy votes had come from Southern and Border states and the District of Columbia, but he also received twenty-six votes west of the Mississippi (excluding Southern and Border states). He was weakest east of the Mississippi (again, excluding Southern and Border states), receiving only twelve votes there. He received no votes from Illinois, Ohio, Pennsylvania, New York, and Massachusetts, but was supported by "new look" leaders in Michigan, Minnesota, and Wisconsin. Because he received votes in all sections, he was a national choice, and certainly as much a Western as a Southern candidate. He could have given up half his Southern and Border state votes and still have won. Butler's advocation of a midterm convention and his thinking about a party constitution had not cost him Southern support. His constitution was never publicized, so the South had no reason to see Butler in a bad light. He was perceived as a personable candidate, identified with Mitchell-Stevenson moderation, who made statements which Southerners could only find soothing. It would later be revealed that Butler had signed a pledge in New Orleans to this effect:

I do not consider the question of segregation a political issue. I see no reason for any chairman of our party at any level to project segregation into our political discussions. As

54

a lawyer, and if I were to be party chairman, I would consider it not to be a matter subject to political debate or political discussion. [signed Paul M. Butler]

I have not discussed any issues in any context with either Gov. Williams or Sen. Humphrys [*sic*] which may be subject to difference of opinion among members of our party. [signed P. M. Butler][22]

Truman had opposed Butler and favored DiSalle. The old professionals (James Curley, represented by a proxy, was still the national committeeman from Massachusetts), who opposed Butler and favored DiSalle or Finnegan, resented most of all that Butler's "rise in the party was as a reformer."[23] Lyndon Johnson, coveting the 1956 nomination, wanted a non-Stevenson chairman. A back disorder kept him in Washington and he dispatched Sam Rayburn to New Orleans. Rayburn, travelling by train, arrived late and unsuccessfully urged postponement of the vote for chairman.[24] On the other hand, Butler was aided by the support of Congressman Michael Kirwan of Ohio, chairman of the Democratic Congressional Campaign Committee.[25]

Butler also had genuine support from his National Committee colleagues, with whom he had served over two years. For three weeks he had been in contact with ninety-four of the one hundred and five National Committee members. Butler came from the ranks of the electing body, and his selection was seen as the first undictated selection of a national chairman since 1912.[26] Neil Staebler of Michigan worked with Gerald Heaney of Minnesota and Iris Blitch, Georgia national committeewoman, to get support from National Committee members against "the bosses and big city states." They believed Butler would be good in building party organization, and in moving away from the ineffectiveness of the old politics toward a new approach. They secured a number of second-choice pledges for Butler if a second ballot were needed, and several of these votes actually went to Butler on the first ballot.[27]

Stephen Mitchell, who insisted that both Stevenson and he had taken no part in the selection process, proclaimed that undictated choice had occurred, rather than selection by "a presidential candidate," or "a few big city leaders."[28] In spite of Mitchell's words, Butler was widely viewed as his favorite for chairman, and Butler's election was seen as a victory for the Stevenson forces, even if Finnegan or DiSalle would still have been acceptable.[29] Mitchell favored Butler as his successor, particularly after Finnegan's health became a problem, and worked arduously for his election.[30] Likewise, Butler was Adlai Stevenson's first choice at New Orleans and "this word got around, even though Stevenson maintained a neutral position."[31]

By December, 1954, Butler had attracted considerable attention from national political leaders. His energy and innovation, during his first years as national committeeman from Indiana, helped him establish the new leadership image Stevenson and Mitchell felt the party needed. They saw Butler as a reformer with a professional touch, as a symbol of the "New Politics," before that term came to mean so many things. Paul Butler had gained their support for national chairman.

Stephen Mitchell would vacate the chairmanship January 1, 1955. Butler went to Washington in December, before assuming his duties. He returned to South Bend for a January 20 fete, a bipartisan community affair with special tributes coming from such close friends as former Governor Henry Schricker and Reverend John Cavanaugh, C.S.C., President of Notre Dame University.[32]

Butler believed that the chairmanship should be a full-time job. This meant that he would give up his law practice and reside in Washington.[33] Butler took an apartment in the Mayflower Hotel, two blocks from Democratic National Committee offices, but his family remained in South Bend. He was grateful for the recent practice of providing a $25,000 annual salary for the national chairman. As the father of five children (aged 14-20), he would accept the salary.[34] Butler felt justified in this decision because he wanted to be a full-time chairman, and would have no other income upon giving up his law practice. Butler would receive no additional living expenses, no limousine, but would be reimbursed for transportation when on speaking trips for party business.[35] In 1959, several of Butler's critics (including a part-time official of the National Committee who maintained a lucrative business) alleged that he cost the National Committee $50,000 annually in expenses. This figure was supposed to include his salary and a $400 monthly payment for his apartment (actually paid from Butler's salary), as well as frequent airplanes trips to South Bend. His critics suggested that Butler should be forced out as chairman by drying up the funds which supported him and buying him off with a good job elsewhere.[36]

Butler was most vulnerable, if at all, on the charge of frequent trips to South Bend at party expense. Because his family had remained there, he desired to return as often as possible. He also liked to attend Notre Dame football games, at home or away; he once listed his hobbies in this order: following the Notre Dame team and politics. During his chairmanship, he was still able to pursue both hobbies—he saw a good many Notre Dame road games, and missed only one home game.[37] In his first year in office, he probably spent parts of forty-three days in South Bend, often just overnight. Some of this time was occupied by local political meetings, dinners, and elections in which Butler maintained interest. Nine days of a Christmas vacation represented the longest stay in South Bend. Butler's South Bend trips had decreased somewhat by 1956, then by 1958 his South Bend schedule resembled his 1955 schedule. However, Butler seldom travelled to South Bend only to return to Washington. He maintained an active speaking schedule during his chairmanship, and most visits to South Bend were stopover visits between Washington and party or public engagements throughout the United States. His critics also failed to note that the time Butler spent with his family in South Bend was the only real vacation from his job, and he seldom had more than a few days away from his Washington office.[38]

Along with a view of his job as full-time, Butler conceived his role as national chairman as that of an activist. He wanted to extend his already established pattern of activity as Indiana's national committeeman. In April, 1955, Butler was able to report to National Committee members that he had travelled about 26,000 miles during the first three months of his chairmanship to fourteen states, where he gave thirty-six speeches, and had participated in fifteen television programs and many press conferences. He had received many invitations from party officials, but said he would come without invitation if circumstances warranted it. A year later he similarly reported that to date he had travelled 122,000 miles. In 1956 his travel totaled 63,000 miles; in 1957, 62,000; and in 1958, 73,000. By December, 1959, he had journeyed 350,000 miles, an average of 70,000 miles a year.[39] This extensive travel was one means of giving visibility to the chairmanship, and in the long run strengthened the power and reach of the office.

In devotion to the principles of full-time duty and vigorous activity, which Butler had set for himself, he compiled a remarkable record for a national chairman. Just as in Indiana politics, Butler expected from those with whom he was associated at national headquarters similar devotion to duty. This was not always forthcoming from colleagues who had different interests and concepts of party service, and different styles and activity patterns would lead to conflicts between the national chairman and others.

Over what kind of establishment would Paul Butler preside as national chairman? He told the South Bend *Tribune* that the Democratic National Committee employed sixty people, had a $700,000 annual budget, and received two or three hundred letters a day.[40] A staffing table for a July 31, 1954, revision of that year's budget showed fifty-five authorized positions, fifteen in the chairman's office (including the Speakers' Bureau and Young Democrat Clubs, leaving seven for the actual operation of the chairman's office), sixteen in the treasurer's office, thirteen in Public Affairs, and eleven for Political Activities, Women's Division, and the Democratic Senatorial

Campaign Committee.[41] For the 1956 campaign the staff was increased to about one hundred eighty, and then dropped back to forty-nine as financial problems were foreseen from the campaign deficit. Then in late 1957, there were sixty-seven employees, as well as eleven for the *Democratic Digest*. Volunteers also contributed 19,000 hours of work, worth $35,000, according to Butler. By convention time in 1960 strength increased to eighty-six with various campaign committees to provide more help after the convention.[42]

In December, 1958, Butler told the National Convention that National Committee staff members, who had absolutely no fringe benefits, had received no salary increases during his chairmanship, a period in which federal governmental employees had an increase of 17.5%. Consequently, staff members had been given salary increases of 5-10%, depending on length of service.[43]

Expenses for the National Committee in 1954 were actually $1,110,260 because about $500,000 was expended for the congressional elections, in addition to the $700,000 budget for the National Committee. Butler also inherited a $100,152 deficit. For 1955 expenses amounted to $976,884, more than had been budgeted, but there was still an ending balance of $149,387 for the year. In 1954 the payroll represented the largest output (except for donations to candidates for Congress), $352,662. $70,534 was budgeted for travel and transportation; $46,497 for supplies and equipment; $40,125 for telephone and telegram expenses; and $37,070 for rent. Expenses for January, 1955, Butler's first month as chairman, were $56,498, with payroll consuming $23,615. These 1955 and 1956 expenses are recorded in party records:

	1955	1956
January	$ 56,000	$129,000
February	100,000	137,000
May	64,000	97,000
June	76,000	77,000
July	64,000	90,000
August	88,000	220,000
October	76,000	967,000
November	69,000	452,000

The difference in the level of expenditures for the two years is accounted for by the 1956 presidential election. The fluctuation in monthly expenditures for 1955 reflected changes in staff size, varying travel and telephone costs, and costs of an April party dinner.[44]

Beginning the 1956 campaign with a deficit, the National Committee had $372,000 in unpaid bills by the end of November, $287,000 representing debts of the Stevenson-Kefauver Committee. Austerity was reflected in the payroll decline, but still the deficit rose to

$660,000 by May, 1957. Receipts for 1957 were $825,000 and disbursements $818,000. Office expenses for April, 1957, were pared to $53,000. The demands of the 1958 congressional campaign increased the deficit to $750,000, even though the National Committee received $903,000 in 1958. Butler wanted that debt retired in thirty days, relying on the 750 Club, whereby 750 contributors of $1,000 each would erase the deficit, but only gradually in 1959 was the deficit reduced to $316,000. By November, 1959, the National Committee had spent $851,000 for its operation, and Butler pleaded for contributions to meet payroll, rent, and printing costs at headquarters. Its activities would increase for the 1960 campaign; and, as the financial cycle repeated itself, that campaign would leave an unprecedented deficit of $3,820,000, which would no longer be Paul Butler's concern.[45]

Butler had inherited the 1954 election deficit, and had planned for election expenditures in 1956, 1958, and 1960, not always spending as much as desired. He became aware of the importance of fundraising, and his programs in that area of leadership will be given more attention after discussion of other matters.

Personnel at the National Committee office were carried over from the previous regime with a few changes at the top level. Vice chairman India Edwards, secretary Dorothy Vrendenburg, deputy chairman and *Democratic Digest* editor Clayton Fritchey, publicity director Sam Brightman, research director Philip Stern, general counsel Harold Leventhal, and Women's Division director Katie Louchheim continued under the new chairman. A year later, Fritchey, Brightman, and Stern were referred to as Butler's brain trust.[46] Mitchell highly commended Fritchey, who was being paid $15,000 a year plus expenses of $200 per month. Fritchey had been promised $25,000 when the party could afford it. Mitchell also advised Butler that Charles Murphy, who had served from 1947 to 1953 as administrative assistant, then as special counsel to President Truman, had been serving as the National Committee's special counsel since early 1954. In effect, Murphy had been a liaison person between Truman and the National Committee. He had been billing the party about $2,000 a month for services and expenses.[47]

At Butler's first National Committee meeting in January, 1955, Matthew McCloskey was elected treasurer, and at an April meeting Governor G. Mennen Williams of Michigan was elected chairman of the Nationalities Division. Butler announced at the April meeting that although Hyman Raskin had left his position as deputy chairman in December, he had come to Washington several times to advise Butler. Raskin's position was still vacant. By 1960 there would be simply six vice chairmen, and no deputy chairman. The 1955 secretary and treasurer were still in office in 1960, as was the general counsel and parliamentarian, Congressman Clarence Cannon. By that time Katie Louchheim had become a vice chairman and Sam Brightman played a slightly different role. Butler also made new appointments with Evelyn Chavoor and Paul Willis.[48]

Miss Chavoor had worked six years with Congresswoman Helen Douglass of California, and then for one year in the National Committee's Research Bureau. When she learned that Butler wanted her to return to headquarters as assistant to the chairman (the first woman in such a position), she was hesitant, but Hyman Raskin and California's national committeeman Paul Ziffren told her she would like working for Butler; as it turned out, she did, developing great respect and affection for him. She had never met Butler and assumed he would want someone from Indiana in that position. She tried the job for what she thought would be three months, but remained for two years. She worked closely with Butler on all matters relating to his activities and responsibilities as chairman. She was particularly responsible for the administrative functions of the headquarters, supervised correspondence, and made arrangements for National Committee meetings and functions. She also helped prepare for the 1956 convention, and later arranged for establishment of the Stevenson-Kefauver headquarters.[49]

For over two years, in Indiana, as Butler prepared for the intra-party contests and the 1954 campaign, Professor Willis had gathered political intelligence, given speeches, conducted research, written speeches for Butler, and worked on proposals Butler had used in his work as national committeeman. In relying on Willis' professional skills and loyalty in factional matters, Butler had communicated frequently with him in 1953 and 1954. During December, 1954, and January, 1955, Butler recruited Willis as his assistant in an amusing manner, entirely by telephone. Butler would call weekly with reports of what he was doing, and would describe the people being urged on him as assistants. In late January, 1955, Butler finally asked, "You wouldn't consider coming up here as my assistant, would you?" So Willis was recruited to do about what he had been doing in Indiana for two years, on a broader scale, and also to travel with Butler. Willis symbolized to a great extent what Butler wanted his chairmanship to project. Willis remained in the position two years, and was then appointed to the Advisory Committee on Political Organization, where he remained until its demise in 1961.[50]

Butler lived in a state of antagonism with two of those who served at the top level with him from 1955 through 1960—Katie Louchheim and Matthew McCloskey. Stephen Mitchell had asked Butler to retain Mrs. Louchheim as Women's Division director, a position for which she was paid on a *per diem* basis to cover expenses for her time (which was full-time). Others had advised Butler that he might have difficulties with Mrs. Louchheim, and he later regretted his decision to retain her. He may have threatened her with dismissal, but she had influential supporters such as Lyndon Johnson, and was popular among grass roots Democrats.[51] She shared jokes with McCloskey and other National Committee personnel who did not like Butler's policies, personality, or office austerity, even while she shared many of Butler's views on party programs. At the 1960 convention she believed Butler caused the microphones to be shut off when she addressed the delegates. She has recounted the grimness of a party tour taken with Butler and others. While she liked to travel, and would perhaps have preferred to travel most of the time, she wanted to do so in more style than Butler allowed himself.[52]

Butler also threatened to see that McCloskey would be replaced if he did not cooperate, but McCloskey also had influential friends, such as Pennsylvania Governor and National Committeeman David Lawrence. It might also have been difficult to find anyone willing to take on the vexatious task of serving as treasurer. Given his views on motivation for party service, Butler probably found McCloskey's continuing contracting business less than desirable. McCloskey's reminder that Butler was friendly with an official of the American Truckers' Association, and that Butler should use this relationship to secure contributions for the Democratic Party was likely unwelcome, even if Butler had attempted influence with Congress on behalf of the trucking industry.[53] Butler also felt that McCloskey spent too much time with his business in Philadelphia, and not enough time at his office in Washington. Many letters went to McCloskey in Philadelphia; and, at one point, when accusing McCloskey of refusing a request for a conference, Butler charged that even though McCloskey had been in Washington, he had not been in party headquarters for five months. Butler advised him not to let the party suffer too long from such behavior. Butler also filed newspaper clippings alleging racial discrimination by McCloskey's contracting firm. Noting that he and McCloskey had "widely differing views concerning our financial problems," Butler, in effect, accused McCloskey of having a defeatist attitude and of wanting to close down National Committee headquarters and suspend publication of the *Democratic Digest* because of the party deficit.[54] McCloskey responded that Butler's charges were not "very Christian-like," and that he was not a defeatist who had suggested closing national headquarters, although he doubted the *Digest* was worth its cost.[55]

With many members of the National Committee itself, Butler developed a certain rapport. Since he came from their ranks, and since they were mobilized for his election, National Committee members continued to treat Butler as "one of us." And apart from those few with

61

whom good relations proved impossible, Butler pursued a course which was solicitous toward National Committee members. At his first National Committee meeting, he pledged closest cooperation and understanding between the chairman and the members of the group. Open criticism and airing of differences of opinion were urged, and the use of party headquarters on Washington visits was offered.[56] Butler's efforts at communication in preparation for committee meetings, his provisions for comfort, and his distribution of information for those unable to attend meetings were favorably noted. Butler was credited with fostering better acquaintances, exchange of ideas, and party unity.[57]

While Butler expected National Committee members to pay their travel and other expenses, he established new rules making it possible for them to attend fund-raising dinners free. On the eve of the 1956 convention, he informed members that each had been assigned an air-conditioned automobile with driver because of the cooperation of the Chicago host committee and the Ford Motor Company. A similar arrangement prevailed in 1960.[58]

Butler also supported an apportionment of 1960 convention delegates which made all National Committee members delegates with one-half vote. The National Committee also gave itself a set of formal rules, previously lacking, in 1957.[59]

Whatever his relations with other party leaders, Butler was able to command loyalty from most National Committee members. In 1959, one told Butler, "I am still of the opinion that about 80 percent of our Committee has the greatest of admiration for you personally and for your courage, indefatigability, your imaginative qualities and your many other good points." And the retiring West Virginia national committeewoman in 1960 remembered "the wonderful cooperation and enjoyment" she had received working with Butler and his staff.[60]

NOTES

1. John Bartlow Martin, *Adlai Stevenson and the World: The Life of Adlai Stevenson* (Garden City, New York: Doubleday and Company, 1977), p. 77. In Doyle, *As We Knew Adlai*, pp. 84-85, Mitchell relates that he had agreed to remain chairman only through the 1952 election, but stayed on to help pay off debts and rehabilitate the party, after Stevenson consented to continue as party leader.
2. Martin, *Adlai Stevenson and the World*, p. 125.
3. Johnson to Butler, November 7, 1952, Butler Papers, Box 80.

4. Butler to John W. Leslie, April 20, 1954, Butler Papers, Box 104.
5. Butler to Alfred Scanlan, April 20, 1954; and Stephen Mitchell to Butler, February 19, 1954, Butler Papers, Box 104.
6. Doyle, *As We Knew Adlai*, p. 82; Stevenson to Arthur Schlesinger, Jr., August 14, 1954, *Stevenson Papers*, IV, p. 385; Martin, *Adlai Stevenson and the World*, p. 130.
7. Stevenson to Arthur Schlesinger, Jr., August 16, 1954, *Stevenson Papers*, IV, 385.
8. Wyatt to Butler, August 31, 1954, Butler Papers, Box 104.
9. Butler to Victor H. Fall, September 30, 1954, Butler Papers, Box 104.
10. South Bend *Tribune*, November 28, 1954; New York *Times*, September 19, 1954.
11. Butler to Woodward, October 1, 1954, Butler Papers, Box 104.
12. Woodward to Truman, September 27, 1954, Butler Papers, Box 104.
13. Woodward to Butler, October 5, 1954, Butler Papers, Box 104.
14. Adlai E. Stevenson, *What I Think* (New York: Harper and Brothers Publishers, 1954), pp. 72-75.
15. Butler to Walker, October 7, 1954, Butler Papers, Box 104.
16. Adlai Stevenson to Harry Ashmore, December 23, 1954, *Stevenson Papers*, IV, 445.
17. *Official Report of the Proceedings of the Democratic National Convention, 1956* (Washington: Democratic National Committee, n.d.), pp. 573, 584-600.
18. Butler Papers, Box 204.
19. Washington *Sunday Star* and St. Louis *Post-Dispatch*, both December 5, 1954.
20. New York *Times*, December 6, 1954.
21. Louisville *Courier-Journal*, December 8, 1954.
22. Photocopies of pledges in Butler Papers, Box 154, with release from Publicity Division, Democratic National Committee, September 12, 1959, which says Georgia state chairman John Bell wrote the pledges on the back of a report Stephen Mitchell had given the National Committee, and Butler signed them. Butler gave the pledges because he was asked for his views. He made no deal for support for chairman, he said.
23. Thomas O'Neill, Baltimore *Sun*, March 18, 1960.
24. Alfred Steinberg, *Sam Johnson's Boy: A Close-Up of the President From Texas* (New York: The Macmillan Company, 1968), p. 393.
25. Jack Redding, *Inside the Democratic Party* (Indianapolis: The Bobbs-Merrill Company, 1958), pp. 298-299.
26. Louisville *Times*, December 6, 1954; see Thomas O'Neill, Baltimore *Sun*, March 18, 1960.
27. Interview with Neil Staebler, December 15, 1980.

28. Doyle, *As We Knew Adlai*, p. 87; Washington *Sunday Star*, December 5, 1954.
29. Chicago *Daily News*, December 4, 1954; St. Louis *Post-Dispatch*, December 5, 1954.
30. James Sundquist to the author, October 23, 1974; Walter Johnson to the author, October 29, 1974; interview with Anne Butler, June 10, 1975.
31. Anonymous Stevenson staff member to the author, February 7, 1975.
32. South Bend *Tribune*, January 5 and 16, 1955.
33. He would be forced out of his old law firm in 1956 for "absenteeism."
34. Washington *Sunday Star*, December 5, 1954.
35. Mrs. Butler pointed out that some chairmen had maintained law practices or other businesses.
36. Robert S. Allen and Paul Scott, Philadelphia *Daily News*, July 22, 1959.
37. Biographical statement, n.d., Butler Papers, Box 2; interview with Anne Butler, June 10, 1975.
38. This picture of Butler's South Bend visits has been compiled from his Appointments Book, Butler Papers, Box 196; Engagement Calendar, 1955, Box 188; and from speeches information, Box 150.
39. *Official Report of the Proceedings of the Democratic National Convention, 1956*, pp. 638-639; ibid., p. 772; mileage calculations in Butler Papers, Box 204; biographical statement, Butler Papers, Box 2.
40. South Bend *Tribune*, February 19, 1955.
41. Butler Papers, Box 8.
42. Mary Zirkle to Butler, November 26, 1956, Butler Papers, Box 8; New York *Times*, November 17, 1956; Butler's 1957 report to the National Committee, Butler Papers, Box 165.
43. *Official Report of the 1960 Democratic National Convention and Committee*, p. 556.
44. This financial data can be found in the Butler Papers, Boxes 8 and 103.
45. Mary Zirkle to Butler, November 26, 1956, Butler Papers, Box 8; *Official Report of the 1960 Democratic National Convention and Committee*, pp. 425, 429-430; receipts and disbursements for 1955 and 1957, Butler Papers, Box 8; audit statements of Lybrand, Rose Brothers, and Montgomery, Butler Papers, Box 16; *Official Report of the 1960 Democratic National Convention and Committee*, pp. 553-554, 556, 587, 721; National Committee Press Release, November 8, 1959, Butler Papers, Box 111; Butler's letter in *Democratic Digest*, November, 1959.
46. Hugh Morrow, "The Democrats No. 1 Optimist," p. 28.

47. Mitchell to Butler, December 29, 1954, Butler Papers, Box 3; Mitchell to Butler, December 13, 1954, Box 16.

48. *Official Report of the Proceedings of the Democratic National Convention, 1956*, pp. 642-644. The vice chairmen were Hale Boggs, William L. Dawson, Katie Louchheim, Mike Mansfield, Robert B. Meyner, and G. Mennen Williams.

49. Interview with Evelyn Chavoor, March 13, 1982; Evelyn Chavoor to the author, April 28, 1982.

50. Paul G. Willis to the author, February 8, 1975. The Willis-Butler speech writing and speech making produced the celebrated phrase, "Nixon-Dixon, and Yates," in relation to a public-private power controversy. In 1954 Willis also prepared these words for Butler to use in an Indiana speech describing the Eisenhower Administration—"Never before have so many, promised so much, waited so long for so little." They found their way into an Adlai Stevenson West Coast speech.

51. Interview with Anne Butler, June 10, 1975; Katie Louchheim, *By the Political Sea* (Garden City, New York: Doubleday and Company, 1970), pp. 170-172.

52. Louchheim, *By the Political Sea*, pp. 34-35, 241-242, 46; interview with Anne Butler, June 10, 1975.

53. McCloskey to Butler, October 1, 1956, Butler Papers, Box 16; Ira Haymaker to Butler, July 30, 1955, Butler Papers, Box 4.

54 Butler to McCloskey, November 19, 1957; and July 18, 1957; Butler Papers, Box 16. Harry Truman was advised of the situation, with a copy of Butler's letter to McCloskey. Butler also mentioned the situation in a California speech (Box 142).

55. McCloskey to Butler, August 27, 1957, Butler Papers, Box 16.

56. *Official Report of the Proceedings of the Democratic National Convention, 1956*, pp. 637-638.

57. Willa May Roberts to Butler, May 13, 1957, Butler Papers, Box 108.

58. *Official Report of the 1960 Democratic National Convention and Committee*, pp. 771-772.

59. Ibid., pp. 674, 378-387, 445.

60. Leo C. Graybill to Butler, October 12, 1959; Mrs. Nunley B. Snedegar to Butler, June 23, 1960; Butler Papers, Box 94.

Chapter Four

PARTY LEADERSHIP AND THE LOYAL OPPOSITION

Hubert Humphrey once remarked that even in the best of times the Democratic National Committee was "a frail political child," and especially under a Republican president.[1] On the other hand, Ralph Goldman has observed that while a winning or losing presidential candidate is only a *titular* party leader, the national chairman is the *formal* party leader of the presidential party.[2] As the formal leader of the Democratic Party, with no Democrat in the White House, would Paul Butler see himself as party leader in fact? His past record of energetic activity indicated that he would not be content with playing a quiescent role as national chairman, and his outspokenness following his election caused observers to comment that the new leader would be forceful. Butler's continued forthrightness on such topics as President Eisenhower, and his embroilment in several controversial issues, fortified the image of an activist chairman who believed that in an age of "New Politics," political parties, reflecting voting trends, should be more issue-oriented and less tied to the old pattern in which patronage was dominant.[3] Butler's views on communication, discussed below, also caused him to believe that a national chairman was a party leader with a special role, particularly when there was no Democratic president. His stress on responsible opposition also suggested active leadership.

However, Paul Butler made no very explicit statement as to what he thought a national chairman's leadership role should be until 1959, and by this time his well-publicized disagreement with Democratic congressional leaders and most Southern Democrats showed what kind of leader he wanted to be.[4] His 1959 statement on a chairman's duties deserves careful attention:

> When a party does not have one of its members in the
> White House, the national chairman, as head of the political
> organization, becomes the instrument to communicate to

67

Congress what members of the party in all ranks are thinking.

In the absence of a party member in the White House, the national chairman has a duty to remind all Democrats of our pledges. Party officials have the same responsibility to the public that elected officials have.

This is especially true in my case because I was national chairman when our 1956 convention adopted our latest platform. Hence, I have a double duty to do what I can to see that our pledges are carried out.

Of course, I have no power to tell Congress what it must do. My language has shown respect for the legislative process, for the problems of our leaders in dealing with the differing philosophies of our members, and with the problem created by lack of co-operation from President Eisenhower.

I'm not acting like a whippersnapper trying to run Congress from a downtown party office. But we can't win in 1960 by doing what the Republicans want us to do. We can't let the Republican President set a pattern for us to follow. It's true we mustn't oppose just for the sake of being different from the Republicans. But one weakness of the two-party system is that people say they can see no difference between the parties.

There is plenty of difference between Democrats and Republicans, and we mustn't blur that difference by our failure to act.[5]

In the same year, with specific reference to civil rights, he said, "I have felt it my duty to express what I consider the majority view of the Democrats of the nation . . . ."[6]

Yet, while Butler saw himself as an important national leader of his party, he was realistic in expecting competition. He remarked in 1957 that party leadership was a combination of congressional leaders, governors, and members of the Democratic Advisory Council.[7] His most likely competitor was Adlai Stevenson, the titular party leader during Butler's entire chairmanship, even if Stevenson was a twice-defeated candidate. When faced with the problem of paying off 1952 campaign debts and rebuilding the Democratic Party, Stephen Mitchell asked, "Who could lead this effort better than Adlai Stevenson? He was our greatest asset."[8] Paul David has commented on the uniqueness of the 1954 congressional election campaign because Stevenson, as titular leader and "Chief Mid-Term Campaigner," forced Eisenhower to follow in the same role. David believed 1954 was the first midterm campaign in which the titular leaders of both parties were active, although

Stevenson gave the role more clarity and higher status.[9] Stuart Gerry Brown observed in 1957 that Stevenson had "in effect been President all along."[10]

Stevenson particularly felt his responsibility as titular leader in the foreign affairs area. He thought the role was "a very ambiguous one," with the leader having "no clear and defined authority." Yet after the 1952 election, the determining fact in his mind was that he was party leader until events changed the situation.[11] In 1960, Stevenson said he had never liked the title, "Titular Head," reiterated the limitations of the role, and candidly admitted there were other claiming party leaders inside and outside Congress.[12] But, by this time, after two presidential defeats, Stevenson had less claim to the title of titular head, and fewer Democrats were willing to honor it.

Other 1956 and 1960 presidential contenders saw themselves as party leaders. There was also a living former Democratic president, Harry Truman (who had opposed Butler's election, and who really never accepted Stevenson as party leader), who had to be reckoned with. Stevenson and other Democrats paid Truman much deference.

Then there was the special case of the Democratic congressional leaders, Senator Lyndon Johnson and Representative Sam Rayburn, who headed party majorities after the 1954 elections. Even with a Republican president, Johnson believed the president alone could provide national leadership. Perhaps Johnson only wanted to lead Democrats in the Senate at this moment, although he was a presidential candidate before his 1955 heart attack. Certainly Johnson did not want anyone else leading Senate Democrats; he did not welcome competition from Paul Butler leading the opposition to the Eisenhower Administration in the manner Butler wanted to lead it.[13]

Finally, some members of the Democratic National Committee, although many were Butler supporters, wanted a share of party leadership. It was this desire which had provided Butler so much assistance from his national committee colleagues when he sought the chairmanship. Therefore, he would find means to make them feel they were partners in party leadership.

If it can be assumed that Stevenson would be the most visible Democratic Party leader, 1955-1960, and Butler's strongest competitor, it does not necessarily follow that Butler and Stevenson competed intensely for party leadership. They did not, in spite of Stevenson's attempt to remove Butler from office at the 1956 Convention. That this was the case stemmed from the similar views Butler and Stevenson had about "loyal opposition," and the similar positions they took on public policy questions during the Eisenhower Administration, when other Democrats avoided certain issues.

The concept of loyal opposition is grounded firmly only in nations which maintain a high level of democratic consensus, where losing political parties do not resort to revolution, nor winning parties to repression. This concept of loyal opposition distinguishes between the present rulers, or government, and the continuing regime. Only loyalty to the latter is mandatory. In the form of organized political party opposition, the loyal opposition is always ready to assume governing responsibility.[14]

Policy alternatives to the program of the Eisenhower Administration would be the essence of any loyal opposition as far as Butler and Stevenson were concerned. Butler began his chairmanship by stressing the important role the opposition played in the American political system. Especially since the Democrats controlled Congress, the opposition should guide the majority and inform the people. As a result, representative institutions would be strengthened.[15] The process of communication, which Butler stressed in party matters, would inform congressional leaders what rank and file Democrats thought about political issues. Of course, Butler made it clear that he was the instrument of such communication. Loyal opposition did not mean opposition for its own sake, just to be different, but to show voters that there were important policy differences between Democrats and Republicans.[16]

> We have a political philosophy and we want to project our political philosophy openly and fully and completely so that the American people can understand it, and if they believe in it, support it, and if they don't believe in it support some other political party and some other political philosophy.[17]

Butler clearly saw the Democratic Advisory Council, authorized in 1956, as an aid to responsible opposition.[18]

Stevenson assumed that "the duty of a loyal opposition is to oppose," therefore reasons must be given in the form of criticism if opposition is to be effective.[19] While there were similarities between the parties, Stevenson believed that elections tended to emphasize political divisions. But loyal opposition involved such a "choosing up of sides."[20]

In addition to ordinary forces working for political consensus, the Eisenhower bipartisan style of political leadership, which resulted in some blurring of party and ideological differences during the 1950s, and to which Johnson and Rayburn contributed, limited the effect of the loyal opposition Butler and Stevenson advocated. Issues were not as important as other factors in determining voter choice in presidential elections. Also, the early Eisenhower years coincided with the period of

"McCarthyism," which has been analyzed largely in terms of a damper on dissent, rather than an effective silencer of dissent. Opposition was sometimes treated as disloyalty.[21] Stevenson had probed that phenomenon in the 1954 campaign. He noted that criticism was often viewed as radical nonconformity, which suggested disloyalty, which in turn suggested treason. He saw this trend contradictory to genuine conservatism, and totalitarian in its repudiation of the liberal tradition of critical inquiry and discussion. Criticism rested on a base of mutual trust, while in 1954 Stevenson found many examples of "truly un-American violence."[22]

Stephen Mitchell had taken a defiant stand against Senator Joseph McCarthy in 1954, and refused to appear with McCarthy before the Irish Fellowship Club of Chicago. As both partisan Democrat and Catholic, Mitchell condemned McCarthy for disgracing Irish Catholics.[23] In December, 1954, the *Democratic Digest* featured an article, "How Eisenhower and Nixon Kept Communism Out of the Campaign,"[24] which quoted Vice President Richard Nixon extensively on the "communist issue." The following year Chairman Butler invited Republican National Chairman Leonard W. Hall to view a Democratic National Committee exhibit, "The Chamber of Smears," which suggested Republicans had tried to portray Democrats as "soft on communism" and as "the war party" in 1954.[25] When Nixon spoke on the Notre Dame campus in 1956, Butler verbally attacked Nixon—a Notre Dame professor said Butler's remarks were "un-Christian." Butler responded, "Notre Dame does not do herself proud when she gives platform and prestige to men in our public life of such character as Nixon . . . he is much less to be admired and respected than Joe McCarthy."[26]

Particularly in the foreign policy debate of the 1950s, the loyal opposition notion, which Stevenson and Butler adhered to, would be tested against the concept of a bipartisan foreign policy. To many Americans bipartisanship in foreign affairs, especially as developed after World War II, simply meant "politics stops at the water's edge," or "Americans do not divide on questions involving the nation's existence," or "once foreign policy is made all must rally behind the President." This type of thinking suggests a consensus similar to that believed to be essential for the existence of democracy itself; thus in the McCarthy period, charges of treason might easily follow criticism. Certainly the concept of a bipartisan foreign policy was ambiguous enough to cause presidents to expect unqualified support and to put opponents on the defensive. The ambiguity also enabled leaders like Stevenson and Butler to probe deeply into what bipartisanship meant in relation to loyal opposition.

71

With an interest in foreign affairs, Stevenson keenly felt responsibility as an opposition leader in this field, realizing that such opposition might differ from domestic policy opposition. Yet a Democratic opposition could not ignore what it perceived to be mistakes in foreign policy formation, even if foreign policy was not a good field for Democratic electoral success in the 1950s. When Walter Lippmann wondered whether Democratic congressional leaders had properly acted as the opposition, Stevenson doubted that they could ever do their duty because public ignorance was so prevalent in an area where initiative rested with presidents anyway.[27]

Stevenson believed that the 1954 campaign for congressional elections had sorely tested and indeed imperiled the sense of unity in America. While feeling that unity was necessary in a responsible discussion of foreign policy, he wanted to avoid unity and bipartisanship becoming ends in themselves.[28] In 1952 President Truman had warned Stevenson that Republicans were turning bipartisanship in foreign policy into a partisan matter because of unpopular Republican ideas in domestic policy.[29] Early in 1954 Stevenson informed Averell Harriman that he did not want to give bipartisan support to the foreign policy of Secretary of State John Foster Dulles. He was afraid that Dulles expected Democrats to support what the Administration had previously decided.[30] While Stevenson believed that Democrats and Republicans should cooperate in foreign policy so as to not perish together, he did not want "principles deemed essential to national honor" sacrificed merely for harmony. Bipartisanship could not mean coerced unity, restriction of discussion, or suppression of criticism. Rather it should result in "the elimination of domestic politics from the conduct of foreign affairs." He believed Republicans had manipulated foreign policy for domestic political purposes and had historically hindered unity because of intra-party divisions.[31]

In 1957 Dulles persuaded Eisenhower to invite Stevenson's participation in a NATO conference. Stevenson felt his talents would be employed, but that he would be given little credit for his efforts. Stevenson resolved only to serve as a consultant since he could not commit the Democratic Party to a program not of its making.[32]

In May, 1960, Stevenson's views on responsible foreign policy criticism were highlighted after the collapse of a Paris summit conference following the shooting down of a U-2 surveillance plane over Russia. At the time Senate Leader Lyndon Johnson was campaigning for the presidential nomination "as the Democratic Party's chief apostle of non-partisanship in times of national crisis."[33] Stevenson responded to the ensuing events at a local party dinner in Chicago. While paying proper respects to unity in a crisis situation,

72

and to the Presidency, he asserted that the United States had provided Russian leaders with the tools for wrecking the summit conference. Citing the clumsiness of the Eisenhower Administration in foreign affairs, and perceiving blunders and lies in the U-2 incident, Stevenson told his audience, "We cannot sweep this whole sorry mess under the rug in the name of national unity." A responsible opposition should "expose and criticize carelessness and mistakes," an obligation to all Americans and America's allies. It would not do for Republicans to say "that in this grave crisis we must all rally around the President in the name of national unity."[34]

Paul Butler was essentially a politician first trained in local organizational politics and concerned with domestic affairs, although his pre-World War II activities in regard to American intervention should not be overlooked. Butler said he was "certainly not well informed in the field of foreign policy," and would leave foreign policy statements to Democratic Senator Walter George, Chairman of the Senate Foreign Relations Committee.[35] Although Butler dealt little with the details of foreign affairs, he communicated a widely publicized philosophy of loyal opposition, which complemented Adlai Stevenson's attempts to educate the public. Early in his chairmanship Butler enunciated his position that Democrats, as the opposition, had no business formulating foreign policy; indeed, Democrats should try to uphold presidential policy, but they still had the obligation to criticize that policy for the "best interests of the country."[36] On the eve of the 1956 election, Butler insisted that Democrats had to keep people informed on foreign policy issues (Eisenhower had just addressed the nation on the Suez crisis) since the United States lacked positive and dynamic leadership in foreign as well as domestic affairs. With the Mideast in turmoil, the European alliance crumbling, American prestige low among her allies, and several times at the brink of war, the American people needed such a corrective.[37]

Even more than Stevenson, who doubted the wisdom of too much Democratic involvement with foreign policy, Butler probed the ambiguities in the popular version of a bipartisan foreign policy which held that once policy was formulated ranks should be closed. Butler argued that Eisenhower had to provide some incentive for Democrats to have a genuine bipartisan attitude. In practice, Butler charged, the President had ignored the true principles of such an approach; he had not sufficiently included Democrats in the formulation of foreign policy, and Democrats could not be expected to blindly uphold his policy.[38] When Republican National Chairman Leonard Hall publicly asked Butler if bipartisanship would be carried into the 1956 election by Democrats, Butler replied that Eisenhower had not followed the doctrine himself, since he had not consulted with Democrats. Any existing

73

bipartisanship was due to the patience and efforts of congressional Democrats.[39] In a 1958 Indiana speech, Butler accused Eisenhower of killing bipartisanship in spite of strong support from congressional Democrats. Therefore, "the Democratic Party reserves the right to dissent from administrative policy when it feels that that policy is dangerous to the best interests of the United States."[40]

Butler was not only resentful of what he saw as the failure of Republicans to involve Democrats in foreign policy formulation, but also, like Truman and Stevenson, of Republican attempts to use foreign policy issues for domestic political purposes, and especially to accuse Democrats of being "soft on communism."

He saw John F. Dulles as a man who preached bipartisanship while leading "partisan wrangling over foreign policy." If Republicans really wanted bipartisanship, they should not campaign against "the war party."[41] Butler tried to blunt the charge that Democrats had lost millions of people to communism by retorting that Republican immigration policy negated any idea of liberation of captive peoples, and that communism had gained because Eisenhower had made foreign policy a part-time job.[42]

After Stevenson had proposed the postponement of H-Bomb tests during the 1956 campaign, Butler opened himself to charges of appeasement by supporting Stevenson. Stevenson had tried to contribute to the cause of peace, which could not be accomplished "by rushing blindly forward in the arms race," while Eisenhower was trying to "blackout discussion" on H-Bomb tests.[43]

By 1958 Butler found three successive elections in which "The Republicans have given us an example of cynical, amoral use of foreign policy . . . in the primitive and provocative terms of disloyalty and treason . . . ." He rhetorically asked, "Is it reasonable to expect Democrats to remain silent on the issue of foreign policy in the interest of national unity while the Republicans attempt to update the 'he got us out of Korea' theme?"[44] Then in 1960, reverting to his own theme of softness, Butler said Eisenhower had had "too soft an attitude toward Russia in the past two years," and had been too trusting of Krushchev.[45]

When it came to criticism of President Dwight Eisenhower, even most Democrats considered him sacrosanct. Much of Paul Butler's reputation as a national chairman came from his tendency to treat the President as just another Republican politician.[46] As one of Butler's South Bend colleagues put it, "Some criticized even the Pope of Rome, but no one dared criticize Ike—except Paul Butler."[47] Butler began this criticism immediately upon his election as chairman, charging that Eisenhower lacked the capacity to govern and unite the nation, and did not let up until the end of his work in 1960.[48] He repeatedly speculated

74

that Eisenhower would not be a candidate in 1956, or that he would resign if reelected. After the President suffered a heart attack in 1955, Butler tried to make Eisenhower's health a major issue, arguing that a part-time presidency was a threat to the American governmental system; he also accused Eisenhower of "abandonment of leadership" in order to remain popular. According to Butler, "The American people will never elect a President who, at sixty-five, has had a serious heart attack and who is unable to be a full-time Chief Executive." Republican leaders had pressured Eisenhower to seek reelection without regard for his health.[49] Earlier, Butler had suggested that because White House life was hard on Mrs. Eisenhower, whose health was poor, the President might not be a candidate for reelection. The family wanted relief from the pressures of public life. Butler promised, however, not to make Mamie's health a campaign issue.[50] After Eisenhower had surgery in June, 1956, and announced the next day that he would seek reelection, Butler said Eisenhower's health had been propagandized in a "new science of politico-medicine."[51]

Following the 1956 election, Butler noted that criticisms of Eisenhower, "which some Democrats have been making for years," were catching up with the President.[52] In 1960 Butler apologized for any implication he might have made that Eisenhower was to blame for the deaths of nineteen Navy bandsmen, flown to Brazil to entertain at a presidential dinner. Butler had called it a political show.[53]

Butler filed much of the adverse criticism he received for his attacks on Eisenhower. He undoubtedly expected criticism, and his defense was related to his views on loyal opposition. He had said that he would not put the President on a pedestal; he did, however, respect the President and the man, and would deal with issues and not dwell on personalities. But, Butler warned, "We have only one President," and poor judgment could not be attributed to presidential advisors.[54] Butler felt the old tradition of criticizing the President's actions, without personal attack, was worthy of maintenance. Republicans could not put every bit of criticism down as a personal attack on Eisenhower, especially since the same Republicans had failed to honor Franklin Roosevelt and Harry Truman. Democrats could be the responsible, critical opposition, which was the best correction for presidential misguidance. In Congress Democrats should neither join with Eisenhower or fight him, but should state a majority program and enact it.[55]

Democratic congressional leaders Lyndon Johnson and Sam Rayburn did not share Paul Butler's enthusiasm for criticism of Eisenhower, nor did they practice Butler's style of political leadership. The whole business of opposition was seen more in terms of accommodation than as necessary conflict. After the 1952 election,

Rayburn advocated cooperation with the President, and Johnson reiterated that he did not accept the idea that it is the business of the opposition to oppose. Their strategy of not directly attacking Eisenhower, in turn, drew the President to them.[56] Even after the Democrats regained congressional control in 1954, Johnson announced continuation of the cooperation doctrine, and Eisenhower appeared grateful. Later in 1955, Adlai Stevenson, content that the congressional leaders had not opposed merely for opposition's sake, praised them for their cooperation. Both parties had to be coalition parties.[57] But to the displeasure of Johnson and Rayburn, the Democratic National Committee staff issued a criticism of Eisenhower's State of the Union Message just after Butler became chairman.[58] Butler had not consulted the congressional leaders in advance, and this incident may have brought about the rather frequent meetings of Butler with Johnson and Rayburn, often breakfasts in the latter's apartment, which became part of the pattern of Butler's life after he settled in at party headquarters.[59] Probably at this point, a pretty close relationship existed between Butler and Rayburn, as between Butler and Stevenson, but Katie Louchheim said Butler and Johnson were always at odds, often for no discernible reason. She also noted that Butler was one of the few people unafraid of Johnson, but then Butler was afraid of no one.[60]

Butler appeared willing to talk to Democratic members of Congress and to engage in the amenities which could give his relations with other Washington Democrats an auspicious beginning. When Butler congratulated congressional Democrats on their 1955 performance, most agreed with him that spending money on the 1956 campaign was preferable to holding a congressional adjournment breakfast, which Republicans had made fashionable. In 1955 a Senator and a Representative were appointed vice chairmen of the Democratic National Committee.[61]

But by 1956, Butler was offended by Johnson's desire to accommodate Eisenhower, while Butler was proclaiming the basic campaign issues.[62] This period was a turning point in relations between Butler and the congressional leaders, and Adlai Stevenson was also affected by his second defeat. Democrats held only narrow congressional margins; and, while some liberal Democrats argued that congressional moderation had lost the presidential contest, Johnson's reaction indicated he believed Paul Butler and Adlai Stevenson were responsible for defeat. Johnson promised to wait for presidential proposals, rather than to advance a Democratic program, and pledged Democrats to support of Eisenhower when he was right, and to opposition when he was wrong.[63] Demands from liberal presidential Democrats for pursuance of a party program in Congress (or implementation of the 1956 platform), and a stressing of party differences in preparation for the 1960 election, were rejected by Johnson, even after the 1958 congressional elections produced large Democratic margins. Johnson did not accept the argument that the opposition had to necessarily oppose, especially in the manner suggested by issue-oriented liberals. Making sure of the votes needed to pass a bill and avoiding a presidential veto were more important than pursuing numerous legislative items which might show Democratic divisions. His reaction to a 1957 Advisory Committee on Political Organization recommendation on the possibility of publicizing departures of Democratic legislators from the platform is obvious.[64]

David Broder has given an important analysis of Johnson's consensual politics, which, while essentially an explanation of his behavior while president, also works well for his legislative leadership period, and going beyond the institutional constraints of the Senate, takes into account Johnson's political socialization in a one-party Southern state—a background quite different from Paul Butler's two-party Indiana.[65]

In 1957 Butler and Johnson did not publicize their differences over proper party leadership style, as in 1959, when their fight became open. Yet the wrangling over creation of the Democratic Advisory Council (DAC), and refusal of the congressional leaders to serve on that body indirectly brought the question of leadership differences into play. From this time, the Butler-congressional leader struggle would be related to the DAC, civil rights issues, and Southern Democrats. When any of these three topics became prominent, the leadership struggle issue was inflamed. As the DAC and Butler became more concerned with civil rights, and as civil rights became a major political issue, the Butler-Johnson differences became more obvious. Since relationships were often intricate, it is difficult to separate the leadership struggle from the DAC, civil rights, and the South, but a separation will be attempted where possible, and these latter topics will be discussed below. Attention will now be focused on the Butler-Johnson public feuding over party leadership philosophy, methods, style, and personality.

By 1958, Adlai Stevenson, who had alternated between believing the Democrats could not survive merely as a congressional party and praising Johnson's party management, reported that Johnson, at a party dinner, privately "complained incessantly about Butler, the Democratic National Committee, the Democratic Advisory Council, and personal matters."[66]

As soon as the 1958 congressional elections, bringing large Democratic gains, were completed, the leadership struggle was intensified. Before the elections, the *Democratic Digest*, which had given Lyndon Johnson occasional publicity, featured letters from congressional leaders on the accomplishments of Congress, and Butler urged these messages as campaign material on party workers.[67] After the Democratic victory, Butler congratulated Sam Rayburn "on the great record of the 85th Congress which contributed to the success of our Party in the elections." Rayburn responded that the victory was even bigger than he had expected, and that he felt even a greater responsibility. Rayburn had already pondered the difficulty of controlling a restless majority, too large.[68]

Butler engaged in a series of speeches on "The Lessons of the 1958 Elections." He told the National Association of Manufacturers the results represented a repudiation of Eisenhower's inadequate leadership and a mandate for liberal, Democratic congressional programs. Having observed Republican tactics in Indiana, Butler commented that you could not successfully campaign against nineteenth century socialism.[69]

The Democratic Advisory Council was scheduled to meet in Washington for work on its "State of the Union Message," and Sam Rayburn, who said he could not attend, warned, "I hope your group does not go into too much specifics on legislation."[70] But the DAC issued an extensive set of legislative demands, prefaced by a statement that responsibility required Democratic action. Particularly since Eisenhower had failed to provide legislative leadership, and with divided party government, congressional Democrats would have to perform the difficult task of leadership, which, in fact, they had already done with effectiveness the previous four years. Rayburn and Johnson were cited for their indicated intention of taking the initiative "in formulating and obtaining consideration of such a comprehensive Democratic program."[71] Lyndon Johnson was enraged, but in his own "State of the Union Message" proposed that congressional Democrats determine their own program without obeisance to the President. This course still might not satisfy liberal Democrats, and could provoke Eisenhower's wrath, since he was pleading for a balanced budget.[72]

The President's new political determination included the threat of vetoes. Johnson soon discovered that Eisenhower's change of tactics, coupled with an increased liberal bloc in the Senate, made the exercise of leadership more difficult than when Eisenhower had seemed more passive, and Johnson more cooperative. But, as Sam Rayburn put it, in defending the leadership method, "We are not here for the principle purpose of passing legislation that the President doesn't like. It is our duty here to pass legislation in the interest of the country, and then let the President do as he pleases . . . ."[73]

Now that Johnson was having leadership difficulties, and was being pressed by Senate liberals for reform in party rules, Butler's opposition became more open. In a civil rights speech in Boston, he urged Congress to implement the *Brown* ruling, and expressed an opinion that Johnson's proposal for conciliation in school segregation cases was inadequate.[74] In addressing a Western states party conference in Denver, Butler noted that some Democrats had accepted the Republican argument that progressive legislation should be forgotten because presidential vetoes could not be overridden. Butler asserted that Republicans should not determine Democratic legislative achievements. This speech was clearly an attack on Johnson, who was then trying to produce a third housing bill that could clear the expected presidential veto. Butler asserted:

> The Democratic Party is not a party of accommodation or attainability of compromise. People who are willing to accommodate themselves and the objectives of the Democratic Party to existing obstacles and obstructions to achievement do not typify the real spirit, the true courage, or the genuine zeal of our Party . . . The Democratic Party is a party of principle."[75]

He repeated the same theme in New York a week later, and in his customary letter in the *Democratic Digest*, pleading for "positive government," as mandated by the 1958 elections, not to be thwarted by veto threats. The DAC followed with its version of the theme.[76]

One of Butler's most controversial public appearances was on the Celebrity Parade program on Washington's Station WMAL-TV, July 5, 1959, with Butler's own Congressman John Brademas and moderator Joseph McCaffrey. The show had been taped June 17, and as early as June 9, McCaffrey told Butler he was setting up a question on civil rights since it was a topic "everyone seems to hit you with."[77] The discussants covered civil rights, Republican duplicity on civil rights, the DAC, national and congressional Democrats, party responsibility (Brademas was a political scientist), youth and the Democratic Party, money in politics, and the 1960 election. McCaffrey knew what questions to ask to elicit controversial responses from Butler. Yet Butler's responses seemed cautious at times with condemnation somewhat balanced with praise. Butler was partly right in accusing newspapers of distorting his remarks, which he later distributed to members of Congress.[78] Perhaps it was the cumulative effect of Butler's recent speeches, or perhaps the emphasis given the congressional situation, but this event clearly brought Butler's feud with congressional leaders to the public's attention.[79]

What had McCaffrey asked, and how had Butler (or Brademas) responded? In answer to a civil rights question, both Butler and

Brademas said there would be a strong civil rights plank in the 1960 platform, and that the Democrats would be united on the issue. National Democrats, unlike Republicans, took the same civil rights stand in every section. What of the division between the national Democratic Party and the congressional Democratic Party? Both Butler and Brademas acknowledged the division. Brademas, praising the DAC and Butler's role in establishing it, thought the Democratic Party would be strengthened in the long run. Butler thought the resolution of questions dividing Democrats would bring about a more nationalistic party. He believed Southern Democrats, protected by congressional seniority, did not represent the national viewpoint. He continued:

> But we have been striving in the Democratic Party to make the party more responsible and more responsive to the needs and demands of the people, and this can only be done on a national basis, and we believe we have to try to influence the Democratic leadership of the Congress to come along with the national program, rather than the more conservative and moderate program which they are trying to follow.

Many of the newer Democratic members of Congress were in contact with the National Committee, Butler said, and had "a feeling that the national program of the Democratic Party must be supported . . . ." Leading Butler on, and mentioning the fate of some vetoed legislation, McCaffrey asked if Democratic congressional majorities were too cautious. Butler answered that the leadership knew that many Democrats around the country were not satisfied with the progress of legislation, but Butler was hopeful that both the attitudes and policies of the leadership would change, with the 1960 election in mind. Democrats won in 1958, not so much because of their congressional record, but because of Eisenhower's lack of aggressive leadership. Now the responsibility rested with the Democratic Congress to enact progressive legislation. Otherwise, victory in 1960 would be difficult. Butler believed the Democratic leaders and members of Congress would react favorably:

> But I have every confidence that the leadership is going to step up the pace of the legislative program in the Congress, and here and there we will be laying a bill upon the President's desk even though knowing in advance that he may veto it and letting it be known and then we will take that issue to the American people.

A few days later, Butler reiterated that congressional leaders were too cautious, and was quoted to the effect that party unity was not served by "abject surrender" to those outside the party, and that the congressional leadership was not above constructive criticism. He said he would not be coerced into resigning by congressional Democrats who were lukewarm to the party platform, and that "We can't win the election of 1960 if we are to ape the Republican Party."[80] At this point, Butler also made the remarks about the leadership role of a national chairman, discussed above.

Butler insisted that he had only made suggestions about legislative strategy, and that he had not attacked Democratic congressional leaders. Perhaps he remembered his advice to Lt. Governor Robert Murphy of Massachusetts that Democrats should not attack other Democrats in public. He wrote Sam Rayburn, "I made no personal attack on any Democrat."[81]

Support and opposition developed as controversy raged for weeks after Butler's Celebrity Parade appearance.[82] Support came from many who held no party or public office; Butler called it grassroots support, and invited newsmen to see these letters. Butler wrote Sam Rayburn that correspondence supported Butler's position $6^1/2$ to 1.[83] The grassroots letters, sometimes accompanied by contributions to the party treasury, expressed liberal feelings and criticisms of Johnson's perceived closeness to Eisenhower and Southern Democrats. Some civil rights interest was shown. Butler's form letter of response asked for support of the Sustaining Membership pledge program "to keep our Party liberal and progressive."

Support also came from some of the California Democratic clubs. The state chairmen of Michigan and Colorado pledged their backing. Montana's national committeeman, who sensed that Butler's television remarks had been milder than those made on other occasions, believed civil rights to be a divisive factor, but also that most Democrats wanted adherence to the party program, rather than any temporary advantage in trying to get along with Eisenhower. The Pennsylvania national committeewoman, who did not always agree with Butler, commended him for his criticism of reactionaries. Carmine De Sapio said New York liked Butler's civil rights ideas. Senator Hubert Humphrey believed Butler's methods to be the only logical course for victory in 1960, and Senator William Proxmire thought Butler's statement on the congressional leadership had been constructive. James Carey, President of the International Union of Electrical, Radio, and Machine Workers, praised Butler's courage, and Walter Reuther responded similarly. Senator John Kennedy did not believe Butler was hurting the chances of a Democratic victory in 1960.[84]

Butler had less support in Congress than from state party officials. Sam Rayburn said the telegrams from members of Congress were 10-1 against Butler. A *Congressional Quarterly* survey showed about 60% of state Democratic governors, chairmen, and national committee members favoring Butler, while a slightly smaller percentage of congressional Democrats preferred Johnson's approach. Senator Spessard Holland agreed that the newspapers may have exaggerated Butler's Celebrity Parade remarks, but he still advised healing and harmony. Senator James Murray angrily broke silence to praise the leadership abilities of Johnson and Rayburn, and to chastise Butler. Senator Mike Mansfield urged Butler to get behind Johnson and Rayburn, since the last three elections had been decided on the basis of the party's congressional record. Indiana Senator Vance Hartke spoke from the Senate floor in defense of Johnson, and Senator Gale McGee said the legislative aim was a long range program, not legislation to elect a president. Governor Edmund Brown of California had agreed to join the DAC, but made it clear he supported Johnson's leadership strategy. However, by December, he was telling Butler that the success of the Democratic Party was in Butler's hands.[85]

Former President Truman wrote Sam Rayburn that Butler was "firing from the hip." Truman believed Butler was trying to organize the 1960 convention for Adlai Stevenson. After privately discussing the situation with Butler in Independence, Missouri, Truman held a press conference in which he said the national chairman should "keep the party together, not tear it apart," and that "Nobody ought to be read out of the party." Yet Truman had suggested some Southern Democrats should leave the party. Four months later, Truman thought Butler "sometimes talks too much . . .We fired the best Chairman we ever had—Frank McKinney." The real bone of contention for Truman was probably that McKinney was his friend and *his* national chairman. As much as Truman agreed with Butler's liberal policy views (and supported DAC statements), and as much as he enjoyed Butler's partisan attacks on Eisenhower and the Republican Party, he never backed Butler as chairman; he supported almost every attempt to eject Butler.[86]

Both Johnson and Rayburn had immediate responses to Butler's Celebrity Parade remarks. Johnson thought Butler was acting like his Republican counterpart, and not like a Democratic chairman. Rayburn said, "Mr. Butler can do the talking and we'll do the acting and make the record."[87]

Relations between Rayburn and Butler had been more cordial than those between Johnson and Butler. Democrats remembererd that Rayburn had intervened with Adlai Stevenson in 1956 to save Butler's chairmanship. Disagreement over the DAC had not strained this relationship too much, although as Butler talked more about civil rights, Rayburn began to tell people, "Mr. Paul Butler knows before now that I know he is talking too much and not very sensibly at that."[88] Then a month before the Celebrity Parade show, Butler had expressed an opinion that there would not likely be a Democratic presidential nominee from the South or Southwest in 1960, because of the civil rights issue.[89] Since Lyndon Johnson was again a candidate for president, Rayburn's pride as both Texan and mentor was hurt. It was probably this incident which most damaged Butler's standing with Rayburn. In response to a letter critical of Butler's pronouncement, Rayburn said, ". . . I think you hit the nail on the head with reference to this man, Butler, who is acting the biggest fool of anybody I can imagine."[90]

After the Celebrity Parade program, Rayburn responded to pro-Butler letters by expressing the belief Congress would establish a good record by enacting legislation for the country's benefit, regardless of the President's action. Rayburn was also aware that there were too few members of the National Committee disposed toward removing Butler as chairman. He advised those who had been solicited for contributions to the Democratic "750 Club" to hold off contributions: "I think it would be interpreted by Butler as your endorsement of his criticism against Congress if you were to send in a thousand dollars now."[91] To many correspondents, Rayburn replied that it looked to him "like this fellow Butler is running wild . . . I think Paul Butler has fallen in the hands of the most radical left-wing elements of the Party—including his Advisory Council and the ADA."[92] Rayburn also feared that Butler had "allowed himself to be passed into the hands of the most radical element of the Democratic Party—that element being led by Paul Ziffren, DNC from California, and others of the Lehman type in New York."[93]

About two weeks after the Celebrity Parade show, Butler, Johnson, and Rayburn met in Rayburn's office, with accounts varying as to whom asked for the meeting. The press was faulted for poor interpretation, and Butler, who said he had not intended to challenge the leadership, noted that he had predicted good legislative results by 1960. The congressional leaders, as part of the "armistice," wanted Butler to remain as chairman.[94]

The controversy between Butler and the legislative leaders, which was intensified by the Celebrity Parade remarks, did abate to some extent after the July armistice arranged in Rayburn's office. More accurately, the controversy found new forms in the maneuvering for the 1960 presidential nomination, particularly since Johnson was a candidate. 1959 ended with the DAC proclaiming that a Democratic Congress had prevented a more rapid deterioration in the State of the Union than that which had occurred, but that a Democratic president was necessary to provide complete leadership.[95] In his letter in the

Democratic Digest, Butler agreed that party unity could not be fostered if one deliberately tried to tear a party apart, but true unity could not come from "compromise of basic principles and beliefs."[96]

NOTES

1. Hubert H. Humphrey, *The Education of a Public Man: My Life and Politics* (Garden City, New York: Doubleday and Company, 1976), p. 364.
2. Ralph M. Goldman, *Search for Consensus: The Story of the Democratic Party* (Philadelphia: Temple University Press, 1979), p. 346.
3. Text of Butler speech at the inaugural luncheon for Governor G. Mennen Williams at Lansing, Michigan, January 1, 1959, Butler Papers, Box 110; text of Butler speech to Southern California Executive Committee Caucus, Los Angeles, California, August 10, 1957, Butler Papers, Box 142.
4. A 1959 biographical statement from the National Committee's Publicity Division stated Butler was "noted for his forthright discussion of national issues . . . and for his outspoken demand for enactment of the Democratic Party's platform."
5. Robert L. Riggs, Louisville *Courier-Journal*, July 19, 1959.
6. Democratic National Committee release, September 12, 1959, Butler Papers, Box 154.
7. Script for Face the Nation, CBS Radio and Television, February 10, 1957, Butler Papers, Box 202.
8. Doyle, *As We Knew Adlai*, p. 85.
9. Paul T. David, "The Changing Party Pattern," *The Antioch Review*, XVI (1956), 333-350.
10. *Stevenson Papers*, VII, 149.
11. Stevenson, *What I Think*, ix and x.
12. *Stevenson Papers*, VII, 464-465.
13. See Ralph K. Huitt, "Democratic Party Leadership in the Senate," *American Political Science Review*, LV (1961), 333-344.
14. Austin Ranney and Willmore Kendall, *Democracy and the American Party System* (New York: Harcourt, Brace and Company, 1956), pp. 107-108.
15. Butler speech at Pittsfield, Massachusetts, March 3, 1955, Butler Papers, Box 146.
16. Robert Riggs, Louisville *Courier-Journal*, July 19, 1959.
17. Excerpts from College News Conference, October 19, 1958, Butler Papers, Box 111.

18. Butler speech to Young Democrats Club, Oklahoma State University, March 10, 1959, Butler Papers, Box 155.
19. Stevenson, *What I Think* , x. But in "Memo to the President: Let's Make the Two-Party System Work," *Look*, September 20, 1955, p. 44, Stevenson places less emphasis on "opposition for opposition's sake."
20. Stevenson, *What I Think*, p. 73.
21. Warren E. Miller and Teresa E. Levitin, *Leadership Change: Presidential Elections from 1952-1976* (Cambridge, Massachusetts: Winthrop Publishers, 1976), p. 51.
22. Stevenson, *What I Think*, pp. 64, 71, 74.
23. Donald F. Crosby, *God, Church, and Flag: Senator Joseph R. McCarthy and the Catholic Church 1950-1957* (Chapel Hill, North Carolina: The University of North Carolina Press, 1978), pp. 77, 151-154.
24. Pp. 13-19.
25. See article on exhibit, "Chamber of Smears," the *Democratic Digest*, March, 1955, pp. 61-70.
26. Butler to Frank O'Malley, June 20, 1957, Butler Papers, Box 1.
27. Stevenson to Lippmann, September 25, 1958, *Stevenson Papers*, VII, 295.
28. Stevenson, *What I Think*, p. 98.
29. Truman to Stevenson, August 16, 1952, *Stevenson Papers* , IV, 46.
30. Stevenson to Harriman, February 4, 1954, ibid, IV, 320-321.
31. Stevenson, *What I Think*, pp. 98-99.
32. Stuart Gerry Brown, *Conscience in Politics: Adlai E. Stevenson in the 1950s* (Syracuse, New York: Syracuse University Press, 1961), pp. 173-188; Stevenson to John F. Dulles, November 3, 1957, *Stevenson Papers*, VII, 98-99.
33. New York *Times*, May 28, 1960.
34. *Stevenson Papers*, VII, 496-499.
35. Script for Meet the Press, NBC TV, February 13, 1955, Butler Papers, Box 202.
36. Butler Papers, Box 202.
37. Butler's text for Pick the Winner, CBS TV and Radio, October 31, 1956, Butler Papers, Box 202.
38. Butler's speech text at Washington and Lee University, February 23, 1955, Butler Papers, Box 146.
39. Butler's speech text for The American Forum, NBC Radio, June 5, 1955, Butler Papers, Box 202.
40. Butler Papers, Box 153.
41. Democratic National Committee release, November 28, 1955, Butler Papers, Box 128.
42. Text for The American Forum, NBC Radio, June 5, 1955, Butler Papers, Box 202; *Washington Post and Times-Herald*, March 23, 1956; Democratic National Committee release, March 7, 1955, Butler Papers, Box 125.

43. *Progress Bulletin*, Pomona, California, Butler Papers, Box 172; The *Daily Oklahoman*, October 8, 1956. From Bonham, Texas, Sam Rayburn agreed with Stevenson "that we must make efforts to stop the building and testing of bigger and more lethal H-bombs our first order of business." (Press release, October 23, 1956, Butler Papers, Box 139).

44. Democratic National Committee release, July 24, 1958, Butler Papers, Box 202.

45. New York *Herald-Tribune*, May 24, 1960.

46. In another comparison of Butler and Adlai Stevenson, a perusal of Stevenson's speeches shows that he did not treat Eisenhower with excessive deference either. Democratic congressional leaders were another case.

47. Interview with anonymous party leader, September 24, 1974.

48. New York *Times*, December 6, 1954.

49. Louisville *Courier-Journal*, March 8, 1956; New York *Post*, May 12, 1956; Democratic National Committee release, February 29, 1956, Butler Papers, Box 119.

50. St. Louis *Post-Dispatch*, March 14, 1955; Arizona *Daily Star*, March 11, 1955. A good many clippings in the Butler Papers, Box 144, refer to Eisenhower's health and reaction to Butler's comments thereon.

51. New York *Times*, June 13, 1956.

52. Butler's letter in the *Democratic Digest*, June, 1957.

53. New York *Times*, March 8, 1960.

54. Texts of speeches at Pittsfield, Massachusetts, March 3, 1955, and at New York City, March 8, 1955, Butler Papers, Box 146.

55. Speech text for National Press Club, February 1, 1955, Butler Papers, Box 146; Script for Meet the Press, NBC TV, February 13, 1955, Butler Papers, Box 202.

56. Steinberg, *Sam Johnson's Boy*, pp. 349-354.

57. Ibid., pp. 394-395; *Stevenson Papers*, IV, 478-479, comments on Lyndon Johnson meeting with Sam Rayburn, Stevenson, and Butler, rationalizing deference to the President; Adlai E. Stevenson, "Memo to the President: Let's Make the Two-Party System Work," *Look*, September 20, 1955, pp. 44.

58. Bone, *Party Committees*, p. 216; Roland Evans and Robert Novak, *Lyndon B. Johnson: The Exercise of Power* (New York: The New American Library, 1966), p. 146.

59. See Appointment Book, January, 1955, to December, 1958, Butler Papers, Box 196.

60. Louchheim, *By the Political Sea*, pp. 170-171.

61. See Butler Papers, Box 85, for notes sent members of Congress on birthdays, and for congratulations sent on reelections; Bone, *Party Committees*, p. 14.

62. The New York *Times Magazine*, July 1, 1956, p. 10.

63. Evans and Novak, *Lyndon B. Johnson*, p. 160.

64. ACPO Recommendation 20-B, 1957, in Paul G. Willis collection. For a general picture of Johnson's leadership views, his objectives and methods, his rationalizations, and the basis for his differences with presidential Democrats see: Huitt, *Democratic Leadership*; Evans and Novak, *Lyndon B. Johnson*, Chapters 8 and 9; Doris Kearns, *Lyndon Johnson and the American Dream* (New York: Harper and Row, Publishers, 1976), Chapter 5; Cornelius P. Cotter and Bernard C. Hennessy, *Politics Without Power: The National Party Committees* (New York: Atherton Press, 1964), pp. 99-100.

65. David S. Broder, *The Party's Over: The Failure of Politics in America* (New York: Harper and Row, Publishers, 1971, 1972), pp. 64-69.

66. Stevenson to Brooks Hays, August 14, 1957, *Stevenson Papers*, VII, 48; Stevenson to Lyndon B. Johnson, August 19, 1957, ibid., VII, 51-52; Stevenson to Mrs. Ronald Tree, February 23, 1958, ibid., VII, 168-169. He also told a critic of Johnson that patience with Southern Democrats, and an understanding of them, would be necessary if the South were to continue solving racial problems (ibid., VII, 68).

67. *Democratic Digest*, February, 1958, p. 3; April, 1958, p. 3; September, 1958, pp. 7-8. See also Butler to Sam Rayburn, September 9, 1958, and Rayburn to Butler, September 17, 1958, in Sam Rayburn Papers, The Sam Rayburn Library, Bonham, Texas (hereafter referred to as Rayburn Papers).

68. Butler to Rayburn, November 12, 1958, and Rayburn to Butler, November 14, 1958, Rayburn Papers; Evans and Novak, *Lyndon B. Johnson*, p. 196. While Lyndon Johnson cited the victory as the fruits of his leadership, Robert E. Baskin, Dallas *Morning News*, November 30, 1958, said Butler had been more in the forefront of the 1958 fight than anyone else.

69. Texts for NAM speech, December 3, 1958, and Manchester, New Hampshire speech, December 13, 1958, Butler Papers, Box 154.

70. Rayburn to Butler, December 2, 1958, Butler Papers, Box 59.

71. *The Democratic Task During the Next Two Years*, a policy statement by the DAC, December 7, 1958, in the author's collection.

72. Steinberg, *Sam Johnson's Boy*, p. 494.

73. Rayburn to D.W. Gilmore, July 9, 1959, Rayburn Papers.

74. Democratic National Committee release for Butler's speech before the Ford Hall Forum, April 26, 1959, Butler Papers, Box 150.

75. Butler speech text, May 16, 1959, Butler Papers, Box 156.

76. New York *Times*, June 15, 1959; *Democratic Digest*, July, 1959.

77. McCaffrey to Butler, June 9, 1959, Butler Papers, Box 12.

78. Marshall McNeil, Washington *News*, July 13, 1959, said that the press quoted Butler badly.
79. See Celebrity Parade, Station WMAL-TV, July 5, 1959, text in Butler Papers, Box 12, for the account which follows.
80. Atlanta *Constitution*, July 10, 1959; Kansas City *Star*, July 12, 1959; Baltimore *Sun*, July 12, 1959.
81. New York *Times*, July 12, 1959; Butler to Murphy, May 8, 1959, Butler Papers, Box 7; Butler to Rayburn, July 15, 1959, Rayburn Papers.
82. There are several boxes of correspondence and newspaper clippings in the Butler Papers on this matter—for instance, Boxes 7, 95, 96, 108, 109, 123, 145, 179, 180, and 181.
83. Butler to Rayburn, July 15, 1959, Rayburn Papers;the Washington *Daily News*, July 21, 1959.
84. Clipping from *Congressional Record*, Butler Papers, Box 123; St. Louis *Post-Dispatch*, September 18, 1959; New York *Times*, July 18, 1959; Emma G. Miller to Butler, July 6, 1959, Butler Papers, Box 109; James Carey to Butler, July 17, 1959, Box 96; Walter Reuther to Butler, August 5, 1959, Box 7; New York *Times*, July 14, 1960.
85. Rayburn to Henry Wade, July 24, 1959, Rayburn Papers; Louisville *Courier-Journal*, July 17, 1959; Holland to Butler, July 17, 1959, Butler Papers, Box 108; Murray to Butler, July 14, 1959, Butler Papers, Box 108; New York *Times*, July 7, 1959; McGee's newsletter, July, 1959, Butler Papers, Box 145; New York *Times*, July 21, 1959; Brown to Butler, December 22, 1959, Butler Papers, Box 6.
86. Robert H. Ferrell (ed.), *Off the Record: The Private Papers of Harry S. Truman* (New York: Harper and Row, Publishers, 1980), p. 381; Louisville *Courier-Journal*, September 11, 1959; excerpts from College News Conference, October 19, 1958, Butler Papers, Box 111; New York *Herald-Tribune*, January 24, 1960; Ferrell, *Off the Record*, pp. 381-382, where Truman tells Dean Acheson that he had never been for Butler for chairman.
87. Chicago *Daily News*, July 7, 1959; New York *Times*, July 7, 1959.
88. Rayburn to Karl G. Hunt, October 25, 1958, Rayburn Papers.
89. Washington *Post*, June 7, 1959.
90. Rayburn to Byron Skelton, June 12, 1959, Rayburn Papers.
91. Rayburn to James Neal, July 17, 1959, Rayburn Papers.
92. Rayburn to Earle B. Mayfield, July 17, 1959, Rayburn Papers.
93. Rayburn to H.M. Ayers, July 17, 1959, Rayburn Papers.
94. New York *Times*, July 25, 1959.
95. *The Decision in 1960: The Need to Elect a Democratic President*, a policy statement by the DAC, December 5-7, 1959, in the author's collection.
96. *Democratic Digest*, December, 1959, and January, 1960.

Chapter Five

CIVIL RIGHTS—PARAMOUNT MORAL ISSUE

From time to time Paul Butler spoke out on a variety of issues. In the end, however, he probably attracted most attention as an advocate of civil rights for black Americans. His attention to this concern placed him in opposition to Republicans, Southern Democrats, and often Democratic congressional leaders, but before the 1960s arrived he had identified the national Democratic Party with a cause which its 1960 platform enunciated clearly—a platform which served as the basis for Kennedy-Johnson civil rights proposals.

Civil rights increasingly became a national issue with political consequences which was the focal point of Butler's troubles with Southern Democrats. The friendly relations which Butler had established with Southern Democrats before and at the time of his election as chairman, relations which he certainly preferred to maintain, persisted for some time. His hopes were expressed in a letter to a retired chairman of the Georgia State Democratic Executive Committee:

> Too few of the people in our party realize that we are all part of a great national political party and you have demonstrated beyond question that our state leaders can, if they only will, convince the rank and file membership of our party that they have an obligation to support and cooperate with the Democratic National Committee.[1]

After Butler made a trip to Georgia, the new state chairman informed him he had made "a splendid impression" on Georgia Democrats, and that those who had met Butler felt he was now a close personal friend, and that Butler's "dynamic leadership" would produce unity and victory in 1956. Meanwhile, the South should not be taken for granted.[2]

But not all problems in the South were so easily handled as those in Georgia. Texas, whose Democratic governor, Allan Shivers, had supported Eisenhower in 1952, posed a complex problem, complicated

89

by the presence and interests of Democratic congressional leaders, Johnson and Rayburn. Butler, seeking a reconciliation with Shivers when other Democrats were criticizing his apostasy and doubting any future loyalty, met with Shivers and Rayburn in Washington. Former chairman Stephen Mitchell announced that to honor Southern loyalists he would challenge the seating of Shivers and other defectors at the 1956 convention, but Butler, Adlai Stevenson, and New York Governor Averell Harriman refused to support Mitchell's position.[3] Butler then went on a much publicized Texas trip, sponsored by the Texas Democratic Advisory Council, and refused to discuss Texas party differences with Shivers. Pamphlets issued by the Advisory Council stressed that Texas Democrats could honor Sam Rayburn by visiting his guest, Paul Butler, a prominent man of integrity, who "although born in Indiana . . . has the Texas spirit and . . . is a Rayburn Democrat."[4] Even though the Advisory Council was a liberal group, Butler was criticized by some, who viewed the trip as appeasement of Shivers. In 1959 a Texas Democrat reviewed this confusing situation for Butler:

> It was you, however, a couple of years later who sneaked off into the Capitol kitchen in Washington with Allan Shivers to cook up a deal whereby he would again, with your approval take over the party in Texas. It was only the loud protests of the loyal Democrats of Texas including me that kept you from consumating the deal you all had planned when you later came to Texas and made a very useful and productive tour.[5]

In four months Shivers said he would support Eisenhower in 1956 again, but the new Texas national committeeman, Lt. Governor Ben Ramsey, would support the Democratic nominee.[6]

Butler's desire for Southern reconciliation was supported by other developments, particularly the actions of the Special Advisory Committee on Rules and Proceedings established in 1953 to handle the loyalty oath problem. It took Chairman Stephen Mitchell a year to carefully appoint the membership and, since the group was to be advisory to the National Committee, few National Committee members served on it. Mitchell remained its chairman, even after Butler became his successor, and Virginia Governor John S. Battle and Minnesota Senator Hubert H. Humphrey served as vice chairmen.[7]

As this committee's work proceeded, some liberal Democrats began to feel that Humphrey and other supposedly liberal colleagues acted like Dixiecrats. On April 16, 1955, the committee decided that the proposed new rules should be attached to the call for the 1956 convention. These moderate proposals placed no real obligation on convention delegates, requiring only members of the National Committee to declare for the party presidential nominee. State parties, in sending delegates to a national convention, incurred an obligation to see that the name of the party nominee or names of party electors were placed on the ballot. Butler was pleased with the committee's work, noting that the proposed rule would "eliminate any necessity for any discussion of the loyalty oath in the 1956 convention, and which may possibly lay the foundation for perfect understanding and good will among the delegates."[8] On December 17, 1955, the National Committee unanimously recommended adoption of the rules by the 1956 convention.

In 1956 Butler was drawn more directly into discussion of civil rights. In a debate with Republican Representative Hugh Scott before the Leadership Conference for Civil Rights in Washington, Butler argued that civil rights supporters should give credit to Franklin Roosevelt and Harry Truman, and that Vice President Richard Nixon had acted partisanly in saying that *Brown v. Board of Education* had been decided under a Republican Chief Justice. He urged President Eisenhower to call leaders together for a biracial conference, and expressed hope for congressional elimination of the poll tax, protection of voting rights, making the Civil Rights Section a division of the Department of Justice, and enactment of an anti-violence measure.[9]

In a speech to the Association of County Commissioners in Savannah, Georgia, Butler made only vague reference to civil rights, but pleaded for the South, which received nothing from the Republican Party, to stay Democratic. He doubted the possibility of a third party or a Southern bolt in 1956 "if we can keep the extremists coming toward the middle." He further predicted that the 1956 platform would feature a moderate civil rights plank without any straddling of the issue. "We're not going to slap our Southern members in the face. We're not going to advocate that the Supreme Court's decision be enforced by guns and bayonets. It's a matter that's in the hands of the courts."[10] In June he told the Michigan CIO convention, "I would oppose brashly reading out of the Democratic Party those states south of the Mason-Dixon line."[11]

Butler had said the platform should state respect for court decisions and that it would be vigorous on civil rights; but when he got to the convention, he criticized Adlai Stevenson for saying the platform should express "unequivocal approval" of the Supreme Court's ruling on segregated schools.[12] The convention decisively rejected credentials committee recommendations against the seating of the regular Mississippi and South Carolina delegations, and adopted a moderate civil rights plank after voting down a strengthening amendment offered by liberals.

Following the 1956 election, civil rights liberals were among those wanting Butler replaced as national chairman, but the political situation surrounding civil rights was beginning to change significantly. Creation of the Democratic Advisory Council by the National Committee's Executive Committee was supported by those who believed the election had been lost in the cities because of lack of a progressive legislative program on the part of congressional Democrats. Butler's friends reported that he was disillusioned by the convention compromises on civil rights. He would later refer to appeasement of the South in 1952 and 1956, and of extreme moderation on racial issues.[13] Response to implementation of *Brown* in the South, on the part of both supporters and opponents, also hastened political readjustment. In its first action, the newly-formed Democratic Advisory Council took a stand for a proposed change in Senate rules designed to weaken filibusters, and urged Congress to follow the Democratic platform on civil rights.[14]

Then during the 1957 Little Rock, Arkansas school integration crisis, Butler told a regional party conference in Raleigh, North Carolina, that threat of a Southern bolt would not keep the Democratic Party from serving all Americans, and that the party would not pull back from recognizing *Brown* as the law of the land. There were immediate demands for Butler's resignation, which he ignored; and the next day, in Oklahoma City, he told another party conference that "the Democratic Party will not be deterred in its stand for civil rights by any threat of a third party in the South."[15] The Democratic Advisory Council, not waiting for its next scheduled meeting, had already responded to Little Rock by telephone communication, partly by criticizing President Eisenhower for failure to exert leadership: "It need hardly be said that the action of Governor Faubus does not represent the position or policy of the Democratic Party."[16] Later the Council directed its staff to investigate the necessity of Congress enacting new civil rights legislation.[17]

Early in 1958, the Democratic National Committee sponsored a two-day Conference on Party Relations for black leaders, the first meeting of its kind, to seek counsel from the assembled participants. Eighty black party officials were invited.[18]

Continuing his emphasis on civil rights, Butler pledged that "the Democratic Party will never fail to stand behind that decision [*Brown*] of the courts," and in 1960 the party would "speak out forthrightly and clearly in support of integration at the earliest possible time."[19]

The Alabama State Democratic Executive Committee had already excoriated Butler and the President for their actions and views on racial matters, one speaker describing the Northern wing of the Democratic Party as the "mulatto wing," but Butler continued to speak out on civil rights and saw to it that not only Southern Democrats would be offended. At Leland Stanford University, he said civil rights should be a bipartisan concern, but Republicans wanted credit for *Brown* and Southern support at the same time. Any time Republican members of Congress decided on a course of bipartisanship, civil rights bills could be enacted. Despite encumbrances from being the only nationally based party, Democrats had the best civil rights record. Butler later added that Republican national chairman Meade Alcorn's research and information on civil rights was as bad as the Republican record of duplicity on human rights. In a talk on party responsibility at Illinois State Normal University, Butler argued that the President should have his Attorney General intervene as *amicus curiae* in the Little Rock school case pending before the Federal Court of Appeals in St. Louis. Butler said this action would aid party responsibility, particularly because the Executive should support the courts on civil rights. Otherwise people would lose faith in government.[20]

Butler had proclaimed that "civil rights is the number one social issue of our times," so he continued to instigate a Democratic-Republican debate.[21] When Republican Chairman Alcorn in a television debate baited Butler with Arkansas Governor Orval Faubus, and chided Butler for once having characterized Faubus as "a great Democrat," Butler responded that the President had to provide moral leadership in racial matters, and Eisenhower had never declared the rightness, legally and morally, of *Brown*. The President should appoint a commission, representative of diverse interests, to discuss civil rights, and "try to bring about a climate of opinion . . . which would provide for a wider and more peaceful and more decent acceptance of this principle as laid down by the Supreme Court." Franklin Roosevelt and Harry Truman had already created the climate which made different racial attitudes possible. Butler proceeded to discuss party realignment, not denying that some congressional Democrats opposed civil rights measures, but asserted that these Democrats did not represent the party majority; as Alcorn had suggested, dissatisfied Democrats would be joining the Republican Party. Butler concluded:

> As a lawyer and as an American I accept the decisions of the Supreme Court as the law of the land and I will fight if necessary in order to sustain that principle that our Supreme Court decisions must be respected as the law of the land by all governors and all citizens.[22]

Two weeks later Butler appeared on the College News Conference television program, further angering Southern Democrats and giving other opponents an opportunity to criticize him. Asked if he agreed with Harry Truman that it would be good for some Southern congressional Democrats and the Solid South to leave the party, Butler answered that Southern committee domination might be a serious matter for Democrats and the nation, and that it would be unfortunate for the South to remain in the party in 1960 just to retain congressional chairmanships. Devotion to the party should be based on conviction on issues, and the racial problem was "a moral issue for the country and it requires moral leadership." The 1960 Democratic platform would brook "no compromise on the integration problem," and "those people in the South who are not deeply dedicated to the policies and beliefs in fact the philosophy of the Democratic Party will have to go their own way." Butler wanted as many Americans as possible believing in Democratic Party principles, but if Southerners did not "want to go along on the racial problem and the whole area of human rights," they would "have to take political asylum wherever they can find it, either in the Republican Party or a third party . . . people should belong to a political party only if they believe in its principles." Butler believed "hundreds of thousands of real solid good Democrats" in the South would still support the party.[23]

At this point Florida Senator George Smathers, chairman of the Senate Democratic Campaign Committee, advised Butler to "pipe down" and get on with the congressional elections, which looked promising for Democrats. Of course, this is what Butler thought he was doing—preparing not only for 1958, but 1960. Harry Truman, whose remarks about Southern Democrats had prompted Butler, now shifted into a conciliatory role, saying he did not agree with Butler and was not reading anyone out of the party. In a speech to the National Press Club, Butler said his intention had not been to read anyone out of the party either; but there should be no compromise on civil rights, "on a problem as clearly and definitely a moral issue as is the race question."[24]

The New York *Post* editorialized that it was tragic that leadership in the civil rights crisis came not from the President, but from Paul Butler, who was risking his political life. Yet, from a political standpoint, Butler believed Democrats could win the 1960 presidential election only by taking a "forthright and positive stand" on civil rights. In fact, Butler's remaining as chairman was attributed to the big election victory in 1958, and his strong civil rights stand, which represented the dominant Northern and Western wings of the Democratic Party.[25]

As a year-end conclusion to the civil rights controversy, the Democratic National Committee resolved a question of national versus state party authority. The Louisiana national committeeman, Camille F. Gravel, Jr., a racial moderate and a party loyalist, had been removed by the Louisiana State Committee. Earl Long, who had lost a congressional primary election to an opponent supported by Gravel, joined segregationists in the removal. Local opinion held that Gravel should have represented Louisiana and not come home to tell people he "represented the national Democratic party."[26] Butler advised that the National Committee judged its members' qualifications, and Gravel was still a member from Louisiana. Speaker Sam Rayburn seemed to agree.[27]

At the December 6 National Committee meeting, the Credentials Committee decided that there was not basis for Gravel's removal, and that the credentials of his replacement, certified by the Louisiana State Committee, should be rejected. Without debate, the full National Committee agreed, 91-15.[28] It then adopted a long resolution praising Butler, who had "lead the Democratic Party to its greatest success in the polls," for operating under adverse conditions, serving as chairman of the Democratic Advisory Council, reorganizing the National Committee, implementing the program of the Advisory Committee on Political Organization, travelling widely, and for "unswerving loyalty to the principles upon which the Party was founded." The resolution continued:

> *Whereas*, the Honorable Paul Butler's speeches on Democratic principles, on the provisions contained in the Democratic platform and on the current issues involving Democratic policies include his forthright utterances on civil rights and the determination of the Democratic Party that the provisions of the Constitution of the United States as interpreted by the Supreme Court shall be enforced and made effective, have attracted the approval of the vast majority of the American people as proved by the recent elections, *Now Therefore*, be it resolved . . . that sincere appreciation and commendation of the unsurpassed services of the Honorable Paul Butler as Chairman of the Committee are hereby expressed.[29]

Although Gravel himself moved to recommit the resolution for deletion of any mention of civil rights, his efforts were unsuccessful.

The following day, the Democratic Advisory Council issued a State of the Union-type statement calling for, along with a wide variety of programs, new civil rights legislation to "aid, assist and encourage the earliest possible reopening of schools now closed, and will prevent

95

the closing of other schools," and for changes in Senate Rule 22, affecting debate.[30]

In April, 1959, Butler gave a major address on civil rights before the Ford Hall Forum in Boston, attempting to subdue his partisanship. He defined human rights as those rights all are endowed with by virtue of God's creation. "They are rights which are founded in the principles of religion and morality." Both Thomas Jefferson and the United Nations had recognized the essentialness to freedom, justice, and peace of governmental recognition of these rights. Republicans had rendered their best service to America when Jeffersonian principles had been observed. Tracing the evolution of concepts of political and economic rights, some of which had been viewed as controversial, Butler once more credited the moral leadership of Franklin and Eleanor Roosevelt, and Harry Truman, for causing a "re-examination of the national conscience," when rights had been denied because of race, creed, or national origin. He cited court decisions which were not the result of any political party's efforts, and praised those Republicans who supported human rights protection, while noting that most Republican officeholders, and a distinct minority of Democrats, had been obstructionists. Butler charged that President Eisenhower was waiting for others to show the way, and had failed to follow other presidents in providing civil rights leadership, even while congressional Democrats were making headway. Looking to the future, Butler believed prejudice was not sectional, but a national problem. Law must be upheld, and the President must label *Brown* morally right. Legislation was also necessary for the implementation of court decisions on segregation, legislation which went beyond Lyndon Johnson's current concept of conciliation in racial matters. The Democratic Party must right wrongs and insist on progressive racial policies because, above all else, this was "the right thing to do morally, as every great body of organized religion in the United States has repeatedly stated . . . the doctrine of the dignity of man is just as true on Monday as it is on Sunday."[31]

By this time, Butler heard directly criticism of his civil rights espousal. One Alabama editor told him, "your alignment with the group that is antagonistic to the fundamental social ideas of the South" was responsible for the inability of Democratic loyalists to raise money for the National Committee.[32] Senator Russell Long indicated that he could not raise funds in Louisiana because of the Gravel incident. On the other hand, an Arkansas loyalist was afraid his contribution to the national party would help Governor Faubus.[33] Butler could only imagine some comments his detractors made. A Texas county official, who felt Republicans were paying Butler to split the Democratic Party, wrote Sam Rayburn:

Sam if there is any way you all can get rid of this S.B. we want him sent to Blanco County. We have what we call the Negro Colony, in the S.E. corner of our county. The Commissioner's Court of Blanco County have promised me if we can get him, they will appoint him Justice of the Peace in this Negro Precinct. Personally I don't think he would make good.[34]

In September Butler faced an embarrassing situation. Governor David Lawrence of Pennsylvania, a member of the National Committee, who had never accepted Butler as chairman and who was often in alignment with factions desiring Butler's ouster, mailed to some National Committee members copies of the pledges concerning segregation which Butler had signed prior to his election in New Orleans. The statements were in the possession of Georgia state chairman John Bell, who had already cited them as sufficient for Butler's expulsion. Butler responded to good political advantage by arguing that opposition to his continuation as chairman was in fact support of segregation: "Apparently Governor Lawrence has joined the Southern segregationists in their effort to remove me as Chairman . . . I had always thought that our views on the issues involving human rights are closely similar." Butler explained the "circumstances" under which he had signed the New Orleans pledges. He had not signed them to get votes, he said, but because Bell had asked for his views. The pledges came shortly after *Brown*, and the issue of segregation was in the domain of the lower federal courts, and "was not a political issue at that time, and men of good will on both sides of the Mason-Dixon line hoped that it would not become one." Butler pointed out that after his election he had also publicly stated that segregation was not a political issue. But Little Rock, resistance to court orders, bombings, school closings, and Republican efforts to claim *Brown* as a political asset had since made segregation a political issue. Since others were responsible for making it such, it deserved frank public discussion. It was his duty to express the majority Democratic view. He still regretted that segregation had become a burning political issue, but his present actions were compatible with his 1954 position.[35]

In preparation for the 1960 presidential campaign, Butler compiled speech material almost entirely on civil rights and the sit-ins of the late 1950s.[36] He spoke to several college mock political conventions, and stressed civil rights at all of them. A liberal Democratic candidate would "be committed to championing the cause of human rights and individual dignity with every ounce of strength at his command," *because human rights was the "greatest moral issue facing the American people today."*[37] At DePauw University in Indiana, Butler traced the history of sit-ins, arguing that they were not "un-American," or "communistic," as some had charged. Individual rights and dignity came from a divine source. Most religious groups approved of non-violent demonstrations. He admonished students and faculty: "In everything that we do in our daily lives remember the teachings of Jesus Christ, Mahatma Gandhi, and Martin Luther King. Love and non-violence is the way. 'May God bless each of you' were their final instructions."[38]

At a National Editorial Association meeting in Atlanta, Butler pleaded for the press to show leadership appropriate to the challenges offered by the civil rights struggle. Newspapers had moved too slowly in the battle for civil rights, and many had failed to measure up to their responsibility of shaping public opinion. Butler also praised several Southern newspapers for leadership in communities where racial tensions were sharpest.[39]

In September, 1959, the Democratic National Committee recommended readoption of the 1956 convention loyalty rules, even though some Southern states were threatening to employ independent presidential electors in 1960. Early in 1960, Butler announced that he would try to prevent the seating of convention delegates from these states, but the 1960 convention readopted the old compromise rules. There was no real conflict over loyalty or civil rights in Los Angeles, and a Southern attempt to weaken a strong civil rights platform failed.[40]

As a member of the Democratic National Committee, and as chairman, Paul Butler had pursued what seemed to be at times a contradictory course. He had stressed party unity and followed a policy of conciliation toward Southern Democrats while at the same time advocating nationalistic party devices which would upset them. Not surprisingly, to those who remembered his earlier conciliatory mood, he appeared a paradox as he increasingly concerned himself with civil rights and pledged the Democratic Party to a liberal civil rights program as a response to what Butler called the leading moral issue of the day. He privately told Lyndon Johnson that he would have to face up to the civil rights problem.[41] Some individuals said Butler had betrayed them, and others said he played politics. While he made political enemies by his insistence on civil rights, he also helped guarantee his survival as chairman, for a while longer, by making it politically difficult for Northern Democrats to directly oppose him. One Butler critic said, "Butler has managed to make it a fight between himself and Faubus; on that basis, he can't possibly lose."[42]

Yet to many American leaders of the late 1950s who saw swift developments and responded accordingly, there was plausibility in Butler's argument that, after 1954, civil rights progressed from a legal to a highly political issue. More importantly, the same Americans usually saw the civil rights issue in moral terms; and, more and more, they noticed that Butler preached with evangelical fervor. Those who knew him in South Bend did not doubt his sincerity on the issue of civil rights, and his perception of it as an essentially moral issue. They pointed out that Butler had shown a concern with civil rights long before *Brown*.[43] A perusal of his public speeches in the 1940s shows his concern with prejudice in American life and his plea for tolerance. This concern fortified his distaste for Hitlerism when many of his contemporaries were less sure. The human rights Butler believed in were, in his thinking, of divine origin, and it was obligatory for government to protect these rights. His encouragement of women in political organization, far beyond tokenism, illustrated another dimension of his human rights thinking. In 1949 Butler sponsored a woman for clerk with a subdivision of the State Highway Department, even though no woman had previously held such a position in Indiana. Law required that vice chairmen of political organization committees be of the opposite sex from chairmen, and they were almost aways women; in St. Joseph County, Paul Butler installed the first woman precinct committeeman, a person who went on to become the first Democratic woman district chairman.[44] The Advisory Committee on Political Organization recommended more female participation in party organization and, among other things, an equal number of women in elected party leadership positions. ACPO employed a black woman, Venice Sprags, as executive secretary, and she implemented several important ACPO recommendations at party headquarters.[45] Finally, as the civil rights issue intensified in the late 1950s, Reverend John Cavanaugh, C.S.C., President of Notre Dame University, and others helped Butler come to see civil rights as so critical a moral issue.[46]

Prior to the 1960 convention, that opposition to John Kennedy which could be attributed to religious prejudice could only reinforce Butler's course in civil rights. The more Paul Butler, the lawyer, saw civil rights not only in legal terms, but also with moral ramifications, the more he acted as a party leader advocating civil rights. As a major spokesman for the Democratic Party, Paul Butler identified the party with a strong civil rights program, before the 1960s. Today, few civil rights supporters would deny it was one of Butler's finest moments in his public leadership career. Yet for all the controversy he aroused by his interest in civil rights, and in spite of his prominence at the time, memories of his role have dimmed. But upon his retirement as chairman, the NAACP remembered his civil rights contribution.[47]

Following the 1960 election, Butler, no longer a party official, analyzed the role of the civil rights question in the election. He attributed Democratic gains from black voters (Richard Nixon still received 32% of the black vote, but in 1956 Eisenhower had received

39%) to "a carefully-planned change of attitude and politics on the part of the Democratic Party nationally." The 1952 and 1956 campaigns had featured "extreme moderation and conservatism on all racial problems" and appeasement of the South. A continuation of that course would have destroyed the Democratic Party as a "vital, positive, liberal, and progressive force," but the party had reverted "to a party of responsibility, daring to be right on the great moral and political issues of our times regardless of the political risks involved." The Democratic National Committee had made four decisions, Butler said, which changed the party's course: (1) it had supported civil rights and progressive legislation; (2) it had used the Democratic Advisory Council to implement such support, as well as the national chairman and other leading Democrats, who urged party members to support these liberal efforts; (3) it had caused the 1960 convention to meet in a liberal and progressive climate and city to adopt its platform; and (4) it had continued to develop techniques, methods, and procedures to insure the adoption of a liberal platform "containing the most forthright and unequivocal statement on civil rights ever made by a political party." Democrats had restored an image of moral right over the opposition. The president-elect and the party were now obligated to carry out Democratic pledges. Butler expected John Kennedy to implement them vigorously.[48]

Paul Butler had pretty well summarized the accomplishments of his chairmanship, and with minimal self-glorification. His political analysis was shrewd, and he might have added that effective politics can also be moral politics.

NOTES

1. Butler to James S. Peters, October 6, 1954, Butler Papers, Box 104.
2. Speech in Augusta, Georgia, April 25, 1955, Butler Papers, Box 147; John S. Bell to Butler, May 5, 1955, Butler Papers, Box 70.
3. Holtzman, *The Loyalty Pledge Controversy*, pp. 24-25; Washington *Star*, May 17, 1955; Steinberg, *Sam Johnson's Boy*, p. 300.
4. *Sam Rayburn and the Democratic Advisory Council of Texas*, Butler Papers, Box 194; Dallas *Morning News*, June 4, 1955.
5. See letters in Butler Papers, Boxes 3, 9, and 40; W.O. Cooper to Butler, July 6, 1959, Rayburn Papers.

6. Democratic National Committee release, October 16, 1955, Butler Papers, Box 115.
7. Holtzman, *The Loyalty Pledge Controversy*, pp. 10-13.
8. Democratic National Committee release, October 16, 1955, Butler Papers, Box 115; Holtzman, *The Loyalty Pledge Controversy*, pp. 16-17.
9. Democratic National Committee release, March 6, 1956, Butler Papers, Box 116; copies of Butler's speech were sent to organizations which had participated in the conference (Butler Papers, Box 69).
10. Louisville *Times*, May 21, 1956; Democratic National Committee release, April 9, 1956, Butler Papers, Box 115; New York *Times*, April 21, 1956.
11. Louisville *Courier-Journal*, December 3, 1958.
12. Butler-Hall Debate, CBS Radio TV, March 25, 1956, Butler Papers, Box 171; newstype strip, August 8, 1956, Butler Papers, Box 171; Chicago *Daily News*, August 11, 1956. For a good perspective on the civil rights issue at the 1956 convention from the standpoint of Eleanor Roosevelt's involvement, see Joseph P. Lash, *Eleanor: The Years Alone* (New York: W.W. Norton and Company, 1972), pp. 246-255. See also Adlai Stevenson to Eleanor Roosevelt, August 9, 1956, and suggested draft of civil rights plank to Butler, August 4, 1956, *Stevenson Papers*, VI, 177-180.
13. New York *Times*, November 27 and 28, 1956; Louisville *Courier-Journal*, December 3, 1958; Democratic National Committee release, November 30, 1960, Butler Papers, Box 204.
14. New York *Times*, February 17 and 18, 1957.
15. New York *Times*, September 18 and 19, 1957.
16. *Democratic Digest*, October, 1957, p. 9.
17. New York *Times*, October 21, 1957.
18. *Democratic Digest*, March, 1958, p. 9; Louchheim, *By the Political Sea*, p. 35; *Official Report of the 1960 Democratic National Convention and Committee*, p. 487.
19. Transcript for Mutual Broadcasting System's Reporters Roundup, May 5, 1958, Butler Papers, Box 124.
20. New York *Times*, January 26, 1958; text of Stanford speech in Butler Papers, Box 151; Democratic National Committee release, October 31, 1958, Box 124; DNC release, July 2, 1958, Butler Papers, Box 124.
21. CBS news release for Face the Nation, February 2, 1958, Butler Papers, Box 124.
22. Excerpts from The Great Game of Politics, CBS Television, October 5, 1958, Butler Papers, Box 164.
23. Excerpts from College News Conference, October 19, 1958, Butler Papers, Box 111.
24. New York *Times*, October 22 and 23, 1958.

25. New York *Post*, October 24, 1958; New York *Times*, November 8 and 17, 1958.
26. Monroe (Louisiana) *Morning World*, October 12, 1958.
27. New York *Times*, October 5, 9, and 10, 1958.
28. *Official Report of the 1960 Democratic National Convention and Committee*, pp. 504-512.
29. Ibid., pp. 512-514.
30. *The Democratic Task During the Next Two Years* , DAC policy statement, December 7, 1958, in author's collection.
31. Democratic National Committee release, April 26, 1959, Butler Papers, Box 150.
32. A copy of M.M. Ayres to Butler, July 9, 1959, Rayburn Papers.
33. Long to Butler, March 16, 1959, Butler Papers, Box 16; Lee Ward to Butler, May 29, 1959, Butler Papers, Box 6.
34. C.H. Stevenson to Rayburn, July 8, 1959, Rayburn Papers.
35. Democratic National Committee release, September 12, 1959, Butler Papers, Box 154.
36. Articles and material for speeches in Butler Papers, Boxes 34, 35, and 36.
37. Democratic National Committee release for speech at Morgan Street College, Baltimore, April 1, 1960, Butler Papers, Box 111; the same idea was stressed at Northwestern University, April 12, 1960, Butler Papers, Box 160.
38. Newspaper story, n.d., Butler Papers, Box 204.
39. Democratic National Committee release, May 7, 1960, Butler Papers, Box 111.
40. *Official Report of the 1960 Democratic National Convention and Committee*, pp. 33-36, 62-98, 662-663; Holtzman, *The Loyalty Pledge Controversy*, pp. 27-29.
41. Interview with Anne Butler, June 10, 1975.
42. Louisville *Courier-Journal*, December 3, 1958.
43. Interview with Marshall Smelser, September 24, 1974.
44. Butler Papers, Box 184; interviews with Freda Noble and Joseph Doran, September 24, 1974.
45. ACPO Recommendation 10, 1955-1956, in Paul G. Willis collection; Neil Staebler to the author, July 6, 1982.
46. Interview with Richard J. Murphy, October 14, 1982.
47. John Morsell's assistant to Butler, July 20, 1960, Butler Papers, Box 6.
48. Democratic National Committee release, Butler speech to Notre Dame Alumni Club of New York, November 30, 1960, Butler Papers, Box 204. In June, 1963, John Kennedy became the first president to call civil rights a moral issue.

Chapter Six

THE DEMOCRATIC ADVISORY COUNCIL

The Democratic Advisory Council (DAC), which came into being after the 1956 election, was a much publicized party device used to present policy alternatives to the program of the Eisenhower Administration, and is still remembered as the prototype of political party policy-making bodies. Paul Butler did not originate the idea of the DAC, but his 1953 proposed midterm party convention conveyed the notion of a policy-making party institution between presidential nominating conventions.

Both biennial conventions and a Party Council were proposed in the 1950 report of the American Political Science Association's Committee on Political Parties.[1] The council of fifty members, meeting annually, could provide liaison between the White House (or the national party organization) and the congressional party organization "on general legislative policy," and "should consider and settle the larger problems of party management," propose preliminary platform drafts, and make recommendations with respect to congressional nominations and apostasy by state and local party organizations (the DAC certainly did follow some of these suggestions, and would probably have liked to have pursued all of them).[2]

The National Committee's Advisory Committee on Political Organization, stressing issue importance, had also recommended creation of a platform committee, which would make policy suggestions to Congress, and wondered if the *Democratic Digest* should not report departures of legislators from the party platform, or minimally stress support of the platform.[3]

The nucleus of the DAC existed in the Finletter Group, described by Theodore H. White as "a loose and changing assembly of former high New Deal officials, businessmen, lawyers, specialists, and professors," named after Thomas Finletter, Secretary of the Air Force under President Truman.[4] The group believed the old New Deal problems had been solved; therefore it focused on new issues and ideas.

103

The Finletter Group was actually not as formal as White described it, and its activities varied from time to time, depending on the issue focus of the moment and the availability of advisors. While not exclusively associated with one Democratic leader, Adlai Stevenson was both its encourager and its primary beneficiary in terms of speech texts, ideas, and 1956 campaign material.[5] As early as 1953, John K. Galbraith suggested to Stevenson that a study committee for formulation of Democratic policy was needed, and Stevenson agreed. Stevenson informed Galbraith that Finletter had explored the possibility and that Charles Murphy, the National Committee's special counsel, thought the body should be established as a National Committee project. Stevenson did not want media mention of any Stevenson Brain Trust so he cautioned for a less formal beginning. Meanwhile, Finletter conducted research when Stevenson requested speech ideas and material.[6]

By the end of 1954, Stevenson wanted a more formal arrangement, with an executive secretary. Looking ahead to 1956, he saw the need for a party program based on careful thought. He insisted that Paul Butler, with whom he had discussed the proposition, should be consulted.[7] Stevenson sometimes joined the Finletter Group, which had been meeting irregularly since 1953. Although at times Stevenson believed the Democrats should avoid much foreign policy discussion, in 1956 he wanted more emphasis on foreign affairs so that party "stature and image" could be developed. During 1955 and 1956, Chairman Butler established several advisory committees for the 1956 campaign—on agriculture, labor, small business, and natural resources, which in some cases issued policy statements.[8]

Of course, Stevenson had believed from the time of his 1952 defeat that Democrats should direct an opposition to the Eisenhower Administration, and initially had some confidence that congressional Democrats would shoulder a good bit of that burden; but after the Democrats regained congressional control, he was disappointed in the leadership's performance. Following his 1956 defeat he still wrestled with the problem of getting Democrats to be an effective opposition, certain that Lyndon Johnson and Sam Rayburn had protected Eisenhower too much. The congressional leaders could not be the only party spokesmen. For a 1960 victory, vigorous criticism of Republicans would have to come from many sources.[9]

This was Stevenson's rationalization for the DAC's creation: presidential campaigns were continuous, and, with the purpose of informing people about issues, the Democratic opposition must be continuous; congressional leaders, with a different function under divided government, could not carry the whole load of opposition; the DAC had helped make it possible for voters to choose wisely, by stating the Democratic case. The DAC could also help ease Stevenson's transition to a new role as a twice-defeated titular leader, yet enable him to play a central role in party leadership.[10]

Following the 1956 defeat Democratic leaders quickly moved to implement Stevenson's concepts. Senator Hubert Humphrey proposed adoption of a sixteen-point legislative program by congressional Democrats, but Johnson and Rayburn preferred waiting to hear Eisenhower's proposals. Then three Stevenson supporters on the National Committee, Jacob Arvey, Paul Ziffren, and David Lawrence, proposed that the National Committee's Executive Committee create an advisory council, and Butler promptly announced its formation. Stevenson accepted membership and claimed some credit for its creation.[11]

Undoubtedly those who insist that Stevenson played an important role in the DAC's formal establishment, in influencing its pronouncements, and in generating financial support for it are correct. They usually give Butler, who served as DAC chairman, credit for strongly supporting its creation, for aiding its development, for encouraging its activities, and, one might add, for prompting its pronouncements by his own well-publicized policy statements.[12] The DAC was an implementation of Butler's belief that the new politics called for increased issue concern and the attraction of issue-oriented party followers. Without saying so, Butler agreed to some extent with the Finletter Group that the old New Deal problems were not the only national concerns. In effect, the belief that the DAC was vital illustrates another area where Stevenson and Butler complemented one another. Butler's role in the DAC will now be more completely examined by reviewing its evolution.

The DAC, unique in being the first formalized policy-making body of the Democratic Party, between conventions, was created by the National Committee's Executive Committee November 27, 1956. Although the document of creation used the term "Advisory Council" in its title, the body of the document referred to "an advisory committee"; consequently, the group was called the Democratic Advisory Committee for awhile, but soon became known as the Democratic Advisory Council. Chairman Butler was authorized to appoint not more than seventeen members, including mayors, governors, members of Congress, and other Democrats to meet with the Executive Committee "to coordinate and advance efforts in behalf of Democratic programs and principles." The chairman would provide adequate staff to enable continual operation for four years. At the same time the Executive Committee reaffirmed support of the 1956 platform and called on congressional Democrats to implement it through legislation, if possible. Domestic and foreign problems obligated Democrats to advance "a plan of action to meet America's most pressing needs," and to take the initiative, even if the Presidency was in the hands of the opposition.[13] This action had been taken by the Executive Committee in spite of the admonition in a party manual that "The duties and powers of the National Committee are derived from the Convention creating it and no Convention has authorized the formulation of proposals which might be construed to be in the nature of platform declarations."[14]

The Executive Committee subsequently authorized twenty members outside its ranks, and Butler invited twenty Democrats to serve, on the basis of problem familiarity, and not representation of interests, he said. Over half were members of Congress, most with party leadership positions—Representatives Sam Rayburn, John W. McCormack, Carl Albert, Michael Kirwan, and Edith Green; Senators Lyndon Johnson, Mike Mansfield, George Smathers, Hubert Humphrey, John Kennedy, and Estes Kefauver. Others asked to serve were Governors Averell Harriman, G. Mennen Williams, Luther Hodges, Ernest McFarland; St. Louis Mayor Raymond Tucker; and Harry Truman, Eleanor Roosevelt, and John Battle, former Virginia governor. Not all those invited to serve accepted—Hodges, Battle, and Mrs. Roosevelt declined (Mrs. Roosevelt because of obligations as a newspaper columnist, although she agreed to serve as a consultant). From the congressional group, only Humphrey and Kefauver joined then, Kennedy not until he became a presidential candidate. Congresswoman Green accepted membership, then withdrew after she learned of Speaker Rayburn's opposition to House members joining the DAC.[15]

Refusal of most congressional nominees to join the DAC was met by pleading, elaboration, and explanation on Butler's part. Butler sought Lyndon Johnson's cooperation, and Johnson had appeared to be favorably disposed to participate in the group's deliberations, but declined after Sam Rayburn's intense opposition was made clear. Both Johnson and Rayburn were in Texas. Johnson sought Rayburn's advice, telling Rayburn he had given careful attention to Butler's telephone calls. He also provided Rayburn with a memorandum with seven points: (1) the DAC proposal opens a hornet's nest and its implementation will result in the defeat of all Democratic legislation and defeat in the 1958 and 1960 elections; (2) Americans will resent professional politicians dictating to their elected representatives; (3) Republicans could not support Democratic legislation of partisan origin; (4) the DAC will deepen party divisions and make it difficult to keep the narrow majorities in line; (5) Republican divisions will be ignored; (6) a small group of appointive officials will presume to exercise the authority of the Democratic National Committee; and (7) congressional responsibility is to constituents, not a party group. Johnson also had five recommendations: (1) the Democratic congressional leadership should politely refuse to serve; (2) the leadership should agree to meet with the DAC to hear its recommendations; (3) the leadership should agree to discuss DAC recommendations with the Senate Democratic Policy Committee and committee chairmen in both houses; (4) DAC advice should not be binding on congressional leaders; (5) Johnson, Mansfield, Rayburn, McCormack, and Albert should sign a proposed letter to Butler, which would state that the congressional leaders had given careful thought to the resolution authorizing the DAC, would welcome advice from any Democratic group, would be happy to meet with the DAC and transmit its suggestions to appropriate congressional centers, but could not serve as members because of obligations to their colleagues, although the spirit in which the resolution had been adopted was appreciated.[16]

Johnson's proposed letter from congressional leaders was apparently sent to Butler, or its main points made known to him. Johnson also wrote Butler that the legislative process was already difficult enough and would be further delayed if an additional group, not created by law, were to intrude.[17] A month later Rayburn answered a letter, extremely critical of the DAC's creation:

> I do not think that there was any effort being made to run Congress, in their way, they were trying to be helpful. Of course, I couldn't join any outside committees because the Members of the House of Representatives expect me to consult with them in making up the program of the House of Representatives.[18]

On December 18, 1956, Butler called the first meeting of the DAC for January 4, 1957, and issued a statement saying the Executive Committee has given the DAC a broad charter, but with no attempt "to dictate to the Congress or to encroach upon its powers," as some interpreters had insisted.[19] Use would be made of the views of congressional leaders and the views of millions of Americans not represented in the congressional Democratic Party. Democratic leadership outside Congress could be rallied behind efforts of congressional leaders to carry out the 1956 platform. Butler said he respected the decision of congressional leaders not to join the DAC, as much as he regretted it; he also accepted the offer of congressional leaders to consult with the DAC.[20]

Expressing his deep respect and affection, Butler sent Rayburn, still in Texas, a copy of this statement, telling Rayburn he understood his attitude toward the DAC. He thanked the Speaker for a telegram in which Rayburn had said, "We would be willing and glad to consult with them at any time or with you as their representative," and invited Rayburn, McCormack, and Albert to meet with the DAC for breakfast the morning of the January 4 council meeting, to which Senate leaders would also be invited. Butler also questioned Rayburn on the possibility of Michael Kirwan, chairman of the House Democratic Congressional Campaign Committee, joining the DAC, along with his Senate counterpart, George Smathers, as preparation for the 1958 elections. Butler told Rayburn that the establishment of the DAC was intended to broaden areas of agreement among Democrats and to rally opinion behind efforts of congressional leaders to enact legislation. More consultation among party leaders would produce a stronger and united party.[21]

Butler wrote Governor Luther Hodges, who had declined DAC membership, that the press had caused the impression that the purpose of the DAC was to encroach on congressional powers and the duties of congressional leaders. Butler told Hodges he had been named to the DAC "because you represent the views of a large number of loyal, patriotic Democrats."[22]

Undaunted by what he thought to be inaccurate press reporting and refusal of half his invitation list, Butler planned for the January 4, 1957, meeting of the DAC. He began thinking of a two-day session to discuss the group's origin, nature, and purpose, and to consider the need for staff, agenda, reference of subjects to study groups, attention to policy matters needing immediate attention, and a foreign policy session with Senators who had been abroad. He believed that if Johnson and Rayburn attended the breakfast session "the political waters which have been muddied by a deliberate attempt by the daily and periodical press to make this movement toward an Advisory Committee appear to be nothing more than a slap in the face at our Congressional leaders" could be cleansed.[23]

Johnson, Rayburn, and McCormack did attend the breakfast session. Relationships between the DAC and congressional leaders were discussed, and agreement reached that the DAC would continue to make advisory policy statements while congressional leaders would consult with the DAC, even while pursuing their own course.[24] The day before, Adlai Stevenson had been less conciliatory than the other parties involved. He believed the Democratic Party needed a base broader than its congressional wing if it were to be an effective opposition, and that members of Congress should welcome new blood. "The Democratic Party is not just a Congressional party, it is a National Party."[25]

Butler continued to keep congressional leaders informed about DAC actions and inquired about possibilities for staffing study committees.[26] In October, 1957, Butler acknowledged that congressional leaders were not prepared to authorize DAC participation by their followers, but he felt that "if we play our cards right, we may win Congressional support and recognition in the not too distant future."[27] However, as shown above, DAC statements on the Little Rock school crisis, Butler's increasing concern with civil rights, and his insistence that congressional leaders be more forthright in dealing with President Eisenhower and in passing liberal legislation all worked to make Butler's hopes unlikely.

Of course, the DAC would always have the support of some individual congressional Democrats, including that of House Majority Leader John McCormack, who inserted DAC material in the *Congressional Record*. Representative Charles Bennett of Florida introduced a House Resolution which embodied the proposals of a DAC statement on a national peace agency. Senator Paul Douglas of Illinois complained that DAC recommendations on civil rights, which he tried to get adopted, had been defeated by Southerners, most of the Republicans, and "by Senator Lyndon Johnson, our Majority Leader."[28] Plans for legislative liaison, bypassing the leadership, were prepared by Charles Murphy in consultation with Butler and others. The DAC was instructed to "render any assistance it can to Democratic members of both houses of Congress in their efforts to obtain passage of legislation in furtherance of Democratic programs and principles."[29] Individual members of Congress were to be invited to attend DAC meetings when the subject matter would be of interest to them. The legislative liaison group met with Senators Joseph Clark and Eugene McCarthy, and planned to meet with others senators. In 1959 the DAC's Administrative Committee invited Senators John Kennedy and Stuart Symington to join the DAC. The liaison group also wanted to secure a congressional man for the DAC staff.[30]

Butler had several meetings with leaders of the House Democratic Study Group, a liberally oriented organization, whose institutionalization after the 1956 election paralleled the development of the DAC, DAC policy pronouncements, and Butler's attacks on the conservatism of Democratic congressional leaders. Resource people like Thomas Finletter and Paul Samuelson not only aided the DAC, but spoke to educational meetings of liberal House Democrats. Representative Frank Thompson, a Study Group leader, when preparing for a 1959 attempt to change the House Rules, thanked the DAC for its assistance.[31]

Butler refused to focus on problems with congressional leaders at the expense of not getting the DAC underway. The January 4, 1957, meeting produced a statement of purpose, the main one being "to further the programs and principles of the Democratic Party." The DAC would be guided by the 1956 platform; but, if events moved swiftly, it would deal with new situations. "We are engaged in an unprecedented effort to make a national political party more responsive and more responsible to its members and to the public. This Council places the maximum strength of the Party behind its own positive programs." While speaking for Democrats not represented in Congress, it would also help Congress carry out the platform. It would propose constructive measures, might agree with Republicans on some issues, and overall would perform the critical function of opposition and afford the Democratic Party "the means of rallying national support and public opinion behind our programs or against unwise programs of the Executive Branch as the case may be."[32] As if to show it meant business, the DAC, at its first meeting, also announced support for a proposed Senate rules change which would curb filibusters, and asked congressional Democrats to scrutinize the Eisenhower Doctrine for the Middle East.[33]

Butler reported in the first issue of the revamped *Democratic Digest* that the DAC had been created in an "effort to make our Party more responsive and more responsible to its members and to the public," illustrated by its action on the filibuster question.[34]

Butler carried on an extensive correspondence with Thomas Finletter in preparation for a February, 1957, meeting of the DAC in San Francisco, in conjunction with a meeting of the Democratic National Committee. In San Francisco, the National Committee formally ratified creation of the DAC, and commended the Executive Committee for its action. In doing this, the National Committee stated that its own function between conventions was to apply the platform to fast-moving events and to formulate and enunciate policy, a function delegated through the Executive Committee to the DAC. Southerners argued against such delegation.[35] Three more policy positions were taken by the DAC in San Francisco, one on civil rights.[36]

In May, 1957, the National Committee and the DAC met together again in Washington, where another Southern move to limit the DAC's effectiveness was put down, and the DAC issued three more policy statements. More importantly, the National Committee approved an operational plan for the DAC—a plan which dealt with origin and purposes, membership, means and methods of operation, use of advisory committees, staff and facilities, and funding.[37] The section on origin and purposes liberally repeated the statement of purposes which had been set forth by the DAC in January. Membership, affected by refusal of congressional leaders to serve, was reduced to include only nine outsiders in addition to Butler and fourteen members of the Executive Committee of the National Committee; Eleanor Roosevelt would serve as a consultant. Butler was *ex officio* chairman of both the Executive Committee and the DAC. The appointive members had only a one-year term, enabling Butler to frequently infuse the DAC with new members.

Butler was also authorized to call DAC meetings and to appoint an Administrative Committee of three, which he would serve as chairman, for purposes of establishing operational policies and exercising general supervision over staff and advisory committees. Thomas Finletter and Philip Perlman were named as the other members of the Administrative Committee. Charles Murphy and Henry Fowler joined the group later.

The DAC was instructed to "continuously study matters of public policy and political activities which are of concern to the Democratic Party," recommend policies, disseminate information, issue public statements, and make non-binding recommendations to the National Committee and the national chairman "with respect to matters within their responsibilities." To further legislative liaison, consultative and assistance functions were suggested.

Advisory committees of five to twenty members, named by the chairman to provide the DAC with expertise and ideas, were authorized to consult Democrats in and out of office, engage in study, and make recommendations for policy and action to the DAC.

The National Committee would provide a staff unit for the work of the DAC and its committees, and the entire National Committee staff facilities and services would assist. Staff provided by the National Committee was initially set to include Charles Tyroler II and Charles Murphy, with their assistants. Funding for staff and activities would come from the National Committee, but earmarked contributions were also encouraged.

How did this operational plan evolve into a structure from 1957 through 1960? In terms of membership, the twenty-five members of 1957 increased to thirty-two by 1960.[38] There were few deletions during this period, but several members were added, such as presidential candidates John Kennedy and Stuart Symington. During four years, Butler recruited enough outsiders to barely outnumber the Executive Committee *ex officio* members.

In May, 1957, the DAC established four advisory committees for party finances, political technology and development, foreign policy, and economic policy, which shifted entirely to public policy areas in time, because the Advisory Committee on Political Organization handled the party areas.[39] It was suggested early in the planning process that membership for advisory committees could be recruited from such groups as women, labor, minorities, business, and agriculture. Since the National Committee was already partly organized along these lines, and had already established its own advisory committees, personnel for DAC advisory committees were already available or could be recruited with ease. Recruitment was also aided by National Committee members, governors, members of Congress, mayors, state chairmen, and intellectuals, such as those who had contributed to the Finletter Group, and these people might as well serve on advisory committees.

Numbers of members on DAC advisory committees and their backgrounds varied according to subject matter. For instance, the Advisory Committee on Science and Technology consisted of seventeen members in December, 1959, sixteen of whom had the title of "Doctor." Such notables as former Secretary of State Dean Acheson, Eleanor Roosevelt, and John K. Galbraith served as chairpersons of advisory committees.[40]

Butler had to consider politics in his appointments. In 1959 he delayed organization of the Advisory Committee on Farm Policy because some felt it was too soon to formulate farm policy for the 1960 election, while others believed it was not prudent to compete with the congressional agricultural committees. When Butler finally made appointments, he had many recommendations from the Farmers' Union leader, James Patton (himself a member of the Advisory Committee on Foreign Affairs), but Butler was determined not to let Farmers' Union people dominate the committee.[41]

Since the raising of earmarked funds for operation of the DAC had been authorized and money already collected, Charles Murphy, National Committee counsel, suggested creation of a New York committee to receive contributions, which could be transferred to the National Committee. This arrangement was necessary because federal law limited individual contributions to the National Committee to $5,000 but a committee organized in New York would not have to file a federal financial report if funds were only collected in New York, and could then transfer money to the National Committee.[42]

The DAC had its own finance committee, which, using the "demands" of its contributors as leverage, asked for additional personnel for the DAC, and for means to distribute DAC publications.[43] Adlai Stevenson solicited funds for the DAC and spoke at fundraising events, such as a dinner honoring Eleanor Roosevelt, which brought in $100,000. In fact, Stevenson's New York City supporters were viewed as the underwriters of the DAC.[44] At times, DAC money helped the National Committee meet its payroll expenses, but on other occasions the DAC asked the National Committee to pay its housekeeping expenses, and officially there was always a subsidy from the National Committee.[45]

In getting its program underway, the DAC spent nearly $18,000 in six months in 1957. These were payroll and professional service expenses, not printing expenditures. A proposed budget for July 1, 1959, through June 30, 1960, projected expenditures of $123,400, of which $90,100 would be utilized for staff, $12,000 for printing and mailing of pamphlets, and $9,000 for housekeeping functions. The executive director would be paid $20,000; the counsel, $12,000; a senior writer and publicist, $12,500; and a senior political scientist, $12,000.[46]

The DAC's three-member Administrative Committee, never publicized much, was used by Butler as an instrument for supervision of DAC activities, as intended by the operational plan. Meeting two or three times a month, the Administrative Committee directed advisory committees as to what topics to pursue, approved pamphlets coming from advisory committees for distribution to the DAC, considered political ramifications of DAC appointments, and implemented plans for congressional liaison. Butler used the Administrative Committee to publicize his own desires, such as wanting no funds accepted for special DAC projects unless paid directly to the National Committee.[47]

Charles Tyroler II was the DAC's only executive director. Since he had supporters, Tyroler survived; but Philip Perlman was at first impatient with Tyroler, believing he had done little to make the DAC an effective party instrument. Adlai Stevenson was not altogether pleased with the DAC's first year's output either. Stevenson may also have learned that Tyroler viewed him as a twice-defeated titular leader, making such an institution as the DAC necessary. It is likely that such criticism of Tyroler lessened as the DAC progressed.[48]

The main work of the DAC, and the activity which attracted the most attention, was its issuance of policy statements. Since its supporters expected policy statements, the DAC immediately had several suggestions for substantive action. Within a year, fifteen statements had been released, and by June, 1960, sixty-one.[49]

Decisions of the DAC relating to public policy were made by majority vote of the membership, while dissenters were guaranteed public access.[50] There was little public disagreement. John Bartlow Martin believed that Truman, Stevenson, and Butler, all trying to control the DAC, created an internal split, but these leaders shared similar policy views.[51] The most likely area for fissures, other than civil rights, was in foreign affairs. Agreeing to serve as chairman of the Advisory Committee on Foreign Policy, former Secretary of State Dean Acheson wanted to help the Democratic Party get "over the foolish attitude of backing away from the Truman administration."[52] Stevenson would have preferred a chairman other than Acheson. In an age when the terms "dove" and "hawk" were not commonly used, Stevenson viewed Acheson as a "saber-rattler," and became anxious over Acheson's military emphasis.[53] In the earlier days Stevenson had wanted Acheson included in the Finletter Group foreign policy discussions, but he also wanted more of George Kennan's "new look" in foreign affairs deliberations.[54] While Kennan was never made a member of the Advisory Committee on Foreign Policy, its files contain an excerpt from the *Congressional Record* featuring anti-Kennan material inserted by Senator J. Allen Frear, Jr.; and an article critical of Kennan written by Congressman Michael Feighan.[55] Kennan's disengagement ideas had earlier been publicly attacked by Acheson.[56] Stevenson also had supporters on the committee, including Barry Bingham, Chester Bowles, Dorothy Fosdick, and William Benton. Benton believed the national interest had to be served at the same time Democrats tried to get the votes of war mothers, nationality groups, and protectionists.[57] Still, the Kennan-Acheson and Stevenson-Acheson divisions were never publicly revealed enough to show a split in DAC ranks.

DAC policy statements evolved from the material gathered by advisory committees, through the drafts prepared by them, on to the final statements of the full council. Single topics might be dealt with by a short statement or a more lengthy document of extensive comment, while some statements had a more general focus, taking on aspects of a State of the Union message, or the basis for a party platform.[58] The statements were mimeographed, released to the media, and usually printed in the *Democratic Digest*.[59] Some, but not all, of the statements were printed as pamphlets, in two different sizes. By July, 1960, seventeen pamphlets were still in print and for sale, and more were promised.[60] They were eventually grouped into four series—Foreign and Military Policy for Peace and Security, Domestic Policies for a Growing and Balanced Economy, Science and Technology, and The Presidency and the Democratic Party. Because of economy measures, forcing a change in pamphlet size, plans to publish each series as a speaker's handbook for the 1960 campaign never materialized.[61]

Butler told fellow Democrats that a DAC policy pronouncement was "front page news throughout the country, and a subject of editorial and columnist comment," and that large-circulation newspapers often printed the texts in full.[62] Use of DAC press releases by newspapers made it appear that a whole party was speaking through a small, industrious group, said columnist Allen Drury.[63] A large clipping collection, illustrating both favorable and unfavorable press response to DAC statements, as well as a collection of letters, accumulated at party headquarters.[64]

Viewing publicity on DAC activities as effective intra-party communication, as well as a means of reaching the general public, Butler described the progress of DAC projects in his reports to National Committee members, and used the *Democratic Digest* to acquaint the party rank and file with texts of policy statements. Readers of the *Digest* were reported to be almost unanimously favorable to these

114

printings. The executive director also believed it important to furnish members of the DAC itself with copies of newspaper columns on DAC activities.[65]

The result of the refusal of congressional leaders, and most Southerners, to serve on the DAC was a series of liberal policy assertions which otherwise would have been impossible, at least without considerably more dissent than that which marked the release of DAC statements. As the 1960 election approached DAC material was increasingly oriented toward possible use in the party platform, and much found its way there. *The Decision in 1960: The Need to Elect a Democratic President*, issued by the DAC in December, 1959, was perceived as a 10,000 word blueprint for the 1960 platform, and it was produced at a session attended by all the party's presidential contenders except Lyndon Johnson.[66] Butler believed the DAC had the role of compiling materials for the platform, and wanted it written before the convention convened so as to not waste time during the proceedings. The DAC's executive director predicted that the DAC, representing the party's liberal majority, would attempt "to select candidates and control the convention in 1960," not directly, but by helping create a liberal platform which a liberal candidate, endorsed in spirit by the DAC, would actively support.[67]

James L. Sundquist has shown how Butler's will was reflected in the 1960 platform. Butler's influence could be traced backward from platform to committee, to drafting subcommittee, to staff putting together the mimeographed draft, to Resolutions Committee chairman, who appointed the staff, and finally to Butler, who selected the chairman (Congressman Chester Bowles). Butler had carefully decided he wanted a platform appropriate to his concept of the Democratic Party, and his appointment of a Resolutions Committee chairman, and the direction he provided the chairman and his staff, ended in a liberal party program for the 1960 election.[68] And having contributed so much to having the DAC recognized as an official policy-making body of the national party, Butler helped fuse DAC activities and platform-making. Sundquist has illustrated quite well the relationship between the DAC and activist liberal Democratic groups in Congress, and the post-platform influence of the DAC on governmental policy in the Kennedy-Johnson period, even though the DAC had vanished by then.[69]

The DAC was publicized on two pages of the 1960 convention program, and that convention formally expressed appreciation for the DAC's services, while authorizing the National Committee to continue the council.[70] Meeting with the Michigan delegation before the convention, however, John Kennedy had refused a request to continue the DAC on the grounds that it would not be proper to have both the president and the DAC speaking on policy.[71] After Kennedy's election, the National Committee let the DAC pass out of existence.

Reflecting the liberalism of the presidential wing of the Democratic Party, the DAC had, nevertheless, been widely recognized for four years as a party policy-making body, and Paul Butler had been closely identified with it from its beginning. He had contributed to its success, not only by his support and efforts to get it underway, but with the direction it took as a party institution, and to some of the language in its pronouncements. These contributions stemmed from Butler's philosophy of responsible opposition parties, which was, in turn, related to his views of the national chairman as a party leader. Emphasizing party policy, and ultimately party differences, was the essence of responsible opposition, along with proper communication with voters and party members. Butler was "the chairman who had the acumen to see the things that were needed to recast the Democratic Party in the right image, and the courage to get them done."[72]

The DAC had not been created to force any issues on Congress, Butler insisted, but was a source of ideas based on "established principles of the Democratic Party." These principles, or majority opinions, were "to be expressed through the DAC as the official position of the Democratic Party." The party not in control of the Executive, in criticizing the incumbent president's policies, and trying to pose alternatives, needed complete information, and the well-thought programs proposed by the DAC constituted a liberal and explicit answer to Republican policies. But since the party had to hold to its liberal views (especially on civil rights), Butler insisted that Democrats would not give up principles for the sake of unity.[73] This philosophy of the use of the DAC as an instrument of party responsibility and opposition was clearly enunciated in the January 4, 1957 statement of purpose of the DAC, as well as in the two State of the Union documents issued by the DAC:

> The Democratic victory in the Congressional elections this autumn provides our party with great opportunities and responsibilities.
>
> All Democrats are concerned about the tasks which face our party in the next two years. We think and talk about them across the nation, consistent with our duties as America's only national political party. We know, moreover, that the measures required of government acquire their true effectiveness only as they rest upon the kind of public understanding and support that comes from full and free discussion.

In accordance with its practice of stating, from time to time, its views on important issues, the Democratic Advisory Council here enumerates the elements of a program it hopes will be adopted during the next two years.[74]

We Democrats are faced with serious responsibilities in the year which lies ahead. We are faced with the responsibility of being a constructive opposition party. We are faced with the responsibility of attaining whatever is attainable in the face of Republican Congressional obstruction and the irascible vetoes of a tired President. But we are also faced with the duty of stating our own alternatives to the Republican drift . . . We have the responsibility of giving the voters a clear choice in 1960 and of making it plain what that choice is.[75]

Adlai Stevenson's 1952 campaign had attracted many amateur reform-minded individuals often found in the new type of political clubs, people who intellectually preferred an issue-oriented political activism.[76] Issue commitment essentially meant changing political parties from neutral interest brokers into sources of positive programs. "Right" policies took precedence over winning votes.[77] To some extent, Butler shared this constituency with Stevenson, particularly the more Butler was recognized as a vocal party spokesman, and the more the DAC, with which Butler was identified, was viewed as a party policy institution. Because Butler and Stevenson had similar views on the importance of issues and policy alternatives contributing to responsible party opposition, these two party leaders worked together in nurturing the DAC and giving it fame which has persisted. The DAC was the capstone of their views and efforts in the field of responsible party opposition.

NOTES

1. *Toward a More Responsible Two-Party System.*
2. Cotter and Hennessy, *Politics Without Power*, pp. 214-15, says Charles Tyroler II admitted APSA influence. Most markings (may have been made by Butler, or by Paul Willis) in the APSA document, in the Butler Papers, Box 81, are in the "Party Council" section.
3. ACPO Recommendation 16-A, 1955-56, and 20-B, 1957, in Paul G. Willis Collection.
4. Theodore H. White, "The Democrats: They're Off and Running for '56," *Collier's*, October 28, 1955, pp. 25-27, 50-55.

5. See Adlai E. Stevenson, *The New America* (New York: Harper and Brothers Publishers, 1957), xx-xxi.

6. Stevenson to Galbraith, October 16, 1953, *Stevenson Papers*, IV, 278-79; Stevenson to Wilson W. Wyatt, October 29, 1953, IV, 280; Stevenson to Finletter, January 15, 1954, IV, 315; Stevenson to Clayton Fritchey, January 28, 1954, IV, 316-17; Stevenson to Robert Tufts, January 30, 1954, IV, 320; Stevenson to Paul Nitze, February 26, 1954, IV, 327; Stevenson to Lloyd K. Garrison, April 6, 1954, IV, 349; Stevenson to Chester Bowles, September 11 and 22, 1954, IV, 392, 399; Stevenson to Finletter, September 22, 1954, IV, 399; and Stevenson to Paul Nitze, October 19, 1954, IV, 418.

7. Stevenson to Thomas Finletter, December 11, 1954, ibid., IV, 441-42; Stevenson to Bernard de Voto, December 28, 1954, IV, 447.

8. Stevenson to Paul Samuelson, March 30, 1955, ibid., IV, 462; Stevenson to Walter H. Heller, June 21, 1955, IV, 509-10; Stevenson to Thomas Finletter, March 14, 1956, VI, 85-86; Bone, *Party Committees*, pp. 62-63.

9. Stevenson to James Boyd, November 20, 1953, *Stevenson Papers* , IV, 287; Stevenson to Eugenie Anderson, July 20, 1955, IV, 532; Stevenson to Mrs. Eugene Meyer, November 27, 1956, VI, 375; Stevenson to Congressman John J. Flint, Jr., January 10, 1957, VI, 406-07.

10. *Stevenson Papers*, VII, 374-79; Brown, *Conscience in Politics*, pp. 224-26.

11. Bone, *Party Committees* , p. 219; *Stevenson Papers*, VI, 374, 376; Stevenson to Richard S. Reynolds, Jr., August 23, 1957, VII, 58-59.

12. Brown, *Conscience in Politics*, pp. 225-26; Cotter and Hennessy, *Politics Without Power*, pp. 213-214.

13. Democratic National Committee Executive Committee Resolution Authorizing Advisory Council, November 27, 1956, Butler Papers, Box 25.

14. Clarence Cannon, *Democratic Manual for the 1956 Democratic National Convention* (Washington, D.C.: Democratic National Committee, 1956), p. 9.

15. Democratic National Committee Release, December 5, 1956, Butler Papers, Box 140; Cotter and Hennessy, *Politics Without Power*, p. 216; Bone, *Party Committees,* p. 222.

16. Lyndon B. Johnson to Rayburn, December 3, 1956, Rayburn Papers.

17. Los Angeles *Examiner*, December 14, 1956.

18. Rayburn to Daniel L. Eckert, January 11, 1957, Rayburn Papers.

19. John Dezell, interview with Butler, n.d., Butler Papers, Box 204. Butler said congressional leaders felt a conflict of duties, but that the press exaggerated the difference of opinion.

20. Statement in Butler Papers, Box 25.
21. Butler to Rayburn, December 26, 1956, Butler Papers, Box 59.
22. Butler to Hodges, December 27, 1956, Butler Papers, Box 59.
23. Butler to Leo C. Graybill, December 26, 1956, Butler Papers, Box 59.
24. New York *Times*, January 6, 1957.
25. *Stevenson Papers*, VI, 402-03.
26. Butler to Sam Rayburn, May 6, 1957, Rayburn Papers.
27. Butler to William Benton, October 31, 1957, Butler Papers, Box 2.
28. McCormack to Butler, June 30, 1959, Butler Papers, Box 59; Douglas to Butler, March 24, 1960, Butler Papers, Box 6.
29. Revised draft, June 10, 1959, Butler Papers, Box 63.
30. *Minutes*, DAC Administration Committee, March 16, August 13, and August 24, 1959, and February 16, 1960, Butler Papers, Box 58.
31. Butler to Congressman Gerald Flynn, February 23, 1960, Butler Papers, Box 3; Thompson to Butler, December 11, 1959, Box 64; Kenneth Kofmehl, "The Institutionalization of a Voting Bloc," *Western Political Quarterly* 17 (1964), 256-72. See James L. Sundquist, *Politics and Policy: The Eisenhower, Kennedy, and Johnson Years* (Washington, D.C.: The Brookings Institution, 1968), pp. 395-415, for an excellent discussion of the relationship between the DAC and Senate and House liberal activist blocs.
32. *Statement On Its Purposes By The Advisory Council*, January 4, 1957, Butler Papers, Box 25. This material on the origins and purposes of the DAC was prepared by Charles Murphy, Counsel for the National Committee, in consultation with Philip Perlman, Butler, and staff members. In May, 1957, this material was worked into an operational plan (Butler to Adlai E. Stevenson, February 1, 1957, Butler Papers, Box 59).
33. Bone, *Party Committees*, pp. 222-23.
34. *Democratic Digest*, February, 1957, pp. 2, 7.
35. *Official Report of the 1960 Democratic National Convention and Committee*, pp. 368-377.
36. See the index, listing DAC policy statements, Butler Papers, Box 25.
37. *The Advisory Council of the Democratic National Committee: Plan of Operations*, adopted May 3 and 5, 1957, Butler Papers, Box 25. See also Butler's agenda for this meeting and minutes of the meeting in Box 25.
38. Membership list in *The Decision in 1960*.
39. See agenda and minutes for the meeting, Butler Papers, Box 25; also Democratic National Committee Release, December, 1959, "Biography of Paul M. Butler," Butler Papers, Box 2.
40. See *DAC Planning Sheet*, March, 1957, Butler Papers, Box 59.

41. Butler to Senator Paul H. Douglas, August 7, 1959, Butler Papers, Box 62; other letters in Box 62.
42. Murphy to Thomas Finletter, October 23, 1957, copy in Butler Papers, Box 59.
43. Robert F. Benjamin to Butler, July 3, 1958, Butler Papers, Box 2.
44. Adlai E. Stevenson to Richard S. Reynolds, Jr., August 23, 1957, *Stevenson Papers*, VII, 58-59; Stevenson to John L. Burling, May 30, 1958, VII, 209; VII, 374-379.
45. Cotter and Hennessy, *Politics Without Power*, p. 224; Robert F. Benjamin to Butler, July 3, 1958, Burtler Papers, Box 2.
46. Mary C. Zirkle to Butler, June 18 and August 23, 1957, Butler Papers, Box 58; budget also in Box 58.
47. See minutes for meetings, February 28, March 9, March 16, August 13, August 24, 1959, and February 16, 1960; Butler Papers, Box 58.
48. Philip Perlman to Thomas Finletter, July 24, 1957, copy in Butler Papers, Box 16; Stevenson to Margaret Halsey, January 29, 1958, *Stevenson Papers*, VII, 155; Brown, *Conscience in Politics*, p. 226; John Dezell, interview with Charles Tyroler, n.d., Butler Papers, Box 204.
49. Titles listed in a DAC index, Butler Papers, Box 25.
50. *The Advisory Council of the Democratic National Committee: Plan of Operations*, adopted May 3 and 5, 1957, Butler Papers, Box 25; *The Democratic Task During the Next Two Years*.
51. Martin, *Adlai Stevenson and the World*, p. 400.
52. David S. McLellan (ed.), *Among Friends: Personàl Letters of Dean Acheson* (New York: Dodd, Mead, and Co., 1980), pp. 123-24.
53. The DAC had charged the Eisenhower Administration with "unilateral disarmament at the expense of our national security." (New York *Times* , October 20, 1957). See Stevenson to Thomas Finletter, October 27, 1959, *Stevenson Papers*, VII, 369; Stevenson to Chester Bowles, January 22, 1958, VII, 151.
54. Stevenson to Lloyd K. Garrison, April 6, 1954, ibid., IV, 349; Stevenson to George Kennan, January 30, 1954, IV, 319.
55. Michael Feighan, "The Kennan Fables," *The Ukrainian Quarterly*, March, 1958.
56. New York *Times*, January 21, 1958.
57. William E. Benton to Butler, August 27, 1957, Butler Papers, Box 2.
58. For the evolution, see Box 58, Butler Papers, Box 59 for civil rights; Box 60 for economic policy, Box 61 for foreign policy, Box 62 for science and technology, and Boxes 63 and 64 for a variety of topics. See Boxes 25 and 59 to compare advisory committee drafts with DAC statements. Compare, for instance, Democratic National Committee Release on the Little Rock

Crisis, September 15, 1957, Butler Papers, Box 143; *A National Peace Agency*, December, 1959, in author's collection; and *The Decision in 1960*.

59. See Butler Papers, Box 25.
60. *Democratic Digest*, July, 1960, p. 19.
61. Dean Acheson to Butler, June 25, 1960, Butler Papers, Box 64.
62. Butler's letter, *Democratic Digest*, February, 1958.
63. New York *Times*, February 9, 1958.
64. See Butler Papers, Boxes 59 and 173.
65. Charles Tyroler to Butler, February 13, 1959, Butler Papers, Box 9; *Democratic Digest*, June, 1959, p. 1.
66. Cotter and Hennessy, *Politics Without Power*, p. 222; New York *Times*, December 6 and 7, 1959.
67. William Benton to Butler, December 8, 1959, Butler Papers, Box 6; New York *Times*, March 8, 1960; *Democratic Digest*, March, 1960; ACPO Recommendations 16, 1955-56; 13, 1957; and 10, 1959, Willis Collections; the Dezell interview with Charles Tyroler; *Official Report of the 1960 Democratic National Convention and Committee*, p. 812.
68. Sundquist, *Politics and Policy*, p. 251; Sundquist to Butler, August 10, 1960, Butler Papers, Box 6.
69. Sundquist, *Politics and Policy*, pp. 395-415.
70. *1960 Democratic National Convention* (in Butler Papers), pp. 42-43; *Official Report of the 1960 Democratic National Convention and Committee*, p. 210.
71. Interview with Neil Staebler, February 22, 1981.
72. James Sundquist to Butler, August 10, 1960, Butler Papers, Box 6.
73. Dezell interview with Butler.
74. *The Democratic Task During the Next Two Years.*
75. *The Decision in 1960.*
76. James Q. Wilson, *The Amateur Democrat* (Chicago: The University of Chicago Press, 1962), pp. 52-58.
77. James Q. Wilson, "Politics and Reform in American Cities," in *American Government Annual 1962-1963* (New York: Holt, Rinehart, and Winston, Inc., 1962), p. 49.

Chapter Seven

COMMUNICATION, FUNDING, AND ORGANIZATION

While he served as Democratic national chairman, Paul Butler's approach to party leadership placed a heavy emphasis on issues in politics, but other aspects of his perception of the role of the party and party leadership led to related emphases and activities. Cotter and Hennessy believed a party chairman in Butler's time could assume the major roles of image-maker, hell-raiser, fund-raiser, campaign manager, and administration, with the ultimate importance of the latter related to a chairman's other responsibilities.[1] Butler undoubtedly fit into this framework well. Apart from his work as publicist for liberal party ideas he constantly stressed, in letters to party members and in speeches to party workers, three things—communication, funding, and organization. Not that these concerns were unrelated to issues. Cotter and Hennessy showed how the out-party chairman could be forced into a policy-making role and be drawn to the media in the process.[2] While the importance of communication to issue discussion and persuasion is obvious, communication was also seen by Butler as the factor rendering party organization effective. In addition to making most party activities possible funding served as a device for intra-party communication. A larger base of contributors of small amounts to the party treasury was considered a communications goal, particularly because sustaining party members would receive the *Democratic Digest*, and could perhaps be drawn into party activity.

A discussion of communication is a proper beginning for an analysis of the several party activities covered in this chapter because Butler often stressed this "catch-all" word, and related it to other party functions. Addressing the American Society of Newspaper Editors, Butler said a national party chairman was the most unhidden persuader in politics, deeply involved in the process of communication because the "new politics" of issues and personality attracted a non-traditional type of citizen.[3] As he told Michigan Democrats:

The extent and nature of the modern means of mass communication, the increased educational level of the population, the increasing importance of nationalizing trends as regards both section and nationality, the expanding participation of citizens in the process of political parties and the growing importance of governmental programs in the Nation's economy and the everyday life of the citizen are all increasing the emphasis on the power of issues, principles and ideas as the forces which are most responsible for the attraction and lasting attachment of new people to the banners of political parties.[4]

During his troubles with congressional leaders, Butler advanced the idea that he, as an out-party chairman, had to function as an instrument to communicate to Congress the thoughts of Democratic Party members.[5] Along with the other interests Butler had shown as an activist National Committee member, 1952-1954, he stressed communication. When congressional district research was discussed at the first Executive Committee meeting he attended, he suggested a Washington party conference on communication and research, and the handbook for precinct workers which he unsuccessfully urged in 1954 was predicated on the base of intra-party communication.[6] Communication, that "catch-all" word, covered, as a minimum, getting facts to the public and informing Democrats on issues and organizational techniques. The DAC and the *Democratic Digest* were important means to these ends.[7] Communication was also related to the emphasis Butler placed on the political party as an agent of responsible opposition. The role of the opposition party was to guide the majority and inform the public; devices to facilitate communication made the Democratic Party more responsive and responsible to its members, as well as the public. Also, as issues (and the party's position on issues) were pressed on party followers, a broad base of energetic workers, the result of increased participation in party activities, would be created.[8] If the central molding force of party organization was communication, the organizational form itself being insufficient, then communication was something more than the means employed by party organization for reaching voters. While the public could be contacted through newspapers, magazines, radio, and television, word-of-mouth information from party workers at the precinct level would be the best communicative approach, especially with a one-party press. The *Democratic Digest* not only reached the public to a limited extent, but aided party workers in reaching voters. Butler said the new *Digest* format for 1957 would be less literary, but more simple and direct for communication with party workers.[9]

124

To Butler's way of thinking communication also meant intra-party awareness, regardless of attempts to inform the public. The new *Digest* format for 1957, while exhibiting a new size and a difference in content, was also noticeable because for the first time the magazine devoted considerable space to what the National Committee, the DAC, and state party organizations were doing, and also featured excerpts from newsletters Democratic congressmen sent their constituents.[10] The central and connecting core of party organization would result from a two-way communicative process necessitated by the need of the national party organizational level to know what was happening at the state and local levels of organization, and by the need of the latter to be aware of what the national organization was undertaking. Communication patterns, with an up and down flow, would be designed to bring about a common understanding of procedures (what to do and how to do it) and issues (what to say and how to say it). Idea exchange would make communication between party organizational levels more effective, which, in turn, would strengthen organization itself. To facilitate two-way communication the Advisory Committee on Political Organization had recommended letting state chairmen serve as non-voting members of the National Committee.[11]

The field service program of the Advisory Committee on Political Organization was designed to serve state party organizations in the communications field, as well as in organization and party activity; through the regional programs, intra-party communication could be improved. One objective of "improved communications within the Party" was supposedly to get frank grass roots criticism of National Committee operations. So that the National Committee could be informed on local sentiment, field representatives of the National Committee would be necessary. This type of feedback would be the essence of two-way communication. The sharing of organizational techniques, experimented with or perfected locally, was another aspect of communication as a mechanism of exchange between levels of party organization.[12]

Efforts at intra-party communication, aimed at broader intra-party coordination, often failed for the same reasons coordination was lacking in the first place. In 1956, for the first time in campaign history, election materials (particularly literature) was prepared in advance of the National Convention and displayed there. County party leaders were also provided with a catalogue to aid in ordering materials. National Committee personnel then tried to ascertain how much material, supposedly based on need, should go to each local area. The result was still a "problem of plain communication," down to state, county, and precinct levels, because much correspondence from the National Committee was ignored and transportation and channeling problems arose. On the other hand, a request for the return of a questionnaire on 1956 election results, sent to county chairmen, produced a good bit of information.[13]

Another aspect of intra-party communication, which Butler stressed, was with National Committee members. This process began with preparation for National Committee meetings, and for what one member called "the comfort and convenience of the committee." She told Butler, "You are doing a wonderful job in keeping your Committee informed," and "the National Committee had the opportunity to become better acquainted and exchange ideas and views that will eventually bring the Party closer together."[14] Part of this preparation for meetings involved distribution of an annotated tentative agenda. For those unable to attend meetings Butler provided materials and explanations of actions taken.[15] These practices helped Butler maintain the support of most National Committee members.

To aid the communicative process, Butler advised state and local political committees that they could utilize national party publicity in the form of news releases, statements on issues, speech texts, fact sheets, cartoons, and *Democratic Digest* materials, but he believed the national headquarters could offer more in the nature of clip sheets on newspaper editorials and issues. (The Advisory Committee on Political Organization recommended that national headquarters send air mail, special delivery bulletins to state headquarters during campaign periods.) At the same time, Butler encouraged state, congressional district, and county party organizations to expand publicity activities. Local committees could make more of media releases on state party activity, while state committees could consider using professional publicity directors, volunteer publicity committees, publications, news bulletins, speaker committees, research committees, and publicity committees for assistance to Democratic state legislators. Butler also believed state and local organizations would benefit from more contact with publishers, editors, and television and radio stations.[16]

Except in a few instances, where such ideas had already been partially implemented, Butler's advice on publicity and communication to state and local party organizations was largely ignored, but at the national level his opportunities to shape publicity practices were greater. In an evaluation of Butler's chairmanship, David Broder noted that Butler's emphasis on communication-educational devices (he cited the use of opinion polls) fit with other ideas Butler had about a national party.[17] Early in his term, Butler hired a New York advertisement agency with a record of television success—Norman, Craig, and Kummel.[18] Still, because newspaper men like Sam Brightman and Clayton Fritchey predominated at national headquarters, the Democrats were less disposed than Republicans to use public relations personnel and techniques.[19]

Butler told Democrats that the dollars they contributed to the National Committee brought about these efforts for publicity and communication: 530,000 address plates (151,000 names representing specific party office and interest group categories), 1,351,000 pieces of mail annually, information releases, arrangements for 400 speeches and 200 media talks each year, daily contact with 10-20 media representatives, weekly releases of news stories and speeches, answering of 15,000 to 25,000 letters per year, and handling about 6 requests from members of Congress for speech material daily.[20]

Many of the speeches and television and radio talks which Butler reported as arranged for by headquarters were his own responsibility. He became somewhat a talk-show celebrity, while extensive travel and speech-making early became party of his pattern of leadership activity, even if many speaking invitations had to be declined. He used the National Committee's research facilities and local party leaders to prepare himself for speaking tours and for careful arrangements, including the mailing of advance materials. Using local party figures to assist him, he also communicated with many of the people he met on these tours. For television and radio appearances, he similarly relied on staff assistance for preparation, and responded to those who complimented his performance. These tours and appearances helped make the chairmanship visible to party followers.[21]

Consideration of the *Democratic Digest* would have to be included in any discussion of communication efforts in the Democratic Party of the 1950s because Paul Butler placed great importance on it as a communicative device. The interest he had shown in the magazine, in his first years as national committeeman from Indiana, did not waiver when he became chairman, and he tried to find ways to make the *Digest* more effective, if less so as a means of reaching the general public, then more so for purposes of intra-party communication. When Butler first came to the chairman's office, Clayton Fritchey, a former newsman and Truman aide, and a person Butler did not get on well with, was head of the National Committee's Public Affairs Division and editor of the *Digest*. In 1957, Sam Brightman became deputy chairman for public affairs and *Digest* editor; Brightman, an old newspaper man, would be the chief conceiver and promoter of the magazine during Butler's remaining tenure. He served with the National Committee from 1947 until 1965.

Throughout its history, the *Democratic Digest* has periodically emerged in a new format, as the "new *Digest*." Such was the case after Butler began National Committee service. The "old" *Digest*, published by the Women's Division, was of a size similar to the *New Republic*, but there the similarity ended, and the magazine had been used especially as a campaign document. Then, in August, 1953, partly in response to what Democrats believed was a one-party press, a "new" *Digest*, the size of the *Reader's Digest*, emerged as a newstand publication, also available by subscription. A content analysis found that, unlike the *Reader's Digest* , most of its articles were original, not reprinted, and emphasis was on what Republicans said and did, not on Democratic positions and activities. This emphasis supposedly recognized the non-ideological character of American political parties and the difficulties in trying to bind party members to a national party program; consequently, the *Digest*, by being anti-Republican, could appeal to the party identification of party workers, creating a bond between them and the national party.[22] It was this form of the *Digest* that Butler sold subscriptions for in Indiana. At a May, 1954 National Committee meeting, Butler introduced a resolution, which was approved, commending the *Digest* and authorizing plans to improve it.[23]

The officers of the *Digest* corporation (Corrupt Practices Laws made a corporation necessary) arranged for assistance in the form of services and funds from the National Committee, with the National Committee to be repaid. By August, 1955, weekly salaries totaled $1,429, which under the pressure of economy were to be reduced to $1,188. Loans from the National Committee were increasingly relied on to pay creditors, but the 1954 congressional election campaign had drained off *Digest* staff. By the time Butler became chairman unpaid loans due the National Committee amounted to $66,000; total unpaid obligations were $166,759.[24] Noting that the *Digest* had lost $144,000 the previous nine months, Butler discussed the situation with the National Committee's Executive Committee in April, 1955. He did not believe the publication had to be self-supporting, since the party could subsidize "the dissemination of information and propaganda," but revision of the *Digest* to cut costs and circulation increases were possibilities.[25] National Committee loans for 1955 totaled $131,000; $98,500 in 1956. By October, 1956, unpaid obligations of the Digest were $333,177. Subscriptions had also increased, from 19,441 in 1953 to 62,602 in late 1956, but since newstand sales fell precipitously, total circulation actually decreased.[26] Some state chairmen (particularly in Southern and Western states) refused to appoint leaders for *Digest* sales, while others complained it was hard to arouse enthusiasm for a partisan magazine in one-party states. One announced he had no intention of becoming a magazine salesman.[27]

Forced into the usual post-election economy by the large 1956 campaign deficit, the National Committee re-examined the *Digest* as an institution worthy of party subsidy, and another "new" *Digest* resulted,

128

with fewer pages and more the size of the pre-1953 magazine. There would no longer be any news agency distribution of the *Digest*, making it more feasible to design the publication for simple and direct communication with party workers.[28]

Party organization people seemed to prefer the change in format, and those who once thought subscriptions could best be obtained by mail solicitation now believed that local party organizations could more effectively find subscribers; this belief was confirmed when the mailing of 392,000 sample copies obtained less than one percent response. With this shift to local subscription implementation, it is not surprising that Butler thought about the possibility of state or regional editors for the *Digest*.[29]

If the new *Digest* was to be sold by precinct workers, it was also designed for their use. The first revised issue reported that a survey had revealed that readers wanted these matters stressed: (1) news not found in the one-party press; (2) news background and interpretation; (3) Democratic Party personalities; (4) facts for use as political ammunition; (5) tips on new political techniques; (6) an easily-read format; (7) brief, crisp, and interesting writing; and (8) a low price.[30] As an intra-party communication device the *Digest* differed from its predecessor by not only attacking Republicans, but by stressing Democratic Party activity at all levels and DAC policy statements. If policy guidance by a national party was worth some effort, the new *Digest* reflected that view. In May, 1957, Butler informed the National Committee that an important responsibility was "to develop the media for our Party to communicate the issues and our stand on the issues and news about Democratic activities to our workers in the precincts," and to increase *Digest* circulation in the process.[31] And the Advisory Committee on Political Organization believed the *Digest* should now become the prime vehicle of communication for the party. The *Digest* had changed from a recruiting medium to a party organization medium, but more positive tools for party workers in the magazine were preferable to ironic criticism of the GOP.[32]

An examination of the first year's issues of the new *Digest* shows emphasis on DAC activities and policy pronouncements, party organization activities and information, fund-raising programs, the importance of intra-party communication, and meetings and actions of the National Committee. This emphasis was Paul Butler's.[33] The new *Digest* provided Butler with an outlet for communication with Democrats, whereas the old *Digest*, with rare exceptions, did not publicize the party chairman or his activities. In fact, Butler's election as chairman had not been mentioned in the *Digest*. Now, Butler's activities, travels, and the essence of his controversial statements on policy were publicized. Moreover, replete with information, interpretation, and opinion, Butler's letter, "Dear Fellow Democrats," was a regular feature. Through the new *Digest*, the party chairman would communicate with party members.

In this manner the pattern for *Digest* content and style was established for the 1957-1960 period, but the old financial and circulation problems persisted. It soon became evident that subscriptions fell far short of goals, that no formal promotion methods existed, and that few states had anyone in charge of directing subscription campaigns.[34] The old pattern of National Committee subsidy persisted. The subscription list was padded by National Committee orders for special programs and groups, and National Committee loans by the end of 1958 totaled $406,900 since 1954.[35] But even if the *Digest* had to be subsidized, it remained an important institution in Butler's concept of intra-party communication and his broader concept of the role he saw for the national Democratic Party. In this context, Butler thought the magazine was a success, and fought to keep it in existence. He monitored the subscription campaign, personally thanked anyone who could sell subscriptions, urged "*Digest* Groups" to tour Washington, and planned that 1956 convention pages would be selected on the basis of their success in selling subscriptions.[36]

In November, 1960, the *Digest* ceased publication as an official party magazine, although a special issue for John Kennedy's inauguration followed. The *Digest* was replaced by a four-page newsletter, the *Democrat*.[37] It had gone the way of several of Butler's legacies, and nothing like the 1953-1957, or the 1957-1960 *Democratic Digest* has since been seen in the party.

Cotter and Hennessy have stressed change in the twentieth century from national party chairmen with prime responsibility in fundraising to party chairmen as publicity leaders and partisan image makers, whereby in the transition financial operations at party headquarters became more bureaucratized, with the treasurer, head of the Finance Division, and the comptroller at Democratic headquarters becoming chief financial administrators.[38]

Paul Butler had demonstrated leadership in party financial affairs as Indiana's national committeeman, partly because the Indiana factional situation forced him into assuming this role. His work with the 1954 congressional campaign dinner, his success in having Indiana meet its financial quota, and his work with Chairman Mitchell in establishing a financial advisory council in Indiana showed his capability and gave him some insight into party financial operations. The closer look he had at party financial conditions, after he became chairman, caused his concerns to grow and led to long discussions with colleagues about the haphazard, inadequate financial planning he thought characterized the Democratic Party.[39]

As national chairman, Butler would focus on two major facets of party finance—the usual deficit of varying proportions and methods for raising money—both viewed against the background of the necessities of the approaching campaign. Butler's remarks at National Committee meetings, his letter in the *Democratic Digest*, and the emphasis given fundraising in the *Digest* all show that in practice he stressed the importance he said funding deserved when he ranked it with communication and organization as essential party goals.[40] The *Digest* steadily stressed both the importance and mechanics of fundraising by publicizing events such as Democratic Party Night and drives such as Dollars for Democrats and the Sustaining Membership Program, and revealed results of financial ventures. Its back cover was often used to advertise financial programs.[41] As already demonstrated, Butler's disagreements with the treasurer, Matthew McCloskey, partly resulted from Butler's feeling that McCloskey devoted too little time to what Butler considered an important party activity.

Still, Butler's concern with party finance did not put him directly into the administration of financial activities, although he speculated about and experimented with different administrative arrangements for six years. In April, 1955, Butler told the National Committee he and McCloskey had not had time to develop any plan for finances, but he recommended a committee on finance to assist the treasurer and financial staff personnel. An advisory committee on fund-raising techniques was later established. At the 1956 convention Butler and McCloskey were ready to announce the appointment of a finance chairman, but declined out of respect for the presidential nominee.[42] In 1957 Butler still wanted a finance committee, and twice the Advisory Committee on Political Organization recommended a permanent finance committee as well as training for fundraisers.[43] Finally, in 1960, Roger L. Stevens, a New York realtor and theatrical producer, was named to head the Democratic National Committee's National Finance Committee. It remained, however, somewhat of a paper organization because McCloskey resented sharing financial authority with the group.[44] Its function was to solicit and obtain contributions so as to pay off the party debt. With at least one member from every state, the Finance Committee became a potential link to state organizations as Finance Committee members, National Committee members, the national chairman, and the treasurer interacted.

Essential to any discussion of Democratic Party fundraising during the 1950s is an understanding of assessments against state parties, or the quota system, because of the heavy reliance on this system as a source of funds, even if results were usually disappointing. Democrats

131

did not formally establish a quota system until 1953, by which time Chairman Mitchell believed the 1952 campaign deficit mandated such action.[45] On the part of state parties there was always some discontent with the manner in which each state's quota was determined. For instance, a formula adopted in January, 1960, which based the assessment on population, wealth, and Democratic congressional strength meant states were penalized for voting Democratic.[46]

Treasurer McCloskey, who saw the National Committee as Father and Mother of state parties, stated on several occasions that the children were not taking very good care of their parents. After his exasperation over the failure of states to meet quotas and the backlog of unpaid assessments, he ceased to be good natured.[47] At first he wanted quota records kept confidential, but later he saw advantage in public shaming of those who were negligent. The Advisory Committee on Political Organization recommended that the status of quotas be published in the *Democratic Digest* as a means of putting pressure on states.[48]

In early 1955 McCloskey reported that seventeen states had not met their combined 1953 and 1954 quotas, and by the time of the 1956 convention he figured that $748,000 remained unpaid from the past three years. By the next spring, bemoaning the lack of state cooperation on quotas, McCloskey said the post-election deficit could be paid off if current assessments of about $882,000 were paid up. Apparently unpaid quotas from previous years had been forgotten. By early 1958 the National Committee needed $1,300,000 to plan a campaign and meet its deficit, so it again stressed quota payment. By the end of 1958 a total of $1,053,000 was owed by the states, after the assessment total had been raised to $1,187,000 for that year. By September, 1958, eleven states had not even paid any of their 1958 quotas; $923,000 was owed.[49]

By this time the quota system, or the game of how much the states owed, was so complicated by the matter of intertwined fund-raising programs that bookkeeping became difficult. From the time quotas were established it had been common practice to credit a state with tickets sold in that state for national party dinners. As the party adopted other fund-raising devices, such as Dollars for Democrats and the Sustaining Membership Program, the state parties expected similar credit. This expectation, which the national party more or less accepted, but with much confusion, caused McCloskey to comment that a realistic assessment was in order.[50] In other words, if quotas were not considered to be in addition to other funds raised in the states, most states were not as much in arrears as it appeared; at the same time, the practice threw Butler's plan to raise money from other sources out of balance, and reduced expected income which had been budgeted. This problem persisted, and was never settled by the time of Butler's departure.

Butler concentrated on other aspects of fundraising, letting McCloskey handle the thorny and generally thankless matter of state quotas. In view of Butler's poor relations with some state party leaders, this was a wise strategy, enabling Butler to work with programs which bypassed hostile leaders to some extent. Meanwhile, McCloskey could lecture state leaders that they should not withhold contributions because of differences over policy positions taken by party leaders and committees.[51] Even so, Butler was sometimes critical of McCloskey's handling of quota problems. State leaders sometimes bargained with McCloskey for adjustments of state quotas, and McCloskey often thought it better to adjust quotas and get some money rather than none. Butler warned that such arrangements needed clearance from him or from the National Committee's State Quota Appeal Board.[52]

Party dinners, with overpriced meals and speeches, had also become a standard fund-raising approach for the Democratic Party, even if these dinners were not always financially successful. With the Democrats out of the White House during Butler's chairmanship, attendance at dinners fluctuated, depending in part on how much victory was anticipated in the approaching campaign.[53] Documents showing income from party dinners, but not listing or not attributing all valid expenses to such dinners, were misleading. McCloskey pointed out that the 1959 Truman Diamond Jubilee Dinner, celebrated in different locations, might have created good will, but that expenses were about equal to receipts of $215,000.[54]

An important explanation for some states not meeting their quotas, or supporting party dinners, in addition to issue differences, was personality and the relationship between Butler and state party leaders—New York and Illinois were two such examples.[55] Could a large group of continuous party contributors of small amounts be reached who could lessen dependence on large contributors, provide alternatives to state assessments, perhaps get around recalcitrant state leaders, and provide funds for expansion of party activities? Several advisors encouraged Butler's desire to experiment, and Dollars for Democrats, the Sustaining Membership Program, and Democratic Party Night came into being. Describing the new finance plan as a program above and beyond the state quota system, Butler promised all levels of party committees a share of the proceeds.[56]

For the next three years Butler would argue that his broadly-based program of small contributions on a continuing basis was necessary because of the size and number of Republican contributions. When Butler proclaimed that Democrats would not rely only on wealthy contributors, he satisfied the self-image of Democrats as the party of the little person, thereby serving propaganda purposes.[57] Going beyond basic operations, the Democratic Party could establish a campaign fund and pay for special services such as party worker training programs.

With the Sustaining Membership Program Butler revived a party experiment of the 1920s.[58] Sustaining members were expected to contribute $10 or more a year to the National Committee. By presenting a card to charter sustaining member Number One, Harry S. Truman, in Independence, Missouri, Butler inaugurated the program in July, 1957, and encouraged it the remainder of his term.[59] Nearly a half million letters were mailed in 1957 to obtain 12,000 sustaining members. The number of party contributors rose from 4,925 in 1955 to 29,437 in 1958, although the total amount contributed dropped from $1,063,660 to $874,601. By 1959 sustaining contributions amounted to $158,323 of the total $1,064,149 income.[60] While Butler's announcement of the program carried some implication that sustaining contributions would be shared with state and local party committees, probably based on an Advisory Committee on Political Organization recommendation that these committees aid in solicitation, the National Committee carefully guarded the funds raised in the only real program featuring direct relations between the National Committee and small contributors. However, the contributions could be credited against state quotas.

Dollars for Democrats, also pushed by the ACPO, began in 1956, following a similar 1952 drive for money.[61] In 1957 Dollars became an annual event for the remainder of Butler's tenure, receiving ample publicity.[62] Although thirty-six state and territorial units were expected to participate in the 1957 drive, October 11 and 12, only twenty-five units did. In 1958 thirty-eight units participated to some extent.[63] Collection of Dollars funds was entirely a local matter, with publicity and materials furnished by the National Committee and distributed through the state committees. Local, state, and national party organizations were to divide the money three ways. The establishment of state steering committees, and congressional district and county chairman by July 1, followed by state workshops, was supposed to get the 1958 drive underway, so that local workers could solicit funds in their neighborhoods from September 26 through September 29, with a goal of 400 workers in each congressional district, each worker reaching 100 homes, and garnering $10,000 per district.[64]

Dollars for Democrats had overhead costs, and did not produce large amounts of money ($100,000 in 1958; $110,000 in 1959; $120,000 in 1960),[65] while problems existed from the beginning. Because of Adlai Stevenson's wishes, state organizations received no funds from Dollars in 1956, and if volunteer groups, active in Stevenson's campaign, collected money, local party groups were denied

134

proceeds.[66] Butler established the three-way division system in 1957; but, in addition to the lack of state cooperation, the National Committee sometimes failed to receive its share of the locally collected funds. Lower level committees might deduct "expenses," or forward whatever amount they chose, creating bookkeeping problems by not specifying what funds forwarded to Washington represented. State leaders were a vital link in the program's success, and might choose not to participate, or not to forward promotional literature.[67]

Even though Dollars for Democrats was supported by bipartisan programs of the American Heritage Foundation and the Advertising Council of America ($10,000,000 of free advertising encouraging bipartisan giving), and by the *Reader's Digest, Newsweek,* the New York *Times,* and Eleanor Roosevelt's "My Day" column, such support in 1958 and 1960 brought in amounts little different from 1959, when these groups offered no support.[68]

Democratic Party Night, another fund-raising approach, began in 1957. Democrats should have fun in politics without making it appear that politics were funny, Butler believed, so party followers were encouraged to hold local fund-raising dinners, featuring varied menus and programs, with some hope of clearing $3 per dinner to be divided three ways by levels of party organization. National headquarters publicized the event and offered suggestions for entertainment (such as a "This Is Your Life" script for prominent local Democrats).[69] With 462 events in 1957, in 44 states, attended by 55,000 Democrats, the National Committee cleared only about $27,000. Nearly one hundred parties made no profits, and nearly another hundred failed to report. In 1959 only $7,454 was forwarded to Washington, but the event continued through 1960.[70]

In spite of unfulfilled goals Democrats heard from Treasurer McCloskey that small contributor programs had helped keep national headquarters functioning for the 1958 congressional campaign, as state quota contributions lagged. Even so, the deficit had mounted to over $750,000, and the Finance Committee recommended establishment of "The 750 Club" to secure 750 contributions of $1,000 each to erase the deficit. The idea had been germinating since 1957, when the deficit was $660,000; then the club would have been called "The 660 Club." The new fund drive was headed by Edward Foley, a former Undersecretary of the Treasury, with Adlai Stevenson as honorary chairman, and Harry Truman and Eleanor Roosevelt as committee members. Contributors were promised special facilities at the 1960 convention.[71] "The 750 Club" had considerable success, raising $501,409, by July 12, 1960, and getting this money from all sections and from some of Butler's factional foes in Indiana. Butler pressed friend and foe alike for contributions.[72]

135

Obviously mass, small contributions were not sufficient for adequate financing of desired Democratic Party programs in the late 1950s, but they helped supplement state quota and larger contributions. Still, reliance on large contributions (those of $500 or more) was as necessary for Democrats as Republicans.[73] But to Paul Butler, and other party financial planners, there were important factors in fundraising apart from total dollars collected. The appeal for mass support was an important factor in Butler's plan for mass communication, for recruitment of party workers, and for strengthening local party organization. Finally, it helped Democrats maintain their image of the "party of the little person."[74]

Party organization, especially its revitalization, was a leading concern of Adlai Stevenson and Stephen Mitchell after the 1952 election; and, as has been demonstrated, Butler was just as interested in revitalized and effective party organization when he was a member of the National Committee. So it should not be surprising that party organization was a matter Butler quickly turned his attention to when he became chairman. He was aware that Republican Chairman Guy Gabrielson had held a school for party workers in 1954, dealing with issues, public relations, organization, precinct work, and voter registration.[75]

At the April, 1955 National Committee meeting, Butler announced plans for the expansion of party services by suggesting the creation of three committees in the areas of finance, organization, and public relations. This scheme fit the pattern Butler was to pursue as chairman, with emphasis on funding, organization, and communications (and issues). He told the National Committee that no formal action on its part was necessary for formation of a "campaign planning committee," but that he would appreciate suggestions from those who had political organizational experience. He believed some state parties had new ideas and techniques which would be valuable to national political organization, but which might not be utilized if they were left unpublicized in the laboratories of state Democratic organizations. Butler advised that the campaign planning committee could meet several times to develop methods and techniques which could "be used fairly generally across the country in the campaign of 1956."[76] In this manner Butler outlined the scope and methods of the Advisory Committee on Political Organization (ACPO), which from 1955 through 1960 played an energetic and creative role in Democratic Party activity, a role which has been somewhat neglected by students of political organization, partly because there was usually no deliberate effort to publicize ACPO recommendations, like those of the DAC, even if its meetings and general activities were known about.[77]

136

In August, 1955, Butler appointed the membership and ACPO had its first meeting in Chicago, October 3-5. Butler chose Neil Staebler, Michigan Democratic state chairman, for ACPO chairman. Butler was impressed with new-style political organization in Michigan, and reciprocally, Staebler had been impressed with Butler's organizational insights when Butler came to the National Committee.[78] Staff assistance was provided by four National Committee employees and Staebler's wife, Burnette. One of the four National Committee employees, Venice Sprags, served as ACPO's executive secretary. The committee began with thirty members and six consultants, representing different levels of party organization, public officials or their assistants, and labor unions; state committee personnel predominated, and a future presidential nominee, George McGovern, then executive secretary of the South Dakota Democratic State Committee, was one of the members.

At the Chicago meeting, Butler outlined the committee's assignment:[79]

1. To review and study past organizational ideas and consider revision, and to devise new ideas.
2. To prepare an instructional program for party workers.
3. To compose and circulate useful and effective manuals, handbooks, films, etc.
4. *To determine the role of both the National Committee and chairman, particularly in relation to state party organization.*

The aim was to make the National Committee a clearinghouse for ideas and a reservoir of information concerning party organization, based on study methods and an assessment of their success. Butler noted that the National Committee had never attempted such a program, but that it was the most important function the Democratic Party could undertake for 1956, by laying the groundwork for the "whole political climate in which Democratic candidates can be elected," including "communicating program to every level of Party organization." Here Butler stressed emphasis on policy, and the concept, spelled out later by ACPO, that communication was the central molding force of organization. Paul Butler had a clear view of what he hoped to accomplish, and of relationships among several phases of party activity, with a focus on policy.

Neil Staebler proceeded to outline the scope of the group's work, with a two-fold responsibility of developing organizational materials and methods for both the 1956 campaign and a long-range program of betterment. He wanted an early 1956 deadline for the committee to complete its advisory function, leaving disposition of recommendations to the National Committee. Staebler mentioned twenty-eight areas the committee would be expected to cover, ranging through Butler's guiding factors of communication, issues, organization, and money. This range included specific matters such as materials, training programs, voter registration, relations with interest groups, clearinghouse acivities, radio and television, opinion surveys, *Democratic Digest* promotion, fundraising, campaign speakers, organizational procedures, and publicity. Ten subcommittees were established to examine these areas.

The recommendations[80] which ACPO made in the next several years show it adequately met its charge to consider a broad range of specific areas. By the use of questionnaires (directed to state chairmen mostly) the subcommittees ascertained what activities state party organizations were actually engaged in, what services and programs they needed, and how they might accept programs ACPO had in mind. The recommendations were usually structured in terms of the objectives of a program, which party levels would be involved in implementing a proposed program, how many people would be involved, how much the program would cost, and who would pay for it.

Although some recommendations came from special subcommittees, such as those on Women and Suburban Areas, most were produced by continuing subcommittees, particularly one on Materials and Methods, and to a lesser extent, one on Party Work and Workers. Committee meetings set a pattern of reviewing the group's most recent recommendations, evaluating established programs, and discussing new ideas. In trying to maximize the effects of its recommendations on the approaching campaign, the committee used a timetable. For instance, its June, 1959 meeting was seen as the one where action would be taken which would do the most good for the 1960 election. Its April, 1960 meeting was used to review things happening in the campaign at a half-way point.[81]

Meetings of ACPO were strenuous working sessions. The first day of the April 20-21, 1956 Washington meeting began at 8:30 a.m. and did not end until 10:00 p.m. for subcommittee members. Breakfast, lunch, and dinner periods were used to receive subcommittee reports or to discuss general topics. Some subcommittees met after each meal session. It was necessary to stagger meetings of subcommittees because ACPO members usually served on more than one. The second day of the meeting offered a lighter schedule, with the morning devoted to subcommittee reports.[82]

ACPO's recommendations in 1955 and 1956 (there were at least thirty-nine) represented a well-formed plan, which was used for the 1956 election; and, with some refinement in 1957, became the basis for operation of elections in 1958 and 1960. Recommendations in the latter years tended to be variations on the older, broad themes, and were based on evaluation of programs which had been tried; successful ventures were continued. The earlier suggestions had not always been as specific as the later ones, and the specificness of the later ones made them more valuable.[83] The real basis was established in 1955 and 1956, and if Butler's suggestion to Neil Staebler that the ACPO should terminate in 1956 (because Butler was uncertain of his tenure)[84] had been effected, ACPO would still have an enviable reputation. ACPO was not disbanded, and after Butler's reelection it advised its own continuation with one-third of the membership to be replaced by the chairman each year. Meetings were to be held twice annually, with members paying their own transportation and lodging costs, and the National Committee providing staff, meals, and meeting space.[85]

Following the 1956 election, ACPO saw that most of what its chairman called its "rather ponderous report" had been acted on, and, after looking at the programs which apparently had been successful, looked to future possibilities and variations. The new suggestions were contained in a report to the National Committee in February, 1957, entitled *A Plan for Democratic Leadership, '58-'60*.[86] Staebler informed the National Committee this plan relied on reason, motivation for political activity, and deeper understanding of why political organization was important. Because a National Committee member raised the question of action on Staebler's report, because it required funds, personnel, and adoption of certain policies, Butler called for a motion for execution, which was unanimously adopted. ACPO was also given a resolution of appreciation. Butler promised speedy implementation, and because one part of the report asked for the appointment of a deputy chairman for political organization, as well as six field representatives, asked for suggestions for appointments.[87] Prior to this National Committee action, Butler informed *Democratic Digest* readers that party professionals had once been quite skeptical of ACPO, expecting much theory and few workable ideas, but that of all the undertakings of his chairmanship, he was proudest of ACPO.[88]

At its organizational beginning, Neil Staebler had specified that ACPO was to be "purely advisory" in function; it would make studies, evaluations, and recommendations to the national chairman, who might implement them directly, or send them to the National Committee for action, especially if additional personnel, expertise, and money would be needed for programs. In theory ACPO would recommend but not implement policy nor administer programs, although recommendations usually suggested which headquarters agencies and individuals should be involved in establishing programs.

After ACPO quickly made a number of important recommendations in 1955, records show that by March, 1956, most of thirty-three suggestions had been approved by Butler and that several programs were underway.[89] Recommendations which called for voter opinion surveys, use of television and radio publicity, voter registration programs, and party worker training courses could be put into effect by private firms, a committee of state chairmen, the National Committee staff, or by state and local organizations. Cooperative agreements were suggested. For instance, professional opinion survey organizations could conduct voter surveys and the Research Division of the National Committee could catalog surveys. Task force members, who helped ACPO prepare a proposal for party worker training courses, could implement this program, if the National Committee financed it. The chairman of ACPO could appoint a committee to revise campaign materials. A Michigan firm could prepare a file case for political clubs, while volunteers could help carry out other programs. With the development of campaign materials, advertising agencies, the National Committee's Research Division, and state and county chairmen would be involved. For a voter registration program, Butler established a National Registration Bureau, as advised by ACPO. With such arrangements Butler predicted that by the time of the 1956 convention most campaign material would be printed and 60-75% of the campaign work completed at national headquarters.[90]

Rarely would ACPO move beyond recommendation to implementation of its own suggestions, but this did occur when a subcommittee, with the help of ACPO's executive secretary Venice Sprags, prepared the *Democratic Precinct Handbook*, probably the 1956 *Democratic Fact Book*, and a handbook for voter registration in 1956.[91] ACPO also established an office at the 1956 convention site where its staff was available to accept ideas on organization and help state leaders with organizational problems.[92]

A more detailed examination of ACPO's recommendations in several of the areas given it for study will show what its work actually involved, how far-reaching its suggested programs were, what changes they brought about, and how its suggestions fit Paul Butler's concept of modern party activity.

ACPO concern with issues is evident from the several recommendations made. In its February, 1957 summary of plans for the 1958 and 1960 campaigns, the committee predicated much of its suggested party effort on the notion of "a common body of information and argument for party members," and called for increased issue discussion through various devices so that party members could be provided with "identifiable Party positions," which would enable association with "the Democratic program."[93] ACPO advocated issue conferences at the local, regional, and national levels, as well as quarterly television town meetings for elected Democratic officials to highlight party issue positions; these national sessions would be related to local and regional conferences so that in a two-way communication process the Democratic Party could "put its trademark" on certain programs and issues. The National Committee followed through in

1957 with this idea of a national television town meeting and local gatherings, while in 1958 district issue conferences were used in the congressional campaign. At other times regional party conferences were used for issue discussion, but Butler was concerned that joining National Committee members and state chairmen in such groups might create voting blocs within the National Committee which could be disadvantageous to other party goals, which, it can be surmised, would include centralization, and might weaken Butler's power.[94]

Issue conferences could also aid in preparing party platforms, and from its beginning ACPO wanted public hearings held by both national and state platform drafters in advance of conventions. A platform review committee, with a continuing watchdog function of seeing how well the platform was being implemented and communicating such data to congressional leaders, was also suggested. By the 1960 convention, the Democratic Party had held regional conferences and pre-platform hearings.[95]

While ACPO stressed the importance of issue prominence in party affairs, it never got into the business of policy statements, leaving that function to the national chairman and the DAC, which interestingly was established without an ACPO recommendation. DAC had its own rather mysterious (but apparently inactive) Advisory Committee on Political Techniques, which would seem to have duplicated ACPO, and once ACPO suggested the lodging of a program with that body, the analysis of published opinion surveys.[96]

ACPO's first recommendation asked for "a comprehensive and extensive program of voter surveys . . . as a means whereby the Democratic National Committee can properly assess those areas, groups, and issues which collectively can provide a Democratic electoral majority in 1956." Issues could be determined by the use of surveys conducted by a professional survey organization. If state party surveys had already been undertaken an attempt would be made to make them available for national use. Research in political motivation, behavior, and voter surveys should reflect the notion of democratic processes based on two-way communication rather than a unilateral influence attempt. This type of research would supplement the more traditional research reflected in compilation of congressional voting records, clipping files, and fact sheets.[97]

ACPO was always interested in campaign materials (as an issue and communications concern, as well as a campaign tool), so some of its early recommendations called for evaluation of materials tested in some states and a screening of campaign novelties. A uniform, national color combination for all campaign materials was desired, along with fliers (rather than more expensive slick-backed pamphlets) and publications such as *Fact Book, How to Argue With a Republican* ,

History of the Democratic Party, campaign biographies, and the platform. Showing a concern for proper utilization of campaign materials, ACPO wanted local party needs determined early in campaigns, with the aid of catalogs and sample distributions, and urged state parties to name a materials coordinator. Butler had complained of campaign materials wasted when state organizations had distributed them no further down the line, or when local organizations left materials unused. In 1956 the National Committee kept track of campaign materials going to state and local organizations and established the principle of these organizatiosn purchasing materials from a supply corporation managed by the National Committee's advertising agency. Part of ACPO's emphasis on campaign material reflected the belief, held also by Paul Butler, that early campaign preparation involved having campaign materials ready for use immediately after the convention, no matter who the nominee would be. Butler failed to get pre-convention cooperation from the several presidential candidates, but did succeed in early preparation of campaign material and early television planning.[98]

Even before the *Democratic Digest* changed its format in 1957 ACPO urged state subscription drives, but a survey revealed that thirty-six states had no interest in such an undertaking. ACPO wanted the new *Digest* to become a house organ fostering two-way communication (Butler's goal) by presenting information on issues, organization, and state party activity, all useful tools for party workers; the *Digest* "should become the number one vehicle of communication for the Party."[99]

ACPO acted extensively in the field of party finance—recommending small contributor programs, which led to Dollars for Democrats and other programs; evaluating the small contributor programs after their institution; and recommending a National Finance Committee.[100]

The work ACPO actually did in preparing precinct worker handbooks and voter registration materials showed that it was interested in implementation of its recommendations, and how important it considered precinct work from the standpoint of effective party organization. Democrats were concerned in the 1950s with how population shifts to the suburbs would affect the Democratic coalition. Fearful that new residents of suburbs would be influenced to go along with Republican neighbors, ACPO developed the Welcome Neighbor program in an effort to retain the support of voters who had been Democrats in the central cities. It was believed this approach could attract new party workers and contributors, as well as hold old voters, and rootless suburbanites could attain meaningful identity. Welcoming new voters and gathering of data concerning them should be a continual process, based on early voter contact. A Welcome Neighbor basket, containing the *Democratic Digest* and other party literature, was proposed. This neighborhood activity would be complemented by voter registration drives, directed from Washington.[101]

ACPO believed that if precinct work, voter registration, and get-out-the-vote techniques were to be effective, training for precinct workers was necessary. The training of precinct workers was one of the ideas Butler specifically presented to ACPO, where it was first received unenthusiastically, the training of party workers being an alien idea to the professionals. Yet Butler said the question most frequently asked him came from precinct committeemen—What are my duties? After a presentation by Professor Morris Collins, University of Georgia, ACPO was won over to one of the most important activities sponsored by the committee.[102] Morris had prepared a precinct training course, twelve hours long, to train instructors, who would, in turn, train precinct workers in six-hour sessions. Local organizations and the trainees were expected to finance the courses, which were instituted in 1956, after half the states reported need for such a program. The National Committee provided instructors and materials. Eventually seven university professors offered training to instructors at the state level. The demand for training instructors was never met, but the eventual success of the program depended on precinct committeemen who had been trainees offering their own courses to other precinct workers in their counties. By August, 1958, twenty-three courses at the state level for the training of instructors had been held in twenty states. In Florida, one hundred thirty-two courses for local workers had been conducted, with plans for three hundred more sessions. In Arizona, twenty-two instructors trained by a professor taught thirty courses for committeemen. By 1959 ACPO was enthusiastic about continuing the precinct worker training courses, believing the effort would be more effective if state parties put a person in charge of the program, and if state chairmen themselves became more involved.[103]

In 1958 ACPO recommended a similar course for state, congressional district, and county party organization leaders, and such a course was inaugurated in September, 1959. The next step was suggestion of a conference for state chairmen and vice chairmen, featuring workshops and general sessions on better organizational and campaign methods, which was also held in September, 1959.[104]

Early in 1956 ACPO asked for a Field Assistants Program, which would have used a small team of workers from the Democratic National Committee and the congressional campaign committees, to organize state conferences for both county committees and state committees. This idea evolved into a program featuring six paid professional field workers who would go into the states to aid state parties in

143

strengthening organization (Republicans had employed over one hundred field workers in the 1956 campaign). Butler emphasized that utilization of these National Committee field workers was the responsibility of state party leaders. The National Committee wanted to assist state and local organizations but had no right to direct or order them. The field workers could assist states in establishing precinct workers training courses and in building an organization up to campaign level on a permanent basis. Butler informed the Missouri national committeeman that field representative would not be spies.[105]

Following the appointment of Drexel A. Sprecher as the deputy chairman for political organization, field service activities began in September, 1957. Sprecher told National Committee members that the field workers, as representatives of the National Committee, could promote better understanding and utilization of national headquarters services and act as consultants to state party leaders on organizational matters. Emphasizing that the field workers were not regional directors, had no staff, and were not party organizers (organization was the business of state parties), Sprecher pointed out that field workers would visit National Committee members and state party leaders, would provide information on National Committee services, and would attempt to learn which nationally-inspired programs were well accepted, which needed adjustment, and how the National Committee could be responsive to state needs. In stressing the importance of intra-party communication, field workers could encourage state leaders to utilize programs which had been successful in other states. Consultation on organizational matters was their most important function. Sprecher did not say so, but the Democrats also wanted field representatives to keep the National Committee informed on local political sentiment.[106]

The six field representatives selected to fulfill these goals had professional political experience; a two-week course at the National Committee offices gave them additional insights into the functions and substance of politics—political trends, opinion polls, voting studies, and publicity.[107] John Doran was one of these field representatives. For eight years after World War II he was active in local party organizational work in South Bend, Indiana, where he came to admire Paul Butler's political style and leadership. During 1956 and 1957, Butler (in what apparently was his special recruiting technique, as with Paul Willis) discussed the work of ACPO and the establishment of field representatives with Doran, and finally asked Doran to become a representative.[108]

In appointing field representatives, Butler sought advice from National Committee members, some members of Congress, and state party leaders in the area to be served (usually eight or nine states), and made every effort to see that the representative selected would be acceptable to party leaders. Before the field representatives went to work, Butler conducted a meeting in each of the geographical areas to which representatives were assigned, and invited National Committee members, state party members, and party leaders from larger cities, to whom Butler explained the field activity services offered, with a precise description of the representatives' functions and the manner in which they were to perform. Thus trust and faith in the field representatives were maximized in the face of skepticism on the part of many state and local organizational leaders. At their two-week training course the representatives were continually warned that they would have to build acceptance and trust among party leaders. If National Committee goals failed of attainment, or caused problems, field representatives were told by Sprecher to stay away from the particular locality while National Committee officials attempted to rectify the situation. While the field representatives were cautioned to serve as consultants, rather than to dictate to state and local organizations, it was made clear that when invited to do so they should offer specific national programs which were aimed at fundamentals in precinct organization and activity or headquarters organization. In practice, field representatives found themselves devoting about fifteen percent of their time to fund-raising activities.[109]

By 1959 ACPO reported that the field representatives had made "tremendous contributions . . . in communicating ideas through the various states and in stimulating and perfecting organization," even if party leaders in some cases had not shown proper appreciation for these contributions. More publicity was desirable. It was believed that the field representatives would perform a vital role in the 1960 campaign if their knowledge of state party personnel and operation were put to good advantage.[110]

More than any other party body, ACPO, of which Butler was so proud, stressed what was the interwoven theme of Butler's chairmanship—communication (and, of course, issues), funding, and organization. Butler began enunciating this program as early as April, 1955, when he announced creation of ACPO. He told the National Committee that he was thinking in terms of three committees to expand National Committee services. Later that year, after Butler outlined ACPO's assignment, Neil Staebler included funding and communication in the committee's scope, so that while focusing on organization, ACPO clearly brought funding and communication within its focus. The central molding force of organization was perceived in terms of communication, and a two-way flow of communication among party organizational levels brought common understanding of procedures and issues. In 1957 Butler was able to announce authorization of the largest program in party history in these areas of focus.[111]

Paul Butler picked the members of ACPO in terms of their backgrounds and with an eye towards their ideas on party organization, and he selected a chairman who shared his views of participative politics. While Butler seldom made formal recommendations to ACPO, the program suggested by the committee reflected and effectively integrated his theme of party management.[112]

ACPO died with Butler's retirement. Candidate Kennedy promised Michigan Democrats that he would continue to build up the party organization, but soon changed his mind, believing that effective organization only existed in Michigan and Minnesota. There was nothing else to build on. Yet ACPO's program was important in the 1958 congressional election, a crucial one for Democrats, and in Kennedy's narrow election margin in 1960.[113] ACPO also affected Republican behavior. After his election in 1965, Chairman Ray Bliss encouraged a course parallel to that taken by ACPO, and improved on it in many ways, according to ACPO's chairman.[114] Many of the GOP programs employed in the 1980s reminded observers of ACPO activities. Some Democrats thought Kennedy acted hastily in dismantling ACPO, and Democratic Party organization continued to be neglected by Democratic presidents. Then in 1978 the Democratic national chairman announced that the first regional party offices would be opened outside Washington since Butler's chairmanship.[115]

NOTES

1. Cotter and Hennessy, *Politics Without Power*, pp. 67, 80.
2. Ibid., p. 105.
3. April 16, 1959, Butler Papers, Box 155.
4. Text of speech of Paul M. Butler, Chairman of the Democratic National Committee at Inaugural Luncheon for Governor G. Mennen Williams, Lansing, Michigan, January 1, 1959, Butler Papers, Box 110.
5. Robert L. Riggs, Louisville *Courier-Journal*, July 19, 1959.
6. Butler's notes on the DNC Executive Committee meeting, March 31 and April 1, 1953, Butler Papers, Box 76.
7. *Democratic Digest*, September, 1957, Butler's letter; Salt Lake *Times*, August 2, 1957.
8. Speech text, Pittsfield, Massachusetts, March 3, 1955, Butler Papers, Box 146; Democratic National Committee Release, speech by Paul M. Butler . . . to the Southern California

Executive Committee Caucus, Los Angeles, California, August 10, 1957, Box 142. See David B. Truman, *The Governmental Process* (New York: Alfred A. Knopf, 1955), pp. 195-199, for a discussion of the tasks of group leaders in maintaining internal group cohesion, and the use of internal group publicity, or propaganda, for that purpose.

9. *Democratic Digest*, February, 1957, Butler's letter; Butler speech, Cleveland, Ohio, March 15, 1955, Butler Papers, Box 147; ACPO Recommendation 45, 1959, Willis collection; New York *Times*, November 17, 1956.

10. See *Democratic Digest*, April, 1959, p. 12, and March, 1959, p. 20.

11. ACPO Recommendation 45, 1959, and 9, 1957, Willis collection.

12. *Democratic Digest*, September, 1957, p. 2, and March, 1959, Butler's letter, April, 1958, Butler's letter, and November, 1957, Butler's letter; Bone, *Party Committees*, p. 237; Butler's Los Angeles speech, August 10, 1957; original charge to the ACPO, October, 1955, Willis collection.

13. Notes in author's collection from a course, "Problems of Political Parties and Electoral Process," taught by Paul G. Willis, Spring, 1957; Democratic National Committee memorandum to county chairmen, February, 1957, Butler Papers, Box 119; Bone, *Party Committees*, p. 81 reports on some feedback on the use of campaign materials in 1954.

14. Willa Mae Roberts to Butler, May 13, 1957, Butler Papers, Box 108.

15. Butler to DNC members, January, 1960, Butler Papers, Box 17; Butler to DNC members, February 28, 1957 and March 4, 1957, Box 67.

16. ACPO Recommendation 45, 1959, Willis collection; notes for a speech, "Telling the Democratic Story," n.d., Butler Papers, Box 147.

17. "The Changing Face of the Party Chairman," *New York Times Magazine*, October 18, 1959, p. 16.

18. Morrow, "The Democrats' No. 1 Optimist," p. 69. See *Official Report of the Proceedings of the Democratic National Convention, 1956*, pp. 795-97, for Butler's emphasis on the use of television and radio; also p. 646 for Butler's intention to expand television and radio use.

19. Bone, *Party Committees*, pp. 87-88.

20. Gladys Watkins to Butler, February 17, 1959, Butler Papers, Box 11; and chairman's report for 1957, February 21, 1958, Box 165; *Democratic Digest*, May, 1958, Butler's letter.

21. For an idea of speeches to the public and party groups, see Butler Papers, Boxes 146, 149, 151, 153, 155, 158, and 202; for an idea of trip preparation and follow-up activities, see

Boxes 37, 38, and 88; Clayton Fritchey to Butler, February 9, 1955, Box 9, and material in Box 86.

22. Bone, *Party Committees*, p. 76; Roger H. Marz, "The Democratic Digest: A Content Analysis," *American Political Science Review* LI (1957), pp. 696-703.

23. *Official Report of the Proceedings of the Democratic National Convention, 1956*, pp. 561-62.

24. *Minutes*, Board of Directors of Democratic Digest Corporation, May 29 and June 12, 1953, Butler Papers, Box 11; Hy Raskin to Stephen MItchell, November 18, 1954; Wesley McCune to Butler, February 10, 1955, and Lyons Moore to Wesley McCune, April 1, 1955, Box 11.

25. *DNC Meeting, April 15, 1955*, Butler Papers, Box 13, pp. 75-76, 96-138.

26. *Democratic Digest Corporation Business Report, June 1, 1953 - October 31, 1956*, Butler Papers, Box 47.

27. *Report, Democratic Digest Organizational Promotion, Regions III and V, November 1, 1956*, Butler Papers, Box 50.

28. Bone, *Party Committees*, p. 77.

29. *General Statement for the President of the Democratic Digest Corporation Concerning the Business Operations of the Corporation as of May 1, 1957* ; Butler Papers, Box 11; Lyons Moore to Butler, January 8, 1957, Box 11; Washington *Post-Times Herald*, May 21, 1957; notes for a speech, "Telling the Democratic Story," n.d., Box 147.

30. *Democratic Digest*, February, 1957.

31. *Official Report of the 1960 Democratic National Convention and Committee*, p. 434.

32. ACPO, *A Plan for Democratic Leadership '58-'60*, and Recommendation 20-B, 1957, Willis collection.

33. *Democratic Digest*, September, 1957, Butler's letter.

34. *Official Report of the 1960 Democratic National Convention and Committee*, pp. 431-42.

35. Memorandum, Lyons Moore to Butler, February 18, 1959, Butler Papers, Box 11.

36. In the Butler Papers, Box 21, see the elaborate binder with subscription quotas, *by county*, for each state; Butler to Dr. W.M. Benefiel, April 8, 1955, Box 1; undated memorandum, Box 115.

37. New York *Times*, November 18 and 22, 1960, and March 12, 1961.

38. Cotter and Hennessy, *Politics Without Power*, pp. 71-73, 178.

39. Interview with Marshall Smelser, September, 1974.

40. *Democratic Digest*, September, 1957, Butler's letter.

41. See issues of the new *Digest*, May, 1957, through May, 1960.

42. *Official Report of the Proceedings of the Democratic National Convention, 1956*, pp. 645, 868.

43. New York *Times*, September 28, 1957; ACPO Recommendations 42 and 43, 1957, and 35, 1959, Willis collection.

44. Herbert Alexander, *Financing the 1960 Election* (Princeton, New Jersey: Citizens' Research Foundation, n.d.), pp. 52-53.

45. Cotter and Hennessy, *Politics Without Power*, p. 180; Bone, *Party Committees*, p. 101.

46. *Official Report of the 1960 Democratic National Convention and Committee*, pp. 727, 732-44.

47. Ibid., 426-27, 452-53, and 554-55.

48. ACPO Recommendations 14 and 47, 1957, Willis collection.

49. Typed notes for an April 15, 1955 meeting, pp. 76-85, Butler Papers, Box 16; *Official Report of the Proceedings of the Democratic National Convention and Committee, 1956*, pp. 426-27, 452-54, 660-61; status reports in Box 16, Butler Papers.

50. *Official Report of the Proceedings of the Democratic National Convention and Committee, 1956*, p. 663; *Official Report of the 1960 Democratic National Convention and Committee*, p. 553.

51. *Official Report of the 1960 Democratic National Convention and Committee*, p. 453.

52. Butler to McCloskey, August 19, 1958, and December 23, 1959, Butler Papers, Box 16.

53. Ronald F. Stinnett, *Dollars, Dinners, and Democrats* (Ames, Iowa: The Iowa State University Press, 1967), pp. 194-205.

54. See material in Box 8, Butler Papers, on dinner expenses; *Official Report of the 1960 Democratic National Convention and Committee*, p. 719.

55. Cotter and Hennessy, *Politics Without Power*, p. 181.

56. *Official Report of the 1960 Democratic National Convention and Committee*, pp. 397-400.

57. Butler's Los Angeles speech, August 10, 1957, p. 4; Cotter and Hennessy, *Politics Without Power*, p. 1.

58. Cotter and Hennessy, *Politics Without Power*, p. 185; ACPO suggested a "sustaining fund," which had antecedents in several states.

59. Democratic National Committee Releases, July 27 and 29, 1957, Butler Papers, Box 142; Butler's letters in the *Democratic Digest*, January and July, 1958.

60. Democratic National Committee Release, November 8, 1959, Butler Papers, Box 111.

61. Democratic National Committee Release, September 15, 1957, Butler Papers, Box 142.

62. See back covers, *Democratic Digest*, September and October, 1957, and Butler's letters, October, 1957, January, 1958, July, 1958, and June, 1959.

149

63. Butler's 1957 report to the DNC, Butler Papers, Box 165; ACPO Recommendation 49, 1957, Willis collection; Bernard Hennessy, *Dollars for Democrats, 1959* (New York: McGraw-Hill Book Company, 1960), p. 3.

64. *Democratic Digest*, July, 1958, p. 12.

65. Cotter and Hennessy, *Politics Without Power*, p. 186.

66. Staff meeting notes, September 27, 1956, Butler Papers, Box 16.

67. Hennessy, *Dollars for Democrats*, pp. 3-4, 19-23.

68. *Official Report of the Proceedings of the Democratic National Convention, 1956*, pp. 755-56; *Democratic Digest*, Butler's letter, April, 1958, August, 1958, p. 23, September, 1958, p. 19, and Butler's letter, June, 1960.

69. *Official Report of the 1960 Democratic National Convention and Committee*, pp. 397-98; "This is Your Political Life" script, Butler Papers, Box 21; *Democratic Digest*, Butler's letter, May, 1957, and October, 1957, p. 13.

70. Sheets on Party Night, Box 21, Butler Papers.

71. *Official Report of the 1960 Democratic National Convention and Committee*, pp. 553-55, 557-59; New York *Times*, July 11, 1957, and January 16, 1959.

72. See Butler Papers, Box 29, for almost day by day progress accounts; Butler to Leonora Gundlach, February 6, 1959, Box 5.

73. Alexander, *Financing the 1960 Election*, pp. 57-59.

74. Hennessy, *Dollars for Democrats*, p. 1.

75. Bone, *Party Committees*, p. 93.

76. *Official Report of the Proceedings of the Democratic National Convention, 1956*, p. 645.

77. The *Democratic Digest* shows this. While ACPO recommendations were not long kept confidential, meetings were open only to DNC members and state chairmen, in addition to ACPO members; Neil Staebler to the author, July 6, 1982.

78. In a speech at the inauguration of Michigan Governor G. Mennen Williams in 1959 (Box 110, Butler Papers), Butler praised Michigan party organization, Neil Staebler, and the issue orientation of the Michigan Democracy.

79. This description of the October, 1955 meeting is based on the official report in the Paul G. Willis collection.

80. These recommendations are in the Willis collection, also.

81. See tentative agenda for the August, 1956 Chicago meeting in Butler Papers, Box 9; Neil Staebler to Paul Willis, May 1, 1959, Willis collection; Neil Staebler to ACPO members, January 20, 1960, Willis collection.

82. Agenda in Willis collection.

83. Neil Staebler to the author, July 6, 1982.

84. Butler to Staebler, August 10, 1956, Butler Papers, Box 9.

85. ACPO Recommendation 8, 1957, Willis collection.
86. In Willis collection.
87. *Official Report of the 1960 Democratic National Convention and Committee*, pp. 387-404.
88. *Democratic Digest*, February, 1957, Butler's letter.
89. Recapitulation of ACPO recommendations in Willis collection.
90. See Willis collection for an idea of implementation of ACPO recommendations; also Neil Staebler to the author, July 6, 1982.
91. Copies in author's collection; Neil Staebler to the author, July 6, 1982; ACPO Recommendation 14, 1955-56, Willis collection.
92. Staebler to Butler, August 8, 1956, Butler Papers, Box 9.
93. Summary in Willis collection.
94. *Official Report of the 1960 Democratic National Convention and Committee*, pp. 403, 479; Butler to Calvin W. Rawlings, November 22, 1957, Butler Papers, Box 1.
95. ACPO Recommendations 16, 16A, 17, and 20, 1955-56; 5, 6, and 13, 1957-58; and 10, 33, and 47, 1959; Willis collection.
96. ACPO Recommendations 22-A, 1955-56; and 6, 1958; Willis Collection.
97. ACPO Recommendations 1 and 1A, 1955-56; 20, 1957-58; and 6, 1958; Willis collection.
98. ACPO Recommendations 6, 8, 11, 11-A, and 11-B, 1955-56; 11, 1957-58; 34, 1959; Willis collection. Notes in author's collection from a course, "Problems of Political Parties and Electoral Process," taught by Paul G. Willis, Spring, 1957. Cotter and Hennessy, *Politics Without Power*, p. 75.
99. ACPO Recommendations 20, 1955-56; 14 and 20-B, 1957-58; and 8, 1958; Willis collection.
100. ACPO Recommendations 15, 1955-56; 4, 14, 42, 43, 44, 47, 49, and 51, 1957-58; 1, 1958; and 4, 5, 6, and 35, 1959; Willis collection.
101. ACPO Recommendations 14 and 19, 1955-56; 1, 1957; and 4, 1958; Willis collection; *Democratic Precinct Handbook*, 1956, in author's collection.
102. Neil Staebler to the author, July 6, 1982.
103. ACPO Recommendation 2, 1955-56, Willis collection; *Official Report of the 1960 Democratic National Convention and Committee*, pp. 474-75; *Democratic Digest*, August, 1958, p. 24; ACPO Recommendation 2, 1959, Willis collection.
104. ACPO Recommendation 2, 1958, Willis collection; *Democratic Digest*, May and September, 1959; ACPO Recommendations 1 and 9, 1959, Willis collection.
105. ACPO Recommendations 4 and 5, 1955-56; Butler's 1957 report to the DNC, Butler Papers, Box 165; Democratic National Committee Release, July 12, 1957, Box 142; Butler to Mark Holloran, October 31, 1957, Box 38.

106. *Official Report of the 1960 Democratic National Convention and Committee*, pp. 471-74; Bone, *Party Committees*, p. 237, says the Democrats needed field men to keep the DNC informed on local sentiment.
107. Butler's 1957 report to the DNC, Butler Papers, Box 165.
108. John P. Doran to the author, November 6, 1974.
109. Ibid.
110. ACPO Recommendations 3 and 45, 1959, Willis collection.
111. *Official Report of the Proceedings of the Democratic National Convention, 1956*, pp. 645-46; report of the October, 1955 ACPO meeting in Willis collection; ACPO, *A Plan for Democratic Leadership '58-'60*, Willis collection; Butler's letters in *Democratic Digest*, April and September, 1957.
112. Neil Staebler to the author, July 6, 1982.
113. Interview with Neil Staebler, February 22, 1981.
114. Neil Staebler to the author, July 6, 1982.
115. Louisville *Courier-Journal*, August 31, 1978.

Chapter Eight

FACTIONAL AND TENURE PROBLEMS

Paul Butler's problems with retaining the national chairman's office, particularly after he barely held on to the job at the 1956 convention, now need to be given attention.[1] Consideration of Indiana political developments during this period is the proper way to begin, not because Butler formally had to be elected to any party office in Indiana to remain as chairman, but because he and many others in politics believed a national chairman needed some sort of local base of power, from which the chairman was supposedly chosen in the first place. At the same time it was believed that triumphs in Washington helped Butler in Indiana. At least four factors complicated the situation: (1) Butler simultaneously held on to his national committeeman's position, and his term would expire in 1956;[2] (2) Democratic factionalism was not quiescent in Indiana while Butler established his programs in Washington, because the McKinney-McHale forces had not given up the factional struggle at all; (3) Butler's mentor, Henry Schricker, was no longer governor, and the state chairman, Charles Skillen, increasingly displeased Butler; (4) from 1953 to 1959, Indiana Democrats held no non-judicial statewide offices. Certainly Butler's attention to factional matters was careful. Both Butler and members of his staff monitored the Indiana political situation, and minutes of state committee meetings show Butler was almost always in attendance.[3]

Butler's necessity to concern himself with politics in South Bend was never so great as it was with state politics. Nevertheless, his appointment book and correspondence show that he maintained some local political interest, and when factional candidates, opposed to the local party organization with which Butler was identified, captured the nominations for two top county offices in 1958, the development was interpreted as a loss for Paul Butler.[4]

Butler also had a strong interest in the career of John Brademas, who in 1958 was elected to a twenty-two year career in the House of Representatives, after losing general election contests in 1954 and 1956. Although Brademas always had organizational support for his congressional nominations, there was hesitancy on the part of a core of party workers to feel enthusiastic about Brademas' candidacy and even to vote for him, particularly in the beginning. Brademas had never held party or public office. One observer reported that Brademas was considered arrogant and too ambitious; some candidates refused to appear on television programs with him. Letters in Butler's papers indicate that several party workers felt that Butler employed the local party slating process to force Brademas on them, when they knew nothing of his background.[5] Perhaps Brademas' ethnic background and life experiences were not similar enough to those of many of his critics to suit them, and he may have lacked some of the political touch more popular candidates exhibited in neighborhood meetings. A graduate of South Bend Central High School, Brademas had received degrees from Harvard and Oxford (where he was Rhodes Scholar for Indiana). After his unsuccessful candidacy for Congress in 1954 he served as an assistant to several members of Congress, and for the 1956 campaign assisted Adlai Stevenson as research person and position paper writer. By 1958 he had become an assistant professor of political science at Saint Mary's College in Notre Dame, Indiana.

Brademas' primary election victories were viewed as Butler victories. In 1958 Butler was home to launch Brademas' general election campaign, and after Brademas won the election Butler asked Sam Rayburn's assistance in getting Brademas assigned to the House Education and Labor Committee. Adlai Stevenson did the same.[6] As Brademas prepared for his reelection campaign in 1960, Butler had Brademas join him on the famous July 5, 1959, Celebrity Parade Program. Paul Butler had a lot to do with getting John Brademas established in a successful and outstanding political career because he stood by Brademas, and supported him enthusiastically, when Brademas was not so popular with all party workers.[7]

One method which Butler used in Indiana factional games was almost constant mention of his name as a candidate for major Indiana office, and his enemies were annoyed by this tactic, partly because they were almost certain he had no serious intentions. Even before he became national chairman Butler was considered a candidate for the Senate in 1956. In 1955 some Lake County Democrats, and others, started a Butler-for-governor campaign. More serious candidates tried to ascertain Butler's intentions.[8] Butler kept political speculators guessing as to his plans. In 1957 Butler hinted at a 1958 race for the Senate, and he made clear that if he ran he would attack the record of incumbent Republican William E. Jenner, calling Jenner an extremist, "breast-beating radical of the Right," before that term was generally used.[9] Democratic Senate hopefuls again pressed Butler on his intentions and suggested that his behavior was keeping several talented candidates away from the race. On March 1, 1958, Butler announced that he would not

154

be a senatorial candidate, but before long he intimated to Frank McKinney that he might seek the gubernatorial nomination in 1960. Butler explained his strategy to State Senator Marshall Kizer, chairman of Butler's congressional district organization, and Butler's choice for the senatorial nomination: "I hope he [McKinney] and his cohorts will take seriously my intimation of interest in the gubernatorial nomination of 1960 and try to make sure that they have me stopped by nominating and electing you as our United States Senator this year."[10] Butler's ploy was unsuccessful.

In state convention nominations, Butler suffered a series of defeats from 1956 through 1960. In 1956 Butler favored a former legislative leader, S. Hugh Dillon, for the Democratic gubernatorial nomination, but Bulter, McKinney, and McHale, each backing his own candidate, saw the nomination go to Terre Haute Mayor Ralph Tucker, who opened his own campaign headquarters separately from the state committee office.[11] In 1958 Butler's choice for the senatorial nomination, Marshall Kizer, lost to Evansville Mayor R. Vance Hartke, a factional foe of Butler, Hartke receiving belated support from Frank McKinney.[12] Butler's favorite for the 1960 gubernatorial nomination, Indiana Secretary of State John R. Walsh, withdrew his candidacy on the eve of the state convention, leaving Butler and others with State Auditor Albert A. Steinwedel as the only candidate with a chance to prevent the nomination of Matthew E. Welsh, suppored by Frank McKinney and Frank McHale. Steinwedel, conservative, favored by many rural township trustees, and supporter of Lyndon Johnson for president, seemed an unlikely Butler candidate. He lost by a two-to-one margin to Welsh, who promptly paid homage to the service of McKinney and McHale to the Democratic Party.[13]

Butler and State Chairman Charles Skillen had both been re-elected, respectively, national committeeman and state chairman in 1956. Butler had kept people guessing as to whether he would seek reelection in 1956, and whether he would resign thereafter, while Skillen sometimes talked of resigning, or was threatened with expulsion. Both survived until 1960, because it would have taken a two-thirds vote of the State Committee to force Skillen out and because it was doubtful Butler could be removed by the state party between national conventions (the Gravel issue). Also, Butler's enemies hesitated to oust Skillen, when Skillen and Butler were not friendly, and Skillen's enemies could not agree on his successor. Only once was Skillen formally challenged, in 1958, by a Butler ally, Griffith Rees, and Skillen won, 15-7.[14] Butler was not a candidate for reelection as national committeeman in 1960, and Alexander Campbell, supported by McKinney and McHale, succeeded Butler. Skillen resigned in August, 1960, left with little to do in Matthew Welsh's gubernatorial campaign.[15] Butler and Skillen may have been unlikely bedfellows after 1954, but bedfellows they were from 1952 to 1960.

When Paul Butler called the 1960 Democratic national convention to order, and had only a few days remaining as both national chairman and national committeeman, he had no real base of power left in Indiana politics. However much they had been related, his state and national political careers ended simultaneously. Indiana Democratic factionalism took a somewhat different course after 1960, and would have, even if Butler had been a participant.

Paul Butler's Indiana Democratic faction articulated against the opposition most clearly in the 1960 gubernatorial nomination campaign, and it was essentially Butler's argument from his early political career—that selfish individuals should not put personal interests above party interests. Butler had argued in 1957 that a bipartisan deal might be in the making whereby Democrats would nominate a weak senatorial candidate in 1958, in exchange for Republican support of a conservative Democratic gubernatorial candidate in 1960. Referring to a sixty-to-one return Frank McKinney had once made on an investment (the Empire Ordnance investment, made also by Frank McHale), Butler said, "I'm inclined to think some people put ahead of picking the best Democratic candidate for senator their interest in the nomination of the candidate for governor in 1960. They would use the party for their own selfish gain. That has been done before by both parties in Indiana."[16] As John Walsh, Butler's choice for governor, campaigned against Matthew Welsh, his denunciation and documentation was based on Butler's perception of his own role in Indiana factionalism—"the complete elimination from positions of power and influence of men who deal across Party lines to gain their selfish ends."[17] Butler perceived McKinney and McHale as old school politicians who preferred control of party organization to party victory without organizational control, and who would deal across party lines in making arrangements which benefited a privileged few, rather than the public interest. "The evidence of McHale-McKinney power and influence in Republican administrations, state, county and city, can be documented amply by careful research."[18]

Using the theme of McKinney-McHale participation in the "bipartisan establishment," John Walsh charged that these leaders had an "unholy alliance with the Republican Party," and that they were a "selfish group, who represent the biggest bank in Indiana, the railroads, and the public utilities, and the Chamber of Commerce."[19] Walsh told one campaign rally, "Bossism has now reared its ugly head in our party and some of those who have been identified for years in bipartisan control of both parties have elected themselves the self-appointed heads of your party and mine."[20] Walsh pointed to state commissions, bipartisan by statutory mandate, where appointments made by a Republican governor had allegedly been based on consultation with McKinney and McHale. Walsh specifically cited the Alcoholic Beverage Commission, the State Highway Commission, and the Public Service Commission, on which sat Ira Haymaker, the Democratic state chairman ousted by Butler's faction in 1952. Haymaker's brother, Jack, had been elected state treasurer in 1958, and the Butler faction wanted to defeat him for renomination. Their reason was made clearer a year later, when Haymaker's Republican successor announced that Haymaker had deposited the entire Indianapolis active checking account of the State of Indiana (fluctuating between 20 and 105 million dollars) in American Fletcher National Bank, which Frank McKinney served as board chairman. The bank had paid one-fourth of one percent interest on the funds into a state depository insurance fund. In an updated bipartisan agreement, the new Republican treasurer decided to leave one-third of the funds in McKinney's bank.[21] Walsh also pointed out that the son of the eventual 1960 Republican gubernatorial candidate was employed in a law firm headed by Alexander Campbell, Butler's replacement as national committeeman. Nor had he forgotten to remind audiences that McHale's law firm was national counsel for Central Newspaper Incorporated, publishers of leading Republican newspapers in Indiana and Arizona, including the Indianapolis *Star* and *News*.[22]

Some years later, the successful gubernatorial candidate responded that while McKinney and McHale were his personal friends, and had offered political and financial support, neither was very active in doing so, and had nothing to do with campaign planning.[23]

Unquestionably the factionalism displayed at the national political level in Paul Butler's efforts to remain national chairman, and those of his opponents to replace him, took on some of the characteristics of Indiana factionalism, which at times was inexplicable; yet the two different political environments produced different patterns. If Butler had significant problems with his tenure before the 1956 convention, they were not well publicized. Supporters of Senator Estes Kefauver's presidential candidacy accused Butler of using national headquarters to further Adlai Stevenson's candidacy, but Butler angrily made his denial.[24] After his election as chairman, Butler had told reporters that Stevenson would have to fight for the 1956 nomination, and on the eve of the convention Cabell Phillips had indicated that Butler might be impatient with Stevenson's moderation on issues.[25] Butler's real problem was with some holdover members of the National Committee staff, and the group Stevenson had assembled for his campaign (many of the same individuals involved in the 1952 election). These advisors, not wanting a repeat of the divided organization Stevenson had in 1952, believed the national chairman should be the campaign manager, but

157

they did not want Butler. Their choice was Stevenson's campaign manager, Pennsylvania Secretary of State James Finnegan, who had been one of Butler's New Orleans challengers.[26]

Butler must have had some intimation of these feelings on the part of Stevenson's friends, because before the convention he advised Neil Staebler that ACPO should terminate at the conclusion of the convention when Butler would submit his resignation "in view of the uncertainty of my own tenure"; Butler had also told the Indiana Democratic State Committee that he would submit his resignation at the close of the convention, but such submissions were standard procedure.[27] Still, Butler was widely perceived as Stevenson's chairman.

During the convention nomination proceedings Butler had agreed with Lyndon Johnson and Sam Rayburn that Stevenson was mistaken in leaving selection of a vice-presidential candidate in the hands of the delegates, but there were no open disputes between Butler and Stevenson. Then, when the National Committee held its post-nomination session, Stevenson informed Butler that he would be replaced by James Finnegan. Two members of the National Committee, Paul Ziffren and Camille Gravel, had already informed Butler, as soon as they had heard the rumor. What happened next was not planned by Paul Butler; he was unprepared for the unfolding events.

A resolution was offered, praising Butler's management and operation of the convention, by Leo Graybill of Montana.[28] Butler then asked the parliamentarian, Representative Clarence Cannon, to take the chair, and heard himself highly praised by one national committeeman after another. Butler responded, "I am sure, however, that you do not realize that you are writing my political epitaph. In a moment, I will submit my resignation as Chairman of the Democratic National Committee, and I urge you to accept it."[29] Butler supposedly cried at this point. Following an interlude of other business, Camille Gravel offered a motion of instruction to Butler that he not offer any resignation at that time. Only George Rock of Colorado voted in the negative. After hearing from the vice-presidential nominee, Butler left the meeting to help escort Adlai Stevenson to the hall. Upon returning, Butler tendered his resignation and introduced Stevenson, who concluded his remarks by saying he intended to name James Finnegan campaign director, but asked for Butler's reelection. Butler was then unanimously reelected by acclamation.

What had brought this surprise conclusion about, apart from an obviously strong support of Butler by National Committee members, which leaves some doubt if Stevenson could have prevented Butler's re-election? After all, Stevenson had set a precedent by having the convention delegates select the vice-presidential nominee. He had also

158

wavered between doing what his staff wanted and feeling sorry for Butler. His behavior confirmed the impressions of those who believed Stevenson lacked decisiveness.[30]

As soon as members of the National Committee had begun rising to praise Butler, Harold Levanthal, National Committee counsel, left the meeting to inform Stevenson of what was happening. Sam Rayburn pleaded with Stevenson, as did others, to retain Butler, and when Butler went to escort Stevenson to the National Committee session he heard of an arrangement which would leave him as chairman, but with real direction of the campaign with Finnegan.[31]

Stevenson's decision to keep Butler as chairman upset Stevenson's advisors. In time, after DAC and Butler's outspokenness on many issues, they came to appreciate Butler as a national chairman, although some still believed Finnegan would have been more effective in the 1956 campaign.[32] Butler put on a good public face, telling a television audience he would really handle nine-tenths of the campaign. Hoping that Butler would work harmoniously, Stevenson wrote Mrs. Roosevelt that he had not really wanted Butler replaced, but Finnegan would have full control over the campaign. After the election Butler said he "had nothing to do with the itinerary of Governor Stevenson. I was not consulted at any time and on a couple of occasions when my advice was volunteered it was ignored."[33]

All campaign operations were centered in Washington, but a trifurcated structure existed, consisting of the Stevenson-Kefauver Committee, Volunteers for Stevenson, and the National Committee. Butler still managed the collecting and spending of most campaign funds, network time allocation, and publicity. He had seen that much of the campaign material was prepared before the convention.[34]

Some of Butler's critics assumed his retention as chairman had been a temporary arrangement for the campaign.[35] However, Butler soon announced that he would remain to help pay off a million dollar campaign deficit, institute economy in headquarters operation, and promote a new-look *Democratic Digest*. Stevenson was talking with individuals who wanted Butler replaced, but was concerned about finding Butler another position.[36]

As attention became focused on the DAC, concern about replacing Butler subsided, and in February, 1957, the National Committee praised Butler's leadership.[37] But later in the year Butler believed that Democratic congressional leaders, Jacob Arvey, Carmine De Sapio, David Lawrence, Frank McKinney, and others, some of whom had met with Harry Truman, wanted former Kentucky Senator Earle Clements, a Lyndon Johnson ally, for chairman. Butler charged that a group of saboteurs, a clique, was trying to capture the party organization for their own selfish aims, power, and control (typical Butler language in organizational disputes), and would weaken the chairman's office to do so.[38] In 1958 there were again rumors of Butler's resignation or replacement, which required only a simple majority vote of the National Committee. Yet in spite of enmity aroused by Butler's civil rights speeches, success in the congressional elections both enhanced Butler's reputation as a political leader and strengthened the northern and western wings of the party, which were somewhat militant on civil rights. Besides, even those who wanted Butler ousted could not agree on a replacement. The year ended with another strong endorsement from the National Committee.[39]

If Butler's tenure situation had improved in 1958, it was further strengthened in February, 1959, when the National Committee, over the objection of the South and the Arvey-De Sapio-Lawrence group, gave Butler and California national committeeman Paul Ziffren a victory in their quest to have the 1960 national convention meet in Los Angeles. It appeared that Butler's hold on his office would probably be secure until the convention met, and, while having few illusions he would last beyond the convention, Butler planned to stay in office until then, hoping to see it adopt a liberal platform and nominate a liberal candidate.[40] In April both Indiana and national political leaders sponsored a testimonial dinner for Butler in South Bend. Charles Murphy came from Washington to read Harry Truman's praises, and Indiana factional foes, such as Senator R. Vance Hartke, were present. Senator A.S. Monroney of Oklahoma, a perpetual Stevenson supporter, was the main speaker.[41]

But after Butler got into his dispute with congressional leaders in July, 1959, talk of his ouster was heard again. Congressional leaders, Truman, Arvey, Lawrence, and others were said to be critical of Butler's expenses as well as his public remarks. They charged that he cost Democrats $50,000 a year, including $400 monthly for his apartment (this was not true—Butler paid for his living quarters out of his salary) and frequent trips to South Bend. They believed Butler could be put out by the stopping of contributions to the hard-pressed National Committee, or perhaps Butler could be bought out with a good job out of politics (a recurring theme, to which Butler sometimes seemed receptive). Sam Rayburn told correspondents there were probably not enough votes on the National Committee to vote Butler out. After Rayburn, Johnson, and Butler had agreed to their "armistice," the congressional leaders publicly stated they wanted Butler to remain as chairman.[42]

When the National Committee met in September, Governor Lawrence circulated copies of the statements concerning segregation which Butler had signed in 1954; Butler responded by linking Lawrence with segregationists. Southerners were actually suspicious of Lawrence because they feared that Harry Truman was his choice for chairman. Lawrence reported there were not enough votes to replace Butler, and wondered who would want the job anyway.[43]

Butler was identified with two other factional disputes at this time. A new apportionment formula for the 1960 convention was adopted by the National Committee over the protests of Jacob Arvey. At the Midwest Democratic Conference, a rebel group, representing 1958 election gains, and encouraged by Butler, chose Frank Theis, national committeeman from Kansas, over the incumbent, Jake More of Iowa, for chairman. By announcing that delegate seating and housing at the 1960 convention would be based on state quota payment promptness, Butler, in his role as convention manager, made more enemies, along with some friends. Butler answered his critics with the argument that this policy was rewarding, rather than punitive.[44]

At the close of 1959 Butler announced that he would definitely resign at the conclusion of the convention, but not a minute before, in keeping with a pledge to National Committee members, that, like Stephen Mitchell, he would announce his planned resignation sufficiently in advance for them to plan accordingly. About this time Butler opened a law office in South Bend. Butler's announced resignation (and the unlikelihood he would be the choice of a presidential nominee anyway) transformed demands for his replacement into criticism of his statements concerning the presidential nomination.[45]

The National Committee met January 22, 1960, and upheld Butler on seating and housing arrangements for the convention. It also defeated a rules change proposal of Jacob Arvey providing that voting strength on the National Committee should be proportionate to convention voting.[46]

Butler continued to publicize his opinion that a liberal and progressive Democratic presidential candidate would best represent the national party and win election. A year earlier he had said Adlai Stevenson was not really a 1960 contender, and would not enter the primaries because he was a two-time loser, just as Butler had seemingly ruled out Lyndon Johnson's candidacy by remarking that because of the civil rights issue a Southern or Southwestern candidate was unlikely. In 1959 Butler had agreed with Republican Chairman Thruston Morton that being Catholic would hurt a presidential candidate (but he also thought voter attitudes on this matter had changed since 1928), a statement interpreted by some observers as ruling out Senator John Kennedy's candidacy. But when early in 1960 a Mister "X" told some Washington reporters that Kennedy would be an early, if not a first-ballot convention winner, many believed Mister "X" was Butler. What was widely perceived as Butler's lack of neutrality was criticized by

161

Truman, Rayburn, Senator Eugene McCarthy, and Senator Hubert Humphrey, the latter busily engaged in Wisconsin and West Virginia primary election campaigns. Humphrey demanded Butler's resignation, and Truman had already warned that Butler talked too much and aided Republicans. Later Truman charged that Butler was splitting the Democratic Party.[47]

Apart from Butler's admiration for Kennedy as a person and as a political figure, he became increasingly concerned with the "religious issue" developing in relation to Kennedy's candidacy. This concern probably weakened Butler's attempt to maintain neutrality among candidates, and strengthened the argument of those who said Butler favored a Catholic candidate. While Butler received mail on Kennedy and the religious issue, he may not, at this point, have had any idea of the real undercurrents. His correspondence showed that most of those saying they could not vote for a Catholic candidate were residents of the South, Texas, and Oklahoma, and many letters were copied from a suggested form on Church of God stationery, written by church officials. Original efforts were often illiterate. Letters to Sam Rayburn, opposing Butler in his dispute with the congressional leadership, revealed these undercurrents. Rayburn's correspondents warned him that many Democrats would not vote for Kennedy. "His religion is a stumbling block." Some saw Butler's publicity devices as part of a campaign to elect a Catholic president. The closest Rayburn came to acknowledging such comments was to reply that there were many good potential candidates and advised a wait-and-see policy. Interestingly enough, there still lingers in South Bend, Indiana, among Democrats, the tale that Reverend John Cavanaugh, Notre Dame's president, Joseph Kennedy, a member of Notre Dame's Lay Board of Trustees, and Butler met and decided to make Kennedy president. On June 22, 1960, Butler told the National Press Club that Kennedy was certain to win the Democratic presidential nomination, but if circumstances denied Kennedy the prize, Catholic voters would punish the Democratic Party.[48]

The more Butler pronounced an early ballot victory for Kennedy at Los Angeles, the more he irritated supporters of other candidates. Adlai Stevenson's followers, annoyed with his indecisiveness about the nomination, could not convince Butler that Stevenson should be treated as a serious candidate in the allocation of convention facilities. Harry Truman's displeasure with the course of events was publicly most noticed. In 1959 Truman had suggested to Sam Rayburn that a few party leaders should lay out the convention and pick the officers, with Rayburn as permanent chairman, but Butler's convention planning did not take Truman's wishes into account, and Truman was ready to settle on Congressman Hale Boggs as chairman.[49]

On the eve of the convention Truman privately accused Butler and the National Committee of unethical conduct in contributing to the Kennedy "bandwagon psychology," but still planned to attend the convention. This resolve soon changed, in spite of Sam Rayburn's plea, when Truman became convinced the convention was "packed." Truman held a press conference on July 2, after he had resigned as a convention delegate, explaining that the convention was becoming a "prearranged affair." Truman supported Senator Stuart Symington of Missouri, but also commended Lyndon Johnson, Governor Chester Bowles of Connecticut, and Governor Robert Meyner of New Jersey, along with several other Democrats, but he wondered if Kennedy was "quite ready for the country, or that the country is ready for you." A final round of pre-convention bickering found Butler denying any convention rigging, Lyndon Johnson saying Butler was Kennedy's advocate, Stevenson's campaign director criticizing Butler, and Truman feeling that Butler's slighting of him had been a "blow to the Presidency."[50]

Meanwhile, through all the pre-convention candidate competition, Butler, with wide powers granted by the National Committee, had more quietly been arranging his own "new look" convention. More so than in 1956, the 1960 convention would have a Butler design, oriented toward a television age, for which Butler received much praise.[51] Early platform preparation had followed ACPO recommendations for pre-platform hearings and issue conferences to bring the party closer to the voters, and to mobilize and integrate party ideas for a whole party view, which might bring about better platform implementation. ACPO had also made recommendations on the nature and timing of the convention. Both ACPO and Butler had urged more participation by women in the convention.[52]

Prior to the opening of the convention, Butler addressed the old National Committee, over half of whose membership had changed already. He expressed his appreciation for the members' help and cooperation. "There are just very, very few members of the Committee with whom I have had any personal antagonism." Even those with whom he had disagreed had been "most ladylike and most gentlemanly" to him. Butler had overlooked pettiness, and hoped the new chairman would be better treated.[53] On the opening day of the convention, July 11, shortly after calling his second and last national convention to order, Butler expanded on this theme in addressing the delegates on behalf of the National Committee.[54] In giving an account of his stewardship, he set forth his understanding of the execution of "the responsibilities and duties of the National Chairmanship." Democrats believed in ideas and in disagreement. A national chairman was not to be denied the privilege and responsibility of any Democrat to follow the

163

dictates of conscience. While he had been told the sole duty of a national chairman was to maintain party unity:

> Unity is a pretty word, and I am all for unity, but what does it mean in this case? Does it mean unity without regard to conviction, without regard to the ideas which already have been the lifeblood of the Democratic Party?
>
> I submit that unity on these terms is only a synonym for sterility and death. There is unity in an ice cube, but not heat. There is unity in the tomb, but no controversy. A unity which rules out principle is a unity which we Democrats cannot afford if our party is to live and if our Nation is to prosper.
>
> The perilous times in which we exist do not allow us the luxury of this kind of unity. The Republican Party has had unity imposed upon it. The results are all too painfully apparent in the wreck of our Nation's foreign policy.

Believing that unity had to be based on principles, rather than men, Butler had tried to make the National Committee "a clearing house for the ideas which we as a responsible people must champion." He emphasized what he believed to be the ultimate issue—the survival of America morally, spiritually, and militarily, considering the rate of decline of American prestige in the world, while the President had engaged in "eight years of golfing and goofing." In reference to the U-2 incident, Butler asked, "who was caught in a demoralizing lie about espionage activities—a Soviet premier, or an American President . . . Would Mr. Krushchev have dared to laugh at Franklin Delano Roosevelt? Would Mr. Chou En-Lai have dared to laugh at Theodore Roosevelt?"

Butler also insisted that if the National Committee had taken a stand on issues, it had not done so on candidates, nor rigged the convention. While admitting personal preferences, Butler said he had "tried to maintain a scrupulous neutrality among the candidates."

Following the nomination of the Kennedy-Johnson ticket, Butler presided over his last National Committee meeting, presenting his final report. David Lawrence walked out of the meeting, but Butler said he had affection and respect for everyone else, regardless of differences of principle and policy, and in spite of the holding back on some state financial quotas. Committee members presented checks and cash earmarked for a vacation for Mr. and Mrs. Butler, then voted Butler a resolution of appreciation, mentioning particularly the DAC, the ACPO, and Butler's leadership in policy, as expressed in the platform. During an interlude, with Kennedy and Johnson present, Butler praised

164

the ticket and called the platform "the greatest political document and statement of political principles and policies that any national political party has ever written in our entire history." Butler continued, "I know at times that I have aroused controversy and dispute and unhappiness in trying to arouse the consciousness of all the members of our Democratic Party to the fact that a Platform is something more than just a statement of policies as a lure for votes." In introducing Lyndon Johnson, he noted their well-publicized differences, and used the occasion to proclaim that Johnson's acceptance of the vice-presidential nomination signaled his acceptance of the platform. Later in these desultory proceedings, following the election of Butler's successor, Butler again stressed the importance of the DAC to the platform. Butler said he had deliberately "chosen the rough road" as chairman, but that his successor would be less controversial.[55]

If Butler felt he had been neutral as to candidates, and others thought he had been partial to Kennedy, the Kennedys thought he had been too neutral to help them enough. There is no evidence that Kennedy ever seriously considered retaining Butler as chairman. Jesse Unruh, Speaker of the California House of Representatives, supposedly secured a pledge from Kennedy, early in 1960, that Butler would be replaced as chairman. Kennedy's top choices to replace Butler (for the long run) were probably two state chairmen, John Bailey of Connecticut and Neil Staebler of Michigan. Staebler was chairman of ACPO and a faithful Butler ally. He was not Catholic, and Kennedy had decided he wanted a non-Catholic chairman, at least during the campaign. The South Bend *Tribune* speculated that Staebler, Butler's friend, was interested in party organization and issue discussion; he would be Kennedy's kind of chairman. The *Tribune* was not aware that Kennedy had already disappointed Michigan Democrats by his position on the DAC and his doubts about maintaining the ACPO. John Bailey would become Kennedy's ultimate choice. For the interim campaign period he chose Senator Henry Jackson of Washington, a Protestant.[56]

Paul Butler left the chairmanship after several battles with Democrats as well as Republicans; leaders and some rank-and-file party members showed their enmity. He had received letters addressed "Chairman Nikita Butler," and had been told, "What a stinkin' rat *you* turned out to be!" Grass roots Democrats and leaders also praised him for maintaining a favorable party image, for setting up a 1960 victory, for loyalty, for courage, for efficiency, for hard work, for dignity, and for giving precinct Democrats confidence. He received poems, retirement cards, and letters saying he had given new respectability to the word "politician." In referring to Butler's letter in the *Democratic Digest*, one correspondent wrote, "I will miss your letter, dear friend."[57]

NOTES

1. Box 124, Butler Papers, contains material Butler collected on his possible resignation and his ability to stay in office.
2. While some believed Butler needed to be reelected national committeeman to remain national chairman, others in Indiana wanted him to remain as national committeeman to keep the position out of McKinney-McHale hands, and not set off any intra-party struggle which would hurt chances for state victory in 1956 (John Carvey to Butler, February 2, 1956; and Marshall Kizer to Butler, December 8, 1954; Butler Papers, Box 17).
3. See Butler Papers, Boxes 2, 75, 80, 83, 105, 106, 169, and 170.
4. South Bend *Tribune*, May 7,1958.
5. Bartholomew, *The Indiana Third Congressional District*, p. 181; Butler Papers, Box 7.
6. South Bend *Tribune*, May 5, 1954; the Elksburg (Indiana) *Truth*, October 1, 1958; Butler to Rayburn, November 12, 1958, Rayburn Papers; *Stevenson Papers*, VII, 316.
7. Interview with Anne Butler, June 10, 1975.
8. South Bend *Tribune*, April 24, 1954; Louisville *Times*, November 16, 1955; Russell E. Wise to Butler, November 29, 1955, Butler Papers, Box 7; Metro Holovachka to Butler, November 10, 1955, and January 3, 1956, Box 54.
9. Democratic National Committee Release, June 28, 1957, Butler Papers, Box 142.
10. James Robb to Butler, December 14, 1957, Butler Papers, Box 108; New York *Times*, March 2, 1958; *Minute Book*, Indiana Democratic State Central Committee, January 15, 1958; Butler to McKinney, April 29, 1958, Butler Papers, Box 17; Butler to Kizer, April 29, 1958, Box 17.
11. Indianapolis *News*, June 25, 26, and 27, 1956; and August 22, 24, 25, 26, and 27, 1956.
12. Ibid., June 23, 24, 25, 1958.
13. Butler to Walsh, October 6, 1959, Butler Papers, Box 95, and November 12, 1959, Box 7; Louisville *Courier-Journal*, June 9 and 26, 1960; Matthew E. Welsh, *View From the State House: Recollections and Reflections, 1961-1965* (Indianapolis: Indiana Historical Bureau, 1981), 32-34, describes the convention.
14. Louisville *Courier-Journal*, February 24 and September 2, 1957; Indianapolis *News*, August 30, 1957, and May 15, 1958; *Minute Book*, Indiana Democratic State Central Committee, May 17, 1958.

15. Lafayette *Journal and Courier*, May 16, 1960; Louisville *Courier-Journal*, August 25, 1960; Welsh, *View From the State House*, pp. 35-37.
16. Louisville *Courier-Journal*, December 14, 1957.
17. Paul Butler to the author, July 5, 1961.
18. Ibid.
19. Louisville *Courier-Journal*, May 18, 1960.
20. Ibid., February 5, 1960.
21. Ibid., May 24, 1961.
22. Ibid., May 18, 1960; Indianapolis *News*, November 2, 1960; interview with receptionist, *Star*, June, 1961.
23. Welsh, *View From the State House*, p. 25.
24. New York *Times*, April 21, 1956. See Butler's views regarding neutrality of DNC officers and staff in relation to presidential candidates, *Official Report of the Proceedings of the Democratic National Convention, 1956*, p. 752.
25. *New York Times Magazine*, July 1, 1956.
26. See Adlai E. Stevenson to Butler, August 4, 1955, *Stevenson Papers*, IV, 540, where Stevenson wishes Butler could get along better with Clayton Fritchey; the letter also shows differences in campaign planning. Member of Stevenson's staff to the author, February 7, 1975; Wilson W. Wyatt to the author, March 15, 1978. Arthur Schlesinger, Jr., described Butler in most unflattering terms (Martin, *Adlai Stevenson and the World*, p. 353). Butler believed that Stevenson had been taken in by the arguments of David Lawrence, Jacob Arvey, Matthew McCloskey, and others, according to Anne Butler.
27. Butler to Staebler, August 10, 1956, Butler Papers, Box 9; *Minute Book*, Indiana Democratic State Central Committee, February 10, 1956.
28. See Box 22, Butler Papers, for letters from ordinary people on both Butler's reelection and his convention management.
29. *Official Report of the Proceedings of the Democratic National Convention, 1956*, p. 856.
30. As late as August 1, Stevenson had indicated that, in drawing up a campaign organizational chart, Butler should be shown as campaign manager (as national chairman) and James Finnegan as Butler's deputy, *Stevenson Papers*, VI, 175.
31. *Official Report of the Proceedings of the Democratic National Convention, 1956*, pp. 838-79, gives the formal account. See also Martin, *Adlai Stevenson and the World*, pp. 352-53 and the New York *Times*, August 19, 1956. The author is indebted to Mrs. Evelyn Chavoor for information on this subject. According to Anne Butler, Sam Rayburn told Stevenson, in regard to Butler's removal, "By God, I won't stand for it."
32. Wilson W. Wyatt to the author, March 15, 1978, and a Stevenson advisor to the author, February 7, 1975.

33. New York *Times*, August 30, 1956; *Stevenson Papers*, VI, 191; Butler to Mrs. Lennard Thomas, November 21, 1956, Butler Papers, Box 19.
34. Bone, *Party Committees*, pp. 59-60. See Cotter and Hennessy, *Politics Without Power*, pp. 126-127, for comparison with Republican organization.
35. See material in Box 11, Butler Papers.
36. New York *Times*, November 27, 1956; Stevenson to James Finnegan, January 11, 1957, *Stevenson Papers*, VII, 409.
37. *Official Report of the 1960 Democratic National Convention and Committee*, pp. 405-11.
38. Butler to Stephen Mitchell, July 25, 1957, Butler Papers, Box 17; New York *Times*, July 12, 1957; Butler's Los Angeles speech, Butler Papers, Box 142.
39. Louisville *Courier-Journal*, December 7, 1958; New York *Times*, October 23, 1958; *Official Report of the 1960 Democratic National Convention and Committee*, pp. 512, 551.
40. New York *Times*, February 28, 1959; Robert Riggs in Louisville *Courier-Journal*, March 8 and July 19, 1959.
41. *Democratic Digest*, June, 1959, p. 11.
42. Philadelphia *Daily News*, July 22, 1959; Rayburn to Byron Skelton, July 17, 1959, Rayburn Papers; New York *Times*, July 25, 1959.
43. Louisville *Courier-Journal*, September 17, 1959; Anderson (South Carolina) *Independent*, September 17, 1959; New York *Times*, September 20, 1959.
44. *Official Report of the 1960 Democratic National Convention and Committee*, pp. 674-95; New York *Times*, September 14 and 20, and November 8 and 20, 1959.
45. New York *Times*, December 31, 1959. Butler to Charles W. McKay, July 25, 1957, Butler Papers, Box 16; South Bend *Tribune*, March 20, 1960.
46. *Official Report of the 1960 Democratic National Convention and Committee*, pp. 724-25, 745-53. From the chart, opposite p. 1, in the *Report*; the *Democratic Digest*, May, 1960, p. 27; and the status reports on financial quotas; Butler Papers, Box 16; an idea of the relationship between convention seating and quota attainments can be obtained. For instance, Maryland and South Dakota, high on the quota accomplishment list, had spots in front of the convention platform; Indiana, with moderate contributions, was off the center of the middle of delegate seats; and Mississippi and Kentucky, low in contributions, were in the rear of the hall.
47. Transcript of Face the Nation, CBS News, January 3, 1960, Butler Papers, Box 12; Washington *Post*, January 25, 1959; Chicago *Sun-Times*, July 14, 1959; New York *Times*, March 17 and 22, 1960; New York *Post*, March 23, 1960; Washington

Daily News, January 25 and March 16, 1960; New York *Herald-Tribune*, April 14, 1960.

48. See Butler Papers, Boxes 92 and 94 on the religious issue; Mrs. William Dyer Moore to Sam Rayburn, July 7, 1959, Rayburn Papers; Mrs. Nona E. Hart to Rayburn, July 10, 1959, Rayburn Papers; interview with party spokesman, September, 1974; New York *Herald-Tribune*, June 23, 1960.

49. Brown, *Conscience in Politics*, p. 288; Truman to Rayburn, July 8, 1959, Rayburn Papers; New York *Times*, January 23, 1960.

50. Truman to Agnes E. Meyer, June 25, 1960, Ferrell, *Off the Record*, pp. 386-87; telegram, Rayburn to Truman, June 29, 1960, Rayburn Papers; Truman to Rayburn, June 30, 1960, Rayburn Papers, statement of Harry S. Truman at press conference, July 2, 1960, Rayburn Papers; Los Angeles *Examiner*, July 4, 1960; Los Angeles *Herald and Express*, July 5, 1960; and Chicago *Sun-Times*, July 8, 1960.

51. *Official Report of the 1960 Democratic National Convention and Committee*, pp. 653-54; scrapbook, Box 187, Butler Papers, and messages and engagements, Box 36; Newark *News*, April 9, 1959.

52. ACPO Recommendations 6 and 10, 1955-56; 13, 1957; 16, 17, and 18, 1957-59; and 10 and 44, 1959; Willis collection. See, also, *Democratic Digest*, June, 1960, p. 20.

53. *Official Report of the 1960 Democratic National Convention and Committee*, pp. 777-78.

54. Ibid., pp. 13-19.

55. Ibid., pp. 779-813.

56. Interview with Neil Staebler, February 22, 1981; Michael J. Kirwan, *How to Succeed in Politics* (New York: Macfadden-Bartell Corp; 1964), p. 62; Louchheim, *By the Political Sea*, pp. 140-41; South Bend *Tribune*, July 14, 1960; Cotter and Hennessy, *Politics Without Power*, p. 87, says Jackson's choice could be explained because he was an old friend and had been suggested as a vice-presidential candidate for Western balance.

57. Both nasty letters from Chicago, January 18, 1958, Butler Papers, Box 3, and June 28, 1960, Box 97; Butler kept bad, as well as good correspondence. See also, letters in Box 6; William Benton to Butler, October 2, 1957, Box 2; Robert Riggs to Butler, July 21, 1960, and Chester Bowles to Butler, September 26, 1960, Box 6.

169

Chapter Nine

POST-CHAIRMAN PERIOD

Paul Butler left Los Angeles with "no assigned part to play in the work of the Democratic Party in this campaign," and he had resolved to avoid the turmoil of Indiana politics. However, he indicated that he would be available, like an old fire horse, and would not very soon be taking the vacation National Committee members had provided for.[1] After the campaign ended, Butler was thanked for speaking, but the record is not extant, save for a joint appearance with Congressman Walter Judd, keynoter of the 1960 Republican convention, before the Chicago convention of the National Stationery and Office Equipment Association. Both speakers agreed that "encroaching communism is the issue of the coming decade," but there agreement stopped. Judd accused Democrats of promising something for nothing, while Butler responded that the United States was militarily and economically weak, and asked the delegates how any small businessman could vote for a Republican Party which catered to big business.[2]

In a more private capacity, Butler tried to deal with what he saw as religious bigotry in the campaign. A thick folder in Butler's Papers[3] contains letters opposing a Catholic nominee and Butler's general response that his correspondents had a right to their views, but that he could not agree with them. Any American had both a right to his religion and a right to hold public office. He received one letter, from Coal Hill, Arkansas, which, while illiterate, still made its point: "canady the man you all apontid as our next present he want make the go for he is a catchic and we americans dont want a catchic as our present we like our freedom and if he is ruler he will do a way with our free to worship and we will have to Join the catchic church i have herd lots of our loil democrats say they would go to nichen rather candady a catlic . . . ."[4] Butler answered with a three-paged letter, which served as a model for response to similar messages. Butler responded to "my fellow American," because he was disturbed, in view of the natural rights of all human beings and the protection of those rights by the American government. Senator Kennedy was anxious to protect every

171

American's freedom to worship, and no one would be forced to join the Catholic Church. Butler asked if, as a Catholic, it would be fair to Baptists and Presbyterians if he were to vote only for Catholics; then he cited the Golden Rule. "Our decisions in such matters as electing a President of our great nation must be made in the mind, not in the heart," Butler admonished.[5]

Paul Butler felt much pride and satisfaction in Kennedy's victory, and much "of which to be proud and about which to be enthusiastic" in the early days of the new administration.[6] In 1959, Butler had told columnist Robert L. Riggs, "I want nothing from the party . . . I want no Cabinet post, no federal judgeship. There's not a thing I want when my term is over."[7] Still, would there be a place for Butler in the new administration? Mrs. Butler remembered that Kennedy asked Butler to be a Cabinet member, but that Butler refused because he required more income than such a position would provide, and therefore needed to return to law practice. In February, 1961, Butler visited with Kennedy in the president's office, and in August Butler was appointed to the St. Lawrence Seaway Development Commission. Remuneration would be $50 a day when the commission met. In September Butler was elected chairman of the commission.[8]

Some of Butler's friends believed that Kennedy treated Butler badly in terms of possible employment, that not only was Butler not given any meaningful appointment but that the Kennedys went out of their way to slight him; he had been too neutral for them in the pre-convention period. However little Butler had to offer, individuals contacted him for possible patronage positions in the Kennedy Administration.[9]

There was a suggestion from James Reston that Butler write a book on his Washington career, but he did not want to write, hurting others by what he might say, just to make money.[10] There were also requests for speeches, and early in February, 1961, Butler addressed the Maryland House of Delegates to testify for civil rights legislation pending there.[11] Butler had always seemed to enjoy addressing college groups during his chairmanship, and an address he gave at Antioch College in May, 1961, was an excellent summation of a philosophy of politics which had pretty well guided his own political career.[12]

To encourage participation in newly-formed political clubs on the Antioch campus, Butler urged "particularly participation in the affairs and activities of political parties," not solely for personal advantages and gains, but for fulfillment of the obligation "imposed by the condition of democratic citizenship and the nature of man as a creature of God." College students had a special obligation to participate and bring their talents to the solutions of social problems, and as all citizens, "to bring the social order into harmony with the moral order."

172

As democracy made increasing demands on the electorate and public officials, political leaders of vision, courage, articulation, and understanding would have to be cultivated if the quality of political life were to improve.

Butler told his audience that a realistic approach to the teaching of politics would highly value the role of partisanship, the two-party system, and party responsibility in democratic government. Probably apprised by Paul Willis of conditions at Indiana University, Butler condemned those academic policies, or "artificial barriers," which prevented or discouraged students and faculty from participation in political activities, and which prohibited political activity and speeches on campuses. Politics in an academic setting was a "unifying discipline . . . never dull or static," one of few fields which offered "possibilities for the satisfaction of the individual's creative urge" and "opportunities for the utilization of power for the creation of good," in creating decent living standards, educational opportunities, slum clearance, adequate medical care, and world peace.

In the real political world, where there were many "affable, dedicated individuals concerned with something more than just themselves," one could experience sheer pleasure from varied associations, which often led to cherished friendships, and made a person more human and sympathetic to others. Academic theory could be wedded to practical reality through the opportunity provided by active collegiate political participation. In retrospect, the Antioch speech seems a fitting farewell address for Paul Butler, who had lived by such principles and seen such advantages as a political practitioner for thirty-five years.

Butler had decided that the practice of law, rather than further political activity or employment, would give him, now fifty-five and the father of three sons in college, sufficient income and some financial stability. When Butler left his old law firm in 1956, his friend, Louis Chapleau, offered him at least a South Bend address, so Butler kept an office with Farabaugh, Chapleau, and Roper a short time, even though not a member of the firm nor active in practice. In 1959, when announcing that he would not serve as national chairman beyond the 1960 convention, Butler opened a law office in South Bend in partnership with his son-in-law, J. Patrick O'Malley. Later Butler announced that the practice would leave O'Malley in South Bend, while Butler would have an office in Washington. Butler never really returned to South Bend, and his wife planned to join him in residence in Washington in 1962.[13]

In March, 1961, Butler was sworn to practice before the United States Supreme Court, and had settled in at his office, 1001 Connecticut Avenue. He and Alfred L. Scanlan, a partner in a firm with Shea and Gardner, appeared with Vermont attorneys before the Supreme Court to argue for a Vermont statute which provided governmental payment of tuition to secondary schools of parents' selection, even if sectarian. The opinion of the Vermont Court of Chancery had tested the facts of the situation against the commands of *People ex rel. Everson v. The Board of Education* , 330 U.S. 1 (1947), and subsequent rulings, concluding that the paying of tuition from public tax monies to sectarian schools could not be justified by the public welfare benefits theory; therefore the practice breached the "wall between Church and State." When the U.S. Supreme Court; denied certiorari, the New York *Herald-Tribune* noted that Butler disagreed with President Kennedy's belief that such laws as that enacted by Vermont were unconstitutional.[14]

Two months before the Supreme Court's action, while addressing a Holy Name Society dinner at St. Jane de Chantal parish, Bethesda, Maryland, Butler had advised that private school aid would not violate the Constitution. Stating the problem for American Catholics—providing their children a minimum Catholic education, which would enable them to swim in the current of the stream of life without losing sight of fundamental Catholic principles—Butler noted concern about the financial ability to maintain parochial schools, and fear that Catholics would have to choose between use of public schools or curtailment of Catholic educational facilities. He noted that the Administrative Board of the National Catholic Welfare Council was opposed to Kennedy's school legislation, which omitted aid to religious schools. Butler's concluding advice was for prudence as Catholics pressed their case for governmental assistance. Some of this argument appeared after Butler's death in an article authored by Butler and Alfred L. Scanlan.[15]

In the next fifteen years, Scanlan would share with Edward Bennett Williams the most active role among members of the Catholic bar of Washington who argued church-state cases.[16] Undoubtedly Butler would have shared that distinction. Years earlier he had vocally opposed the doctrine that religious programs in public schools were unconstitutional. It is not likely that he would have agreed with the Court's rulings concerning prayer and Bible reading in public schools either, nor for that matter with the abortion decision. His positions on several issues would have placed Butler in conflict with many liberals of the 1960s and 1970s. The social issues and his generational Cold War foreign policy views might well have left him less a partisan Democrat.

In another major phase of his legal activity, Butler represented E.I. duPont de Nemours and Company in a hearing before the Food and Drug Administration, where the issue was implementation of the content-labeling law enacted by Congress in 1960.[17] But the most spectacular aspect of Butler's law practice was an arrangement whereby he would have been retained as counsel to the Shah of Iran in the United States for $100,000 annually. Three days before his death Butler talked with the Shah's representative about a plan for travel to Iran and a visit by the Shah, accompanied by Butler, to the United States in 1962.[18]

On December 5, 1961, Paul Butler entered George Washington University Hospital because of "complications arising from a number of medical problems," later specified as a respiratory infection with complications and diabetes. Diabetes had not been diagnosed until the 1950s, although Butler was a non-alcoholic drinking and non-smoking politician before the diagnosis. The chairmanship had become a strain, and he had been ill in 1956 and before the 1960 convention. Butler had apparently been progressing well, and his condition had not been considered serious, when he died of a heart attack the morning of December 30.[19]

Upon learning of Butler's death, President Kennedy issued a statement: "I am most grieved to learn of the untimely death of my friend, Paul Butler. He was a courageous leader of the Democratic Party during some of the Party's most difficult hours. His wise counsel will be sorely missed."[20]

Butler's funeral service was held in Sacred Heart Church on the Notre Dame campus, and he was buried in nearby Cedar Grove Cemetery. Among his mourners was former Governor Henry F. Schricker, with whom Butler had risen in politics from 1948 through 1952. Butler's friend, Reverend John J. Cavanaugh, C.S.C., former president of Notre Dame, conducted the services, noting that Christian charity had been the mainspring of Butler's life—a life proving that a close relationship between religion and politics could exist, and that a practical politician could be a religious man.[21]

Probation of Paul Butler's will,[22] dated February 14, 1941, which left his estate to his wife on the assumption she would support and educate his children, showed that after several years in party service Butler had only begun by the time of his death to re-establish a legal practice and gain financial security for his family. His insurance benefits were small, because he experienced difficulty in obtaining coverage. When the estate was finally settled, assets exceeded debts by only $479.18. The inventory revealed that the assets of about $26,000, consisted mainly of close to $15,000 in stock shares and an interest in his law partnership worth $7,500. Debts included about $17,000 in notes due two South Bend banks. According to Mrs. Butler, one of these notes, for $12,081.24, represented money Butler had borrowed to pay salaries of National Committee employees when party funds had been low, and Butler had never received reimbursement. Personal household furnishings had to be sold to satisfy immediate debts. The practice of politics which did not put self above party had not been financially rewarding, whatever other satisfactions it had given the practitioner.

NOTES

1. See Box 34, Butler Papers, for Butler's campaign role; Butler to W. L. Brasher, August 26, 1960, Box 204; Paul Butler to the author, July 5, 1961.
2. John Moss to Butler, December 5, 1960, Butler Papers, Box 30; Chicago *Tribune*, September 27, 1960.
3. Boxes 57 and 58, Butler Papers, contain articles on alleged Catholic persecution of Protestants in South America, and articles from *Christianity Today*, among others.
4. W.L. Brasher to Butler, August 21, 1960, Butler Papers, Box 204.
5. Butler to W.L. Brasher, August 26, 1960, Butler Papers, Box 204.
6. Release, Address of Paul M. Butler, "Politics and You," Antioch College, May 31, 1961, Butler Papers, Box 166.
7. Louisville *Courier-Journal*, July 19, 1959.
8. Interview with Anne Butler, June 10, 1975; Washington *Star*, February 22, 1961; Release, Office of the White House Press Secretary, August 8, 1961, Butler Papers, Box 114; New York *Times*, September 11, 1961.
9. Interview with Neil Staebler, February 22, 1981; interview with Richard J. Murphy, October 14, 1982; interview with Marshall Smelser, September 24, 1974.
10. Interview with Anne Butler, June 10, 1975; in a similar vein, in 1961, Butler said that he would prefer not to be directly quoted on matters pertaining to Indiana politics because he was "out of politics now and desire to remain out of any controversy or contention with any of our Party leaders anywhere." (Butler to the author, July 5, 1961).
11. Box 5, Butler Papers; the Washington *Post*, February 3, 1961.
12. Antioch speech text, Box 166, Butler Papers.
13. Butler to Robert Eveld, June 20, 1957, Butler Papers, Box 16; interview with Louis Chapleau, June 11, 1975; Butler to Judge J. Frank McLaughlin, March 26, 1957, Butler Papers, Box 4, shows that Butler had been admitted to the practice of law in the territory of Hawaii; South Bend *Tribune*, March 20, 1960; New York *Herald-Tribune*, June 20, 1960; interview with Anne Butler, June 10, 1975.

14. 122 Vt. 177, 167A. 2d 514. *Anderson et al. v. Swart et al.*, 366 U.S. 925 (1961); *Herald-Tribune*, May 16, 1961.
15. Text of speech in Box 166, Butler Papers, dated March 17, 1961; "Wall of Separation—Judicial Gloss on the First Amendment," *Notre Dame Lawyer*, XXXVII (1962).
16. Frank J. Sorauf, *The Wall of Separation: The Constitutional Politics of Church and State* (Princeton: Princeton University Press, 1976), p. 186.
17. New York *Post*, March 6, 1961; interview with Anne Butler, June 10, 1975.
18. Interview with Anne Butler, June 10, 1975; John P. Doran to the author, November 6, 1974; it is, of course, possible that the Kennedy Administration may have helped in this arrangement.
19. Chicago *Tribune*, December 31, 1961; South Bend *Tribune*, December 30, 1961; interview with Mrs. Butler, June 10, 1975.
20. Indianapolis *Times*, December 31, 1961.
21. South Bend *Tribune*, January 3, 1962.
22. Record of will in St. Joseph (Indiana) County Clerk's office, Estate #17748, St. Joseph Superior Court No. 2, In the Matter of the Estate of Paul M. Butler; interview with Anne Butler, June 10, 1975. Butler's adversary, Frank McHale, died in 1975, leaving an estate valued at $3,400,000 (Louisville *Courier-Journal*, February 7, 1975).

EPILOGUE

In an age of political party decline (yet with nationalizing tendencies) and with interest in the revitalization of party organization, political scientists have rediscovered Paul Butler and give him rather high marks for his performance as chairman.[1] In a 1971 criticism of the 1950 report of the American Political Science Association's Committee on Political Parties, Evron Kirkpatrick had cited Butler as "the one party leader who tried to implement its proposals [and] failed completely."[2] Kirkpatrick recalled a paper presented by Daniel M. Ogden, Jr., to a panel of the 1960 meeting of the American Political Science Association, a paper gaining some audience by its publication in at least two versions.[3]

Butler read Ogden's paper, making meaningful markings only with the second and third paragraphs. He questioned whether "practical politicians" (changed to "old professional politicians" by Butler) had ignored the 1950 APSA report or had found the party responsibility theory unsound.[4]

Ogden's paper is a good background against which to analyze Butler's philosophy and goals while chairman. Ogden's thesis was that Butler had become acquainted with the party responsibility theory in 1950 and seriously and literally tried to implement it while chairman. In contrast to this theory, Ogden believed that an "arena of compromise" theory could best support analysis of American political parties. Butler had been successful in gaining support for his programs only when he leaned toward party decentralization and compromise, not when as a "stubborn idealist" he pursued party responsibility beyond the goals of mere liberalism. Ogden offered fourteen points as documentation, including Butler's views on party opposition and his belief that political parties should be united by principle, the "central idea of party responsibility theory." Butler had supposedly been particularly motivated by the APSA's committee report's recommendations on stressing policy, effective opposition, loyalty, party rules, a biennial convention, and a party council.

It is doubtful that Butler read the APSA report as early as 1950, as Ogden claims, but as noted above Butler had been made aware of its

179

arguments and had probably read part of it by 1953. Butler claimed he "followed closely the work and recommendations" of the APSA, and noted the interest political scientists had shown in the DAC.[5] Perhaps Butler did consciously pursue the party responsibility theory to a greater degree than Paul Willis, through his contact with Butler, believed Butler's pragmatism allowed.[6] At least there is much reference in Butler's pronouncements during his chairmanship to the importance of a two-party system in democratic government, to the party opposition concept, to the importance of policy questions in political discussion, to the value of parties united by principle, to party loyalty, and specifically to party responsibility itself. These themes are constant in the rhetoric.[7] If Butler was not the proponent of APSA party responsibility theory, he was the advocate of *some* party responsibility theory. While it may not fit perfectly the rigid model Ogden posits, with his assumption there are only two models for party analysis, a pattern exists which leans toward party responsibility.

However, Butler's party responsibility ideas contained reform notions of widely-based participatory, activist politics, fueled by amateurs drawn to Adlai Stevenson's presidential campaigns. These volunteers had been appealed to by the force of ideas. Butler, who as a local political activist and speaker had emphasized issues in the traditional party setting, was tuned to the "new politics" of issues before he read the APSA report. His political integrity and disgust with those who put "selfish interests" above the good of the party had already shown him aspects of the Indiana political system he found wanting. Party united by principle already appealed to him when he became active in the Draft Stevenson Movement and acquainted with the Michigan Democratic Party in the early 1950s. At the sixth inauguration of Governor G. Mennen Williams Butler spoke about Neil Staebler's Michigan organization and Williams as a leader of "dedicated party government." The new politics of issues and image put a "premium on principles," and party organization based on common principles was "the most winning kind." People were brought to politics by issues, principles, and ideas. The Michigan organization was first and foremost issue-oriented.[8] Likewise, the California party was an inspiration, demonstrating the new techniques of an organization and issues institution.[9] Butler never strayed from his trinity of communication, funding, and organization. The new techniques strengthened organization and made for effective, winning politics.[10]

In his Antioch College speech of 1961, cited above as an excellent summary of Butler's thoughts about the political life (and containing the responsibility theory), Butler argued that theory should be wed to reality. His methods for obtaining this goal were not always the same as those others practiced; consequently they overlooked Butler the pragmatist and realist who wanted to win and valued party unity.[11] When he contrasted politicians and political scientists Kirkpatrick might well have observed that Butler was a politician, not a political scientist.[12]

For Paul Butler politics was "the breath of life . . . It is a great game . . . In this game you play for the greatest prizes and you play for keeps."[13] Indeed politicians play "an honorable role in our society. They are the natural peacemakers of our people. Their supreme task is to . . . prevent society from tearing itself apart."[14] The political party was "one of the principle instruments for the settlement of differences available in our society."[15] But as much as he valued party unity he had also been socialized toward party loyalty; he was an organization man. There was nothing wrong with party diversity, but after deliberation the "law of the majority" prevailed. Once common principles had been established there was "no room for disagreement on basic principle."[16]

No doubt Butler seemed at times contradictory on such matters as the South and civil rights. Yet he often showed more consistency than others. When one considers how much Harry Truman (himself contradictory in a short period of time) riled the South, it was ridiculous for Ogden to set up Butler as a foil for Truman the unifier.

On the party rules and national convention delegate loyalty issues, Ogden saw a Butler victory in 1955 because arena-type methods were employed. While the resolution of the Southern problem was not entirely in Butler's hands he had generally pursued a policy of conciliation with the South (until 1957, when Butler said the situation had changed), as had his allies, Stephen Mitchell and Adlai Stevenson. Yet Ogden was probably not aware of how much Butler had repressed his feelings. At the time Butler had argued for a midterm party convention he had also compiled his party constitution (not publicly revealed), which resulted primarily from Southern recalcitrance in the early 1950s. Paul Willis' constitution draft, with stiff loyalty and centralizing provisions, was accompanied by warnings about what Southern Democrats had done to the party a century before.[17] Still, in 1954 Butler had not shown Southern leaders why they should not support him for chairman, especially against big-city Northern bosses. Butler had most of the votes of Southern and border state members of the National Committee at New Orleans (twenty-seven votes), but he had more votes (thirty-eight) outside the area.

Ogden made use of the Democratic Advisory Council to illustrate Butler's rejection of arena-type compromise. Butler vigorously instituted the DAC, but many others had urged its creation, while its origins preceded the APSA report. Ironically, the report warned that a national chairman, exercising initiative in matters other than

181

presidential campaign management, was likely to have his authority challenged, with ill feeling, rather than harmony, resulting. Butler had been cooperative with congressional leaders in the first two years, and he made great effort to gain congressional leader membership on the DAC, even while his ideas on issues, policy, and common party principles pushed him toward the DAC concept. What Butler faced was the Anglo-American tradition of legislative party independence from political parties.[18] This tradition proved to be an obstacle to the participation of congressional leaders, but not all spokesmen in Congress refused to support the DAC. Then was DAC a failure, and, if so, by whose definition?

Not all political scientists in the 1960s saw the DAC as a failure, and time has made possible a new perspective. Ogden was unable in 1960 to analyze the "success" of the DAC in terms of setting a definite party agenda, contributing to the 1960 Platform, aiding Kennedy's victory, and in providing a basis for the Kennedy-Johnson legislative program. Since Butler's time the out party has routinely engaged in policy pronouncement.[19]

Ogden observed that Butler's program for mass party financing angered urban party leaders, who lagged on state financial quotas. It is doubtful that sustaining membership drives upset urban leaders much, especially since they could ignore their implementation. The sustaining membership contributions could also be credited against state quotas. Many of these leaders were willing to do anything to discredit Butler's leadership. Meeting state quotas had been a problem ever since Stephen Mitchell had established them in 1953; this problem did not originate with Butler's financial scheme, which did not begin until July, 1957.

Apart from any conscious following of the APSA report, Butler had found financial planning inadequate and haphazard before he became chairman. To encourage mass party participation Butler saw broad-based, small contributions as good in themselves. This type of funding fit well into his trinity making for party effectiveness.

Ogden believed Butler was successful with the Advisory Committee on Political Organization, and especially with the party worker training programs, because those who set them up honored party decentralization realities. ACPO chairman Neil Staebler was praised for his group work techniques approach to politics. Butler was again used as a foil to Staebler. Actually, Staebler never heard of Ogden's research until 1982. Staebler has emphatically stressed that he approved of Butler's goals, and that Ogden did not sort out Butler's three-tiered battle for party reform—reform of methods involving increased participation, stress on certain public policy questions, and the loyalty of Southern convention delegates.[20] The Michigan Democratic Party pursued a responsible party theory. Staebler admired Butler's early performance on the National Committee. Staebler helped manage Butler's election as chairman. Staebler was deliberately picked by Butler to head ACPO because they had similar ideas on party reform and organization. Staebler had instituted a sustaining membership program in Michigan, and ACPO recommended it nationally. ACPO alluded to party centralization, and stressed issues as part of communication, discussion, common information, party position, and the Democratic program. It advocated issue conferences and stressed platform hearings. It even desired publicity for congressional Democrats who ignored the party platform.[21]

Ogden saw that the party worker training programs had paid off in the 1960 election, and regretted that ACPO had been abolished after Kennedy became president. Ironically, when Butler suggested the training programs, Staebler and others on the ACPO at first thought the idea impractical. Training was foreign to the thinking of political participants. Indeed Republicans had operated more training programs.[22]

In spite of disclaimers to the effect that ACPO had no intention of intruding into local political matters, centralizing tendencies were all too apparent to some local leaders, and there was much lethargy in terms of setting up training programs.[23] All of ACPO's program, and especially training party workers, was part and parcel of Butler's ideas about participatory politics and the importance of issues, communication, funding, organization, and effectiveness.

As chairman of the Democratic National Committee Paul Butler illustrated the change from chairmen as fundraisers and campaign managers to publicity leaders and partisan image makers, setting the pace for policy discussion. By his performance he exhibited more strength and success than his contemporaries could see. Cotter and Hennessy believed he did this showing some of the "tinge of charisma" James Farley possessed because of the kind of person Butler was, his conception of a national party, and his energy and persistence. With an "intense passion for party ideology and/or loyalty" Butler exploited "opportunities for the development of charismatic and symbolic leadership." His emphasis on issues and common party principles helped provide a focal point for loyalties and enthusiasm.[24]

Reserved, rather than cold, Butler was aware that his leadership style might upset people—"Whereas one of my many faults, and perhaps the most glaring (and ofttimes against my own good) is being too outspoken and positive on some matters . . ."[25] Yet some aspects of this style had impressed people when he advanced in local politics, his judgment being trusted and his honesty and integrity marked. The Indiana phase of his political upbringing, while tempered by a broader experience, explains much of his style as chairman. He never moved from his belief that no practitioner should use political power for selfish interest.

Compared favorably to James Farley, Butler held no governmental position, as Farley had. George McGovern, who reorganized the South Dakota Democratic Party in the 1950s, believes Butler's political organization efforts were well directed. Neil Staebler thinks he "had the best sense of organization and dedication to the Party of any Chairman in the last 50 years."[26] As nationalizing trends in party organization began to appear his Democratic successors made use of party policy agencies. But it was Republican chairmen who followed who were able to employ similar organizational, financial, and worker and candidate training programs to advantage by harnessing the new technology. They enjoyed favorable money conditions, the right issue—ideology context, and a particular political climate.[27]

Paul Willis has suggested that Butler, a party leader during the twilight years of the two-party system, when reform tendencies were different from those of the McGovern Era, served in the dying stages of the old-time Irish Democratic leadership. Neil Staebler believes Butler was the first of the new-type chairman who "marked the watershed in national politics . . . between the backroom-boss manipulative politics and open-door participative politics."[28] Perhaps Butler can best be described as a transitional-type chairman, using the language of the late '60s and the '70s a bit early.[29] He helped prepare his party to govern in a period when party decline began to be noticed. Against a decentralizing tradition he tried to reorient his party. His particular talents and insights were suited for these tasks at that particular moment.

NOTES

1. Sundquist, *Politics and Policy*; David E. Price, *Bringing Back the Parties* (Washington, D.C.: Congressional Quarterly Press, 1984); Robert J. Huckshorn, *Political Parties in America*, 2nd ed. (Monterey, California: Brooks/Cole Publishing Co., 1984), p. 64.
2. Evron M. Kirkpatrick, "Toward a More Responsible Two-Party System: Political Science, Policy Science, or Pseudo-Science?" *American Political Science Review*, LXV (1971), pp. 965-990; the report was *Toward a More Responsible Two-Party System* (Washington, D.C.: American Political Science Association, 1950).

184

3. Daniel M. Ogden, "Party Theory and Political Reality Inside the Democratic Party," paper delivered at the 1960 meeting of the American Political Science Association, New York (Ann Arbor, Michigan: University Microfilm, Inc.); Ogden, "Paul Butler and the Democratic Party," in Robert E. Lane, James D. Barber, and Fred I. Greenstein (eds.), *An Introduction to Political Analysis: Problems in American Government* (Englewood Cliffs, N.J.: Prentice-Hall, Inc., 1962), pp. 64-71; Ogden, "Paul Butler, Party Theory, and the Democratic Party," in John E. Kersell and Marshall W. Conley (eds.), *Comparative Political Problems: Britain, United States, and Canada* (Scarborough, Ontario: Prentice-Hall of Canada, Ltd., 1968), pp. 117-125. Ogden came to the DNC as an APSA National Committee Fellow about the time Butler departed. He interviewed Butler for the paper presented at the APSA panel, on which Butler was supposed to have served, but apparently did not.

4. In Butler Papers, Box 204.

5. Butler to Philip Wilder, June 3, 1960, Butler Papers, Box 9; Report for Year of 1957 of Democratic National Committee by Paul M. Butler, Chairman, to Members of the Democratic National Committee, February 21, 1958, Butler Papers, Box 165.

6. Paul G. Willis to the author, November 17, 1975; Willis had not read Ogden's paper until this time.

7. Beyond the specific programs Butler helped institute see: Speech Text for National Press Club, February 1, 1955, Butler Papers, Box 146; text for Florida speech, March 2, 1955, Box 146; text for Pittsfield, Massachusetts speech, March 3, 1955, Box 146; DNC release, April 11, 1955, Box 76; text for Georgia speech, April 25, 1955, Box 147; *Toledo Blade*, May 26, 1957, Box 173; text of speech for conference on "Party "Responsibility in the 20th Century," Bloomington, Illinois, July 2, 1958, Box 152; text for Wichita, Kansas speech, October 8, 1958, Box 153; text for Oklahoma State University YDC speech, March 10, 1959, Box 155; text for Ford Hall Forum address, April 26, 1959, Box 156; text for Western States Democratic Conference, May 16, 1959, Box 156; text for Antioch speech, May 31, 1961, Box 166.

8. Text of speech of Paul M. Butler at Inaugural Luncheon for Governor G. Mennen Williams, January 1, 1959, Butler Papers, Box 110.

9. Text of speech of Paul M. Butler at Los Angeles, California, August 10, 1957, Butler Papers, Box 142.

10. Two writers in particular, Sidney Hyman and David Broder, had keen insight into what Butler was doing while chairman. See Sidney Hyman, "The Collective Leadership of Paul M. Butler," *The Reporter*, December 24, 1959, p. 8; and David Broder, "The

Changing Face of the Party Chairman," *New York Times Magazine*, October 18, 1959, p. 16.

11. Paul G. Willis to the author, February 8, 1975.

12. Kirkpatrick, "Toward a More Responsible Two-Party System," p. 981.

13. Speech text for National Press Club, February 29, 1956, Butler Papers, Box 149.

14. Script for radio program, WLW (Washington), February 5, 1956, Butler Papers, Box 202.

15. Text for speech, March 2, 1955, Butler Papers, Box 146.

16. Text for Texas speech, June 14, 1955, Butler Papers, Box 149.

17. Paul G. Willis to the author, February 8, 1975. The Constitution draft is in Butler Papers, Box 83. The Constitution draft cites the APSA report.

18. See Cotter and Hennessy, *Politics Without Power*, p. 10, on the constituency orientation of American politics; and Bone, *Party Committees*, pp. 214-18, on policy formulation by national committees.

19. Sundquist, *Politics and Policy*, pp. 395-415; Cotter and Hennessy, *Politics Without Power*, pp. 211-24; Huckshorn, *Political Parties in America*, p. 64; Price, *Bringing Back the Parties*, pp. 264-279., Price also analyzes the APSA report and argues that its recommendations are less visionary today (see pp. 104-107; 263-264).

20. Interview with Neil Staebler, December 15, 1980; Neil Staebler to the author, July 6 and 19, 1982. Staebler believes political scientists have never been able to get a tangible feeling for participatory politics. His Harvard speech, February 13, 1961, Butler Papers, Box 145, credits the success of the Democratic Party in 1958 and 1960 to "a composite of the skillful work of the Congressional Democrats, the firm line developed by the Advisory Council, and the vigorous organization work of the National Chairman, Paul Butler. Butler is one of the unsung heroes of American politics and will eventually be recognized as having turned the Democratic Party around . . ."

21. Sawyer, *The Democratic State Central Committee*; Neil Staebler to the author, July 6 and 19, 1982; ACPO Recommendation No. 20-B (1957), Butler Papers, Box 66. See material above.

22. Daniel M. Ogden, Jr., "The Democratic National Committee in the Campaign of 1960," *Western Political Quarterly*, XIV (1961, Supplement), pp. 27-28; Neil Staebler to the author, July 6, 1982; Bone, *Party Committees*, p. 93.

23. Drexel A. Sprecher, Gordon L. Lippit, and Bernard C. Hennessy, "Training Programs of the Democratic National Committee," *Journal of Social Issues*, XVI (1960), pp. 30-39.

24. Cotter and Hennessy, *Politics Without Power,* pp. 64, 71. Also see Cotter and Hennessy generally, pp. 67-80; and Bone, *Party Committees*, pp. 9-10, 211.

25. Paul G. Willis to the author, February 8, 1975; Butler to Edward F. Voorde, April 25, 1958, Butler Papers, Box 17.

26. Interview with Richard J. Murphy, October 14, 1982; George McGovern to the author, October 4, 1982; Neil Staebler to the author, January 14, 1981.

27. Neil Staebler to the author, July 6, 1982, on how Ray Bliss followed a parallel course and improved on Butler's programs; Price, *Bringing Back the Parties*, pp. 21-50 and 246-54; John F. Bibby and Robert J. Huckshorn, "The Republican Party in American Politics," in Jeff Fischel (ed.), *Parties and Elections in an Anti-Party Age: American Politics and the Crisis of Confidence* (Bloomington, Indiana: Indiana University Press, 1978), pp. 55-65; A. James Reichley, "The Rise of National Parties," in John E. Chubb and Paul E. Peterson (eds.), *The New Direction in American Politics* (Washington, D.C.: The Brookings Institution, 1985), pp. 175-200.

28. Paul G. Willis to the author, September 24, 1977; interview with Neil Staebler, February 22, 1981; Neil Staebler to the author, July 6, 1982.

29. The term "new politics" was used frequently in Butler's speeches. He spoke of the "radical right." He labelled civil rights a "social issue," and clearly saw that racial prejudice was not sectional.

BIBLIOGRAPHICAL NOTE

The extensive notes following each chapter indicate the wide variety of source material employed in the research for this book. Included are many interviews with those who knew Paul M. Butler and party publications in the author's collection. Files of the *Democratic Digest* and pronouncements of the Democratic Advisory Council were helpful.

Those who wish to study the rules, organization, and activities of political parties frequently encounter the problem of party records—they are discarded, lost, or removed as the personal papers of outgoing party officers. Fortunately most of the records of the national Democratic Party, 1955-1960, have been preserved in the Paul M. Butler Papers, deposited by his family in the Archives of the University of Notre Dame. They are essential for any study of this period of Democratic Party activity (the box numbers for this collection are location numbers which are subject to change). Valuable material also was located in the Sam Rayburn Library in Bonham, Texas. Records maintained by Paul G. Willis, including his correspondence, provided precise information which was useful in clarifying several situations. Use was also made of Walter Johnson, Carol Evans, and C. Eric Sears (eds.), *The Papers of Adlai E. Stevenson* (Boston: Little, Brown, 8 vols., 1972-1979).

Especially in the absence of other source material, newspapers (clippings in the Butler Papers, or newspapers in other files) aided an understanding of events and Butler's role in politics. The Louisville *Courier-Journal* did an unusually good job in covering Indiana politics of the 1950s and Butler's career as national chairman.

Two contemporary observers had keen insight when analyzing Butler's goals and methods: David Broder, "The Changing Face of the Party Chairman," *New York Times Magazine*, October 18, 1959, p. 16; and Sidney Hyman, "The Collective Leadership of Paul M. Butler," *The Reporter*, December 24, 1959, p. 8. For information on the Democratic National Committee, Cornelius P. Cotter and Bernard C. Hennessy, *Politics Without Power: The National Party Committees* (New York: Atherton Press, 1964); and Hugh A. Bone, *Party Committees and National Politics* (Seattle: University of Washington Press, 1958), were helpful.

INDEX

191

national committeeman, 25–43;
in 1960 presidential campaign,
161–65, 171–72; parents, 1; post-
chairman activities, 171–175;
reelected national chairman, 158;
relatives in politics, 1; speaking
activities, early, 3–5, 7–8; state
committee member, 15–19;
tenure problems, 153–61; Third
District chairman, 12–13, 15–16;
trinity for winning politics,
123–46; youth and education,
1–2. *See also specific topical
entries*
Butler, Paul, Jr. (son), 3
Butler, William (cousin), 1

Campbell, Alexander, 155, 157
Cannon, Clarence, 60, 158
Carey, James, 81
Carvel, Elbert, 28
Catholic Church: PMB on Catholic
issues, 4, 5; religious issue in
1960, 161–62, 171–72
Cavanaugh, Rev. John, 56, 99, 162,
175
Celebrity Parade Program (1959),
79–83 passim
Chairmanship of PMB: activist
concept, 56–57; criticism of
Eisenhower, 54, 67, 73, 74–75,
80, 164; opposition party leader,
67–69; relations with
congressional leaders, 76–84;
roles of chairman, as seen by
PMB, 123, 146, 182–83;
summary evaluation, 179–84
Chapleau, Louis, 11, 173
Chavoor, Evelyn, 60
Chicago *Tribune*, 6
Christ, Jesus, 98
Civic activities of PMB, 3
Clark, Joseph, 109
Clements, Earl, 159
Collins, Morris, 143
Committee to Defend America by

Aiding the Allies, 5, 7
Congressional Quarterly, 82
Congressional Record, 109, 114
Cotter, Cornelius, *Politics Without
Power: The National Party
Committees*, 130, 183
Croll, Jack, 38–39
Crook, Thurman, 16
Curley, James M., 55

*The Decision in 1960: The Need to
Elect a Democratic President*,
115
The *Democrat*, 130
Democratic Advisory Council
(DAC), 43, 70, 77, 78, 82, 83,
92, 95, 100, 141, 181–182;
congressional leaders oppose,
106–09; creation of, 105–06;
establishment of, 109–13; and
1960 Platform, 115; origins of,
103–05; PMB and, 105–13,
115–16, 117, 181–82; policy
statements of, 113–15, 129; role,
116–17; staff, 112–13
Democratic Digest, 58, 71, 77, 79,
84, 103, 110, 114, 123, 124,
126, 127–30, 132, 159; PMB
and, 30–31, 127, 129–30
Democratic Fact Book, 140
Democratic National Committee,
25–29 passim, 34, 38–43
passim, 52–57 passim, 62, 67,
69, 76, 77, 83, 90–98 passim,
100, 106, 110–15 passim,
124–45 passim, 158–65 passim,
171, 175; Executive Committee,
35–43 passim, 92, 105–07
passim, 110, 124, 128; members
and relations with PMB, 61–62,
159; PMB as member, 1952-
1954, 25, 33–43; staff, and
relations with PMB, 59–61
Democratic National Conventions:
1952, 28, 30, 39, 40, 43; 1956,
40, 43, 62, 90–91, 98, 130, 131,

158

Graybill, Leo, 158
Green, Edith, 106

Hall, Leonard, 71, 73
Harriman, Averell, 53, 90, 106
Hartke, R. Vance, 27, 82, 155, 160
Harvard University, 154
Haymaker, Ira, 15, 17, 18, 157
Haymaker, Jack, 157
Health of PMB, 1; failure of, 175
Heaney, Gerald, 55
Hennessy, Bernard, *Politics Without Power: The National Party Committees*, 130, 183
History of the Democratic Party, 142
Hobson, Rev. Henry W., 6
Hodges, Luther, 106, 108
Holland, Spessard, 82
How to Argue With a Republican, 141
How We Drafted Adlai Stevenson, 28
Humphrey, Hubert H., 36, 38, 67, 81, 90, 105, 106, 162
Hurley, Bishop Joseph P., *Papal Pronouncements and American Foreign Policy*, 6

Illinois State Normal University, 93
Income, *see* Financial affairs of PMB
Indiana bipartisan establishment, 156–57. *See also* McHale, Frank; McKinney, Frank
Indiana Democratic Party, *see* Democratic Party, Indiana
Indiana political culture, 14–15, 183–84
Indiana University, 35, 36, 173
Indianapolis *News*, 17, 32
Indianapolis *Star*, 17, 32
Indianapolis *Times*, 18

Jackson, Henry, 165

Jenner, William E., 154
Johnson, Lyndon B., 26, 61, 69, 78, 82, 83, 98, 106, 108, 109, 115, 155, 158, 160, 161, 163, 164, 165; cooperation with Eisenhower, 72, 75, 76–77, 104, 105; and DAC, 106–07; differences with PMB, 76–77, 78–79, 163; opposed to PMB's election as chairman, 55; part of anti-PMB alliance, 159
Johnson, Walter, 28, 39, 51; *How We Drafted Adlai Stevenson*, 28
Jones, Francis, 2
Jones, Vitus, 1, 2
Jones, Obenchain, and Bulter law firm, 2
Judd, Walter, 171

Kansas City Democratic Midterm Convention (1974), 43
Kefauver, Estes, 38, 106, 157
Kennan, George, 114
Kennedy, John, 35, 36
Kennedy, John F., 81, 99, 100, 130, 164, 174, 175, 182, 183; and ACPO, 146; and DAC, 106, 109, 111, 116; PMB's support of in 1960, 161–63, 165, 171–72; treatment of PMB, 172
Kennedy, Joseph, 162
The Key to Democratic Victory, 34
King, Rev. Martin Luther, Jr., 98
Kirkpatrick, Evron, 179, 181
Kirwan, Michael, 106, 108
Kizer, Marshall, 155

Law practice of PMB, 2–3, 29, 56, 161, 173–75
Lawrence, David, 51, 97, 105, 159, 160–61, 164
Legal preparation of PMB, 1, 2
Lehman, Herbert, 83
Leibowitz, Irving, 24 n61
Leland Stanford University, 93
Levanthal, Harold, 159

194

favors Frank McHale over PMB,
18; Frank McKinney as *his*
chairman, 82; opposes PMB's
election as chairman, 52–53, 55,
69
Tucker, Ralph, 155
Tucker, Raymond, 106
Tyroler, Charles II, 111, 113

U-2 incident (1960), 72–73, 164
Unruh, Jesse, 165

Vote Winner's Note Book, 34
Vrendenburg, Dorothy, 59

Walker, Frank, 53
Walsh, John R., 155, 156, 157
Welsh, Matthew E., 155, 156, 157
Wheeler, Burton K., 7
White, Theodore, 103
The White Committee, *see*
    Committee to Defend America
    by Aiding the Allies
Williams, Edward Bennett, 174
Williams, G. Mennen, 59, 180
Willis, Ann, 35
Willis, Paul G., 32, 35, 173, 180;
    assistant to PMB, 60; and
    Midterm Convention, 35, 36–37,
    38; on PMB as leader, 184;
    recruitment by PMB, 60; rules
    and party constitution, 41–43,
    181; speechwriter, 60, 65 n50
Willkie, Wendell, 12
Wilson, Woodrow, 1
Women in politics, PMB's views
    on, 99, 163
Woodward, Stanley, 52–53
Works Progress Administration
    (WPA), 10
Wyatt, Wilson, 28, 52

Ziffren, Paul, 60, 83, 105, 158, 160

GEORGE C. ROBERTS, Professor of Political Science at Indiana University Northwest, is a native Hoosier who has been studying the unique Indiana political system, in its national setting, for thirty-five years. A graduate of Purdue University, with highest distinction, he earned his graduate degrees at Indiana University. Professor Roberts is editor of the *Proceedings* of the Indiana Academy of the Social Sciences and a co-author of *Apportionment and Reapportionment in Indiana* and *The 1964 Presidential Election in the Southwest.*